TREES

VOLUME TWO
TWO FORESTS

TREES, VOLUME TWO:
TWO FORESTS. First printing.
October 2016. Published by Image Comics,
Inc. Office of publication: 2001 Center Street,
Sixth Floor, Berkeley, CA 94704. Copyright © 2016
Warren Ellis & Jason Howard. Originally published in single
magazine form as TREES #9–14. All rights reserved. TREES, its
logos, and all character likenesses herein are trademarks of Warren
Ellis & Jason Howard unless expressly indicated. Image Comics® and
its logos are registered trademarks and copyrights of Image Comics,
Inc. All rights reserved. No part of this publication may be reproduced
or transmitted, in any form or by any means (except for short excerpts for
review purposes) without the express written permission of Warren Ellis
& Jason Howard or Image Comics, Inc. All names, characters, events,
and locales in this publication are entirely fictional. Any resemblance
to actual persons (living or dead) or events or places, without
satiric intent, is coincidental. Printed in the USA. For information
regarding the CPSIA on this printed material call: 203-
595-3636 and provide reference # RICH–662299.
FOREIGN LICENSING INQUIRIES WRITE TO:
foreignlicensing@imagecomics.com
ISBN 978-1-63215-522-1

WARREN ELLIS
WRITER

JASON HOWARD
ARTIST

FONOGRAFIKS
LETTERING &
BOOK DESIGN

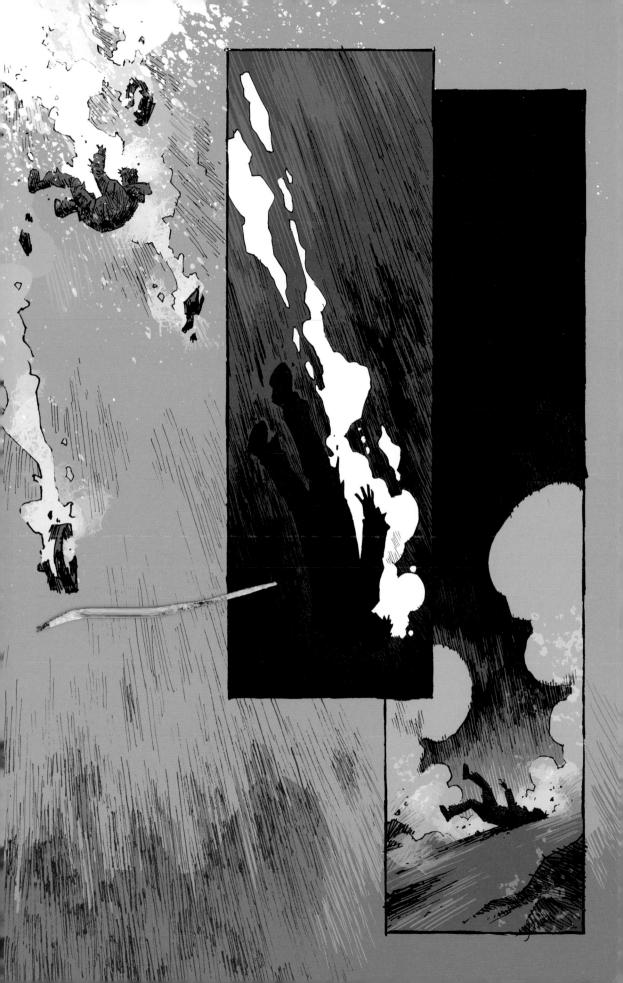

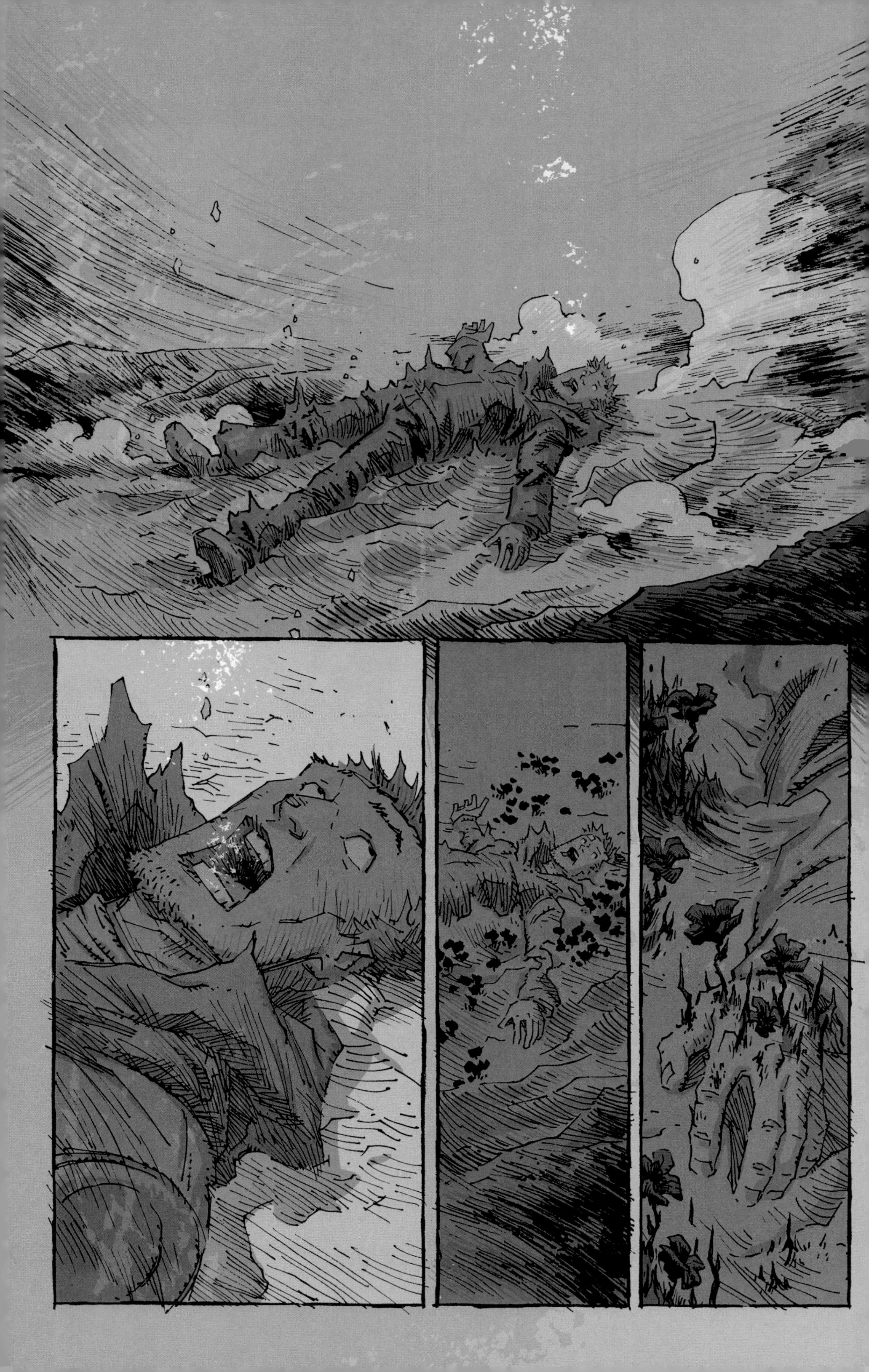

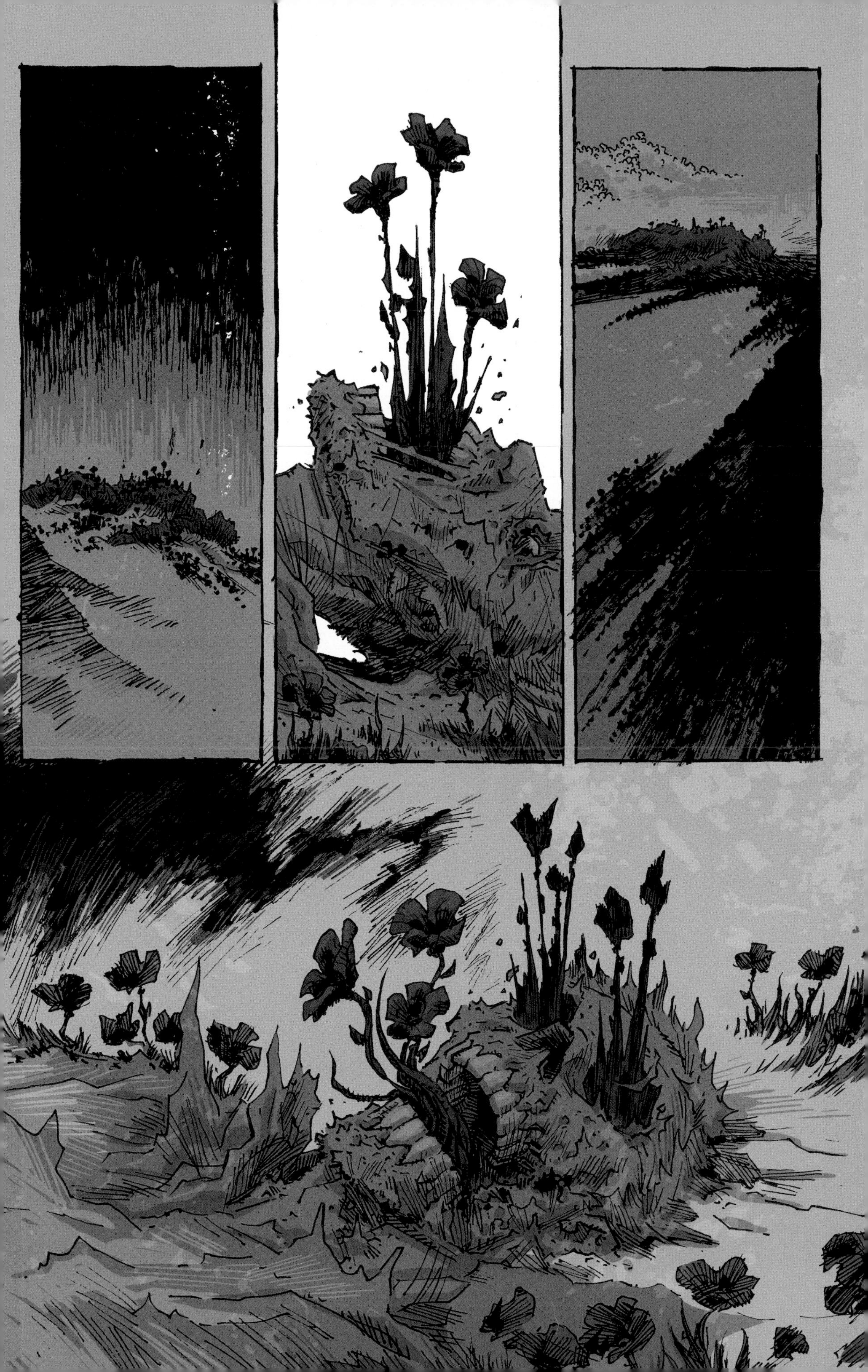

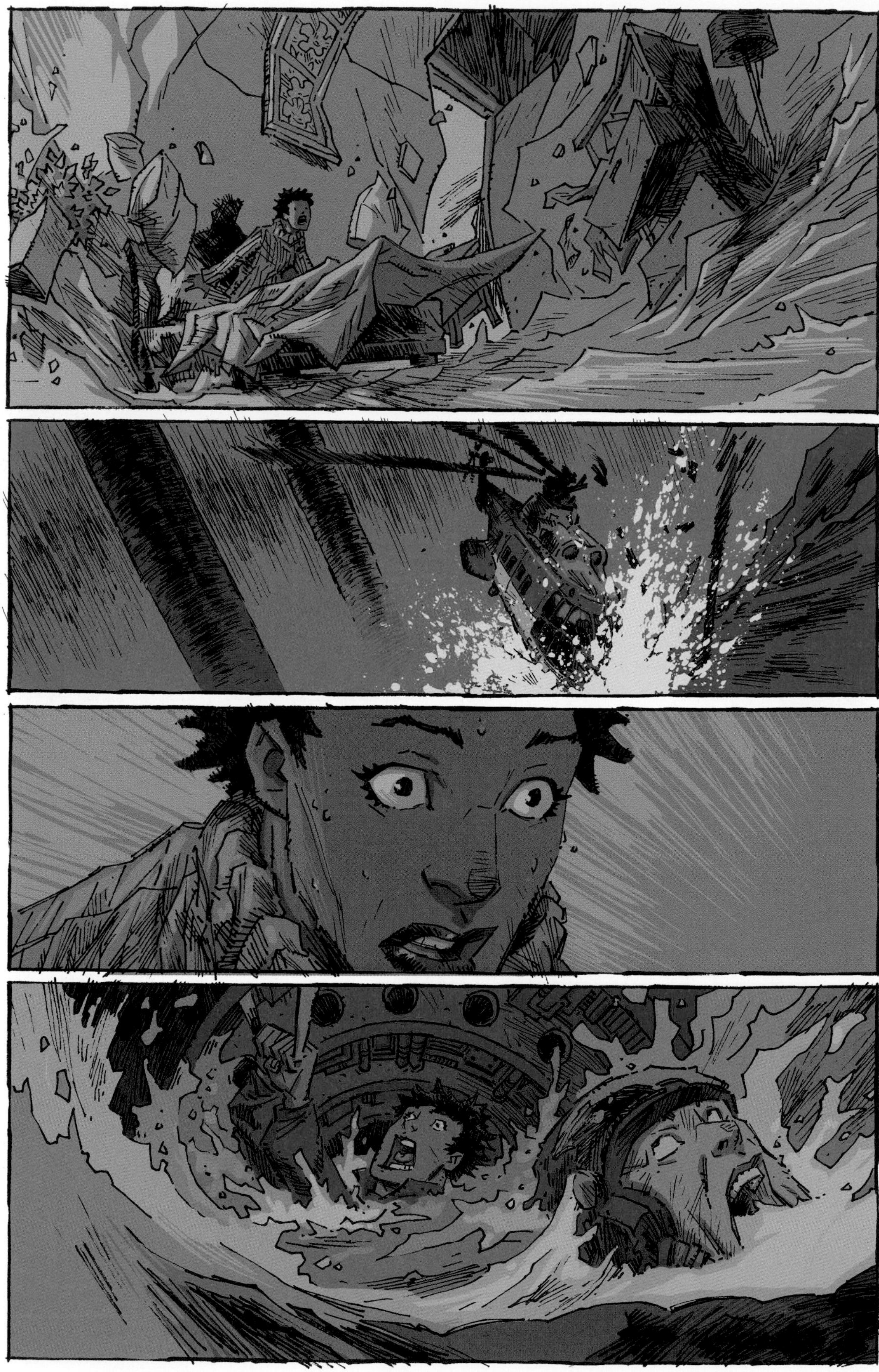

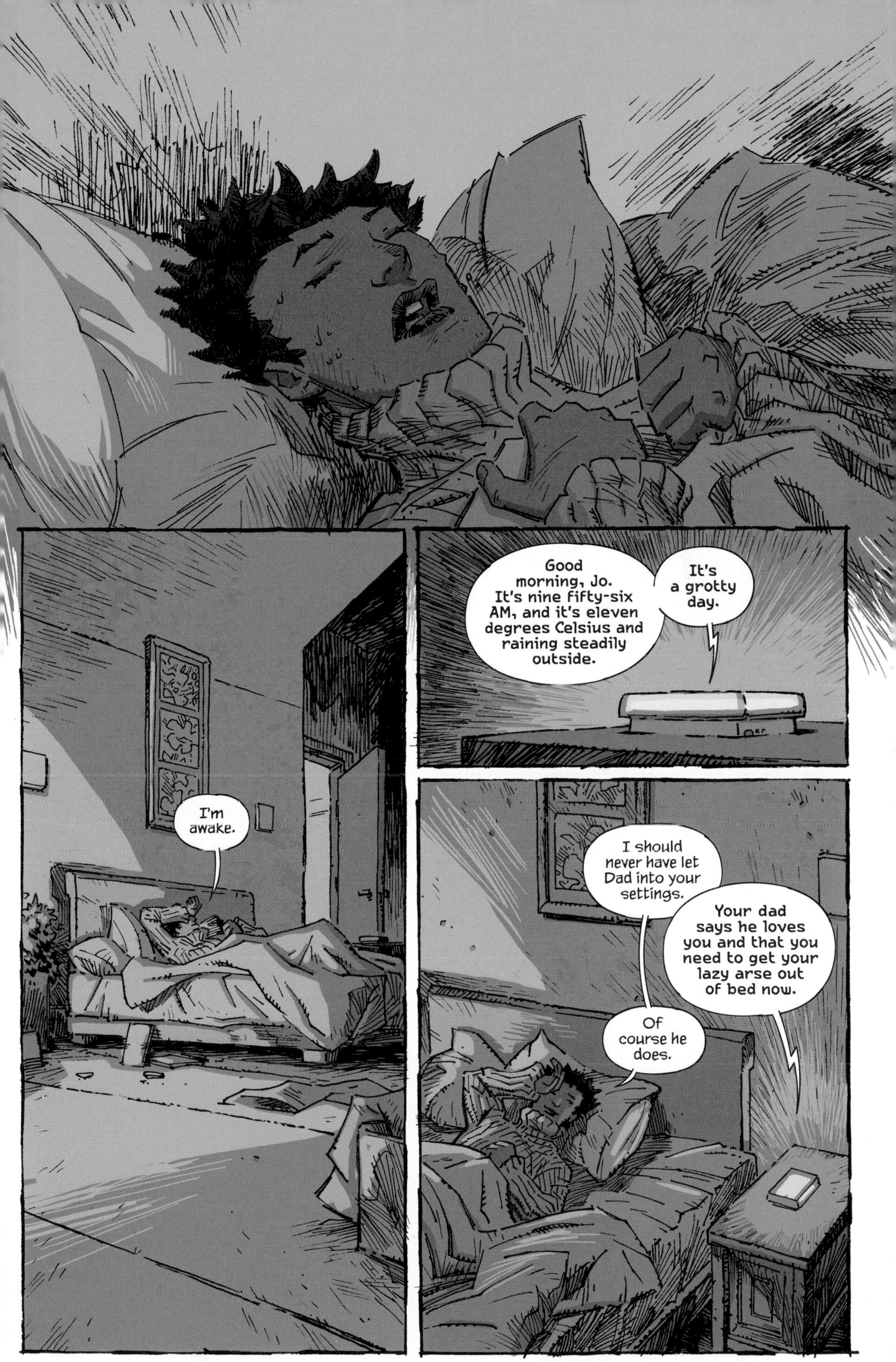
Good morning, Jo. It's nine fifty-six AM, and it's eleven degrees Celsius and raining steadily outside.
It's a grotty day.
I'm awake.
I should never have let Dad into your settings.
Your dad says he loves you and that you need to get your lazy arse out of bed now.
Of course he does.

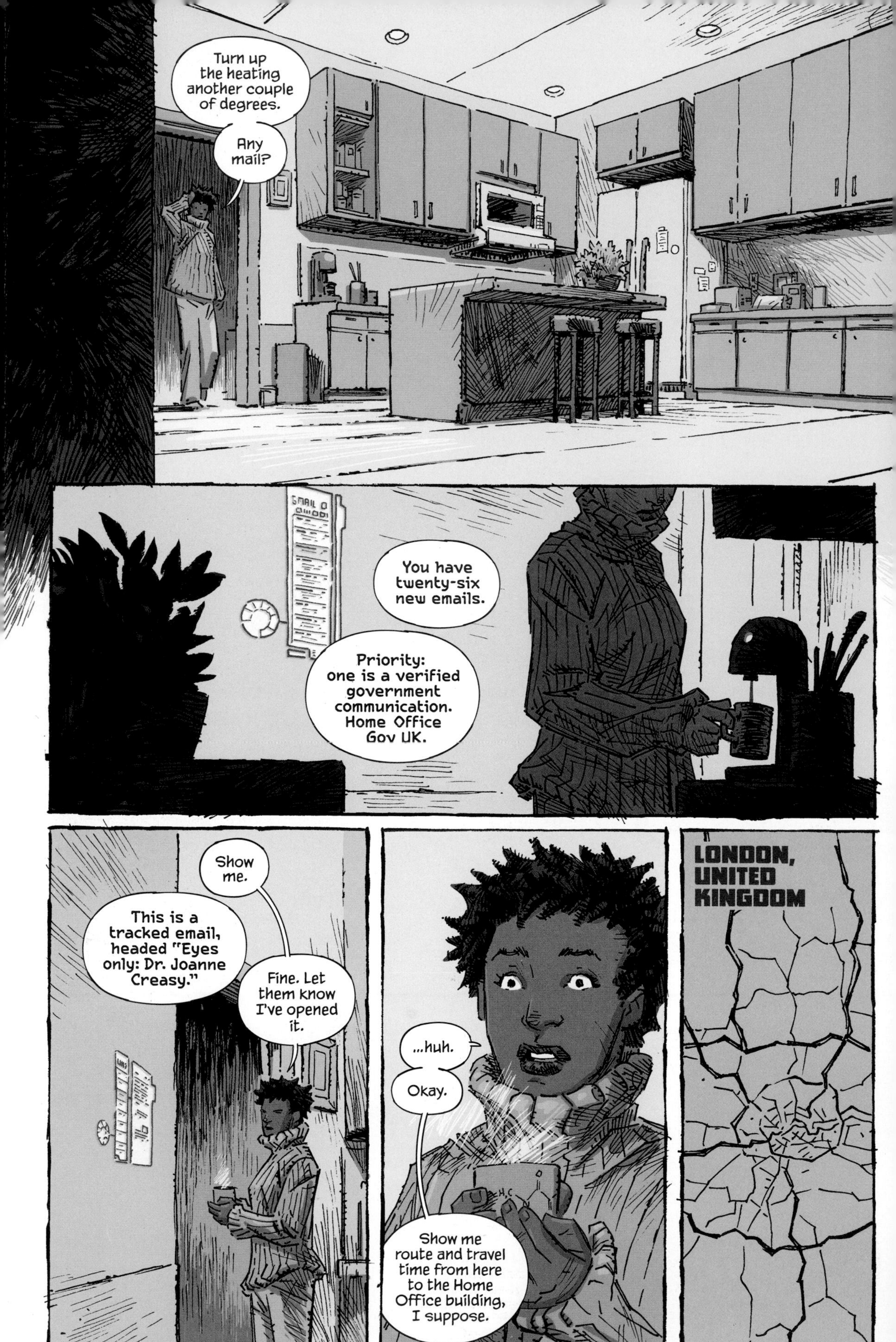
Turn up the heating another couple of degrees.
Any mail?
You have twenty-six new emails.
Priority: one is a verified government communication. Home Office Gov UK.
Show me.
This is a tracked email, headed "Eyes only: Dr. Joanne Creasy."
Fine. Let them know I've opened it.
...huh.
Okay.
Show me route and travel time from here to the Home Office building, I suppose.
LONDON, UNITED KINGDOM

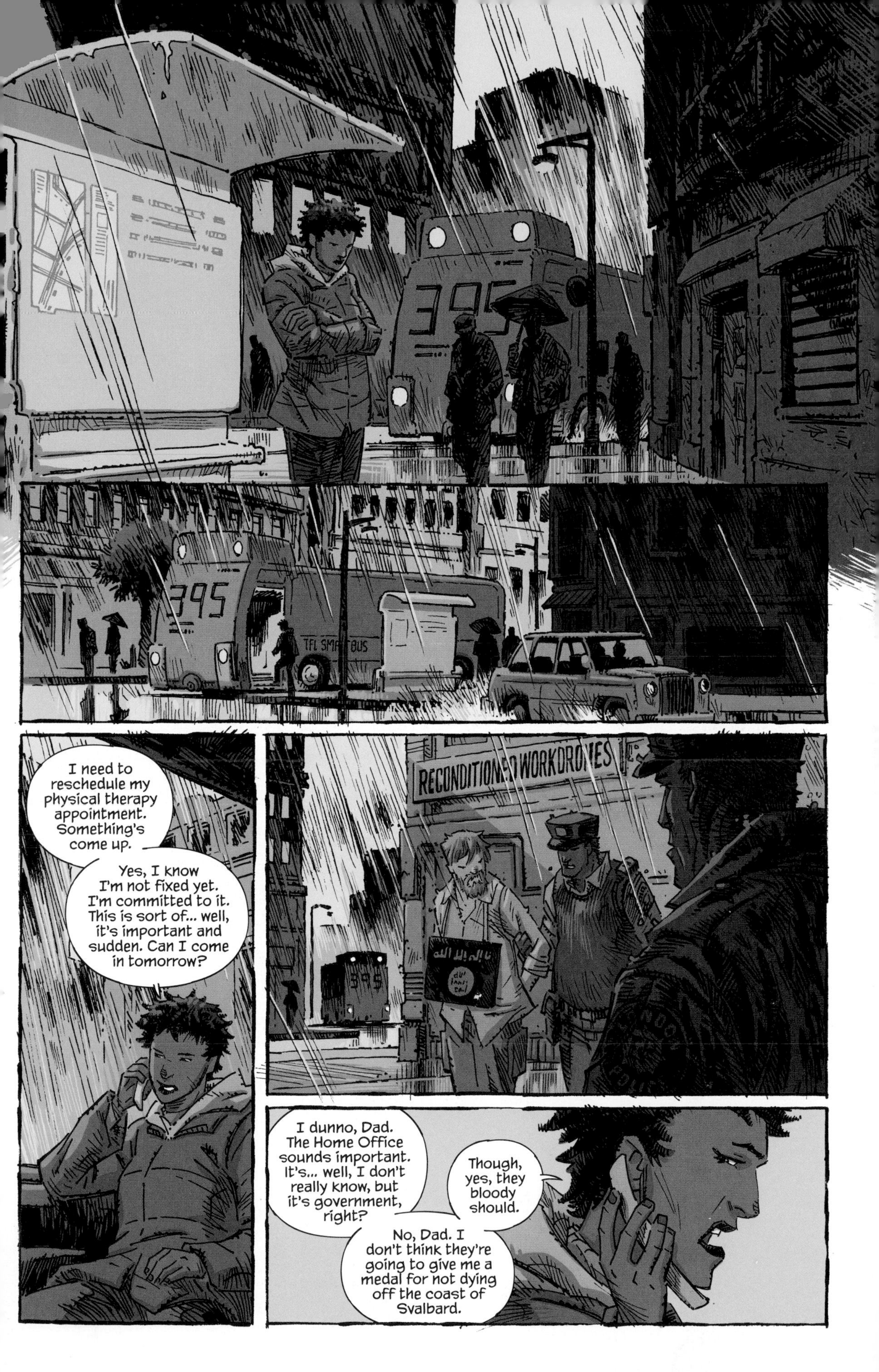
395
395
TFL SMARTBUS
RECONDITIONED WORKDRONES
I need to reschedule my physical therapy appointment. Something's come up.
Yes, I know I'm not fixed yet. I'm committed to it. This is sort of... well, it's important and sudden. Can I come in tomorrow?
I dunno, Dad. The Home Office sounds important. It's... well, I don't really know, but it's government, right?
Though, yes, they bloody should.
No, Dad. I don't think they're going to give me a medal for not dying off the coast of Svalbard.

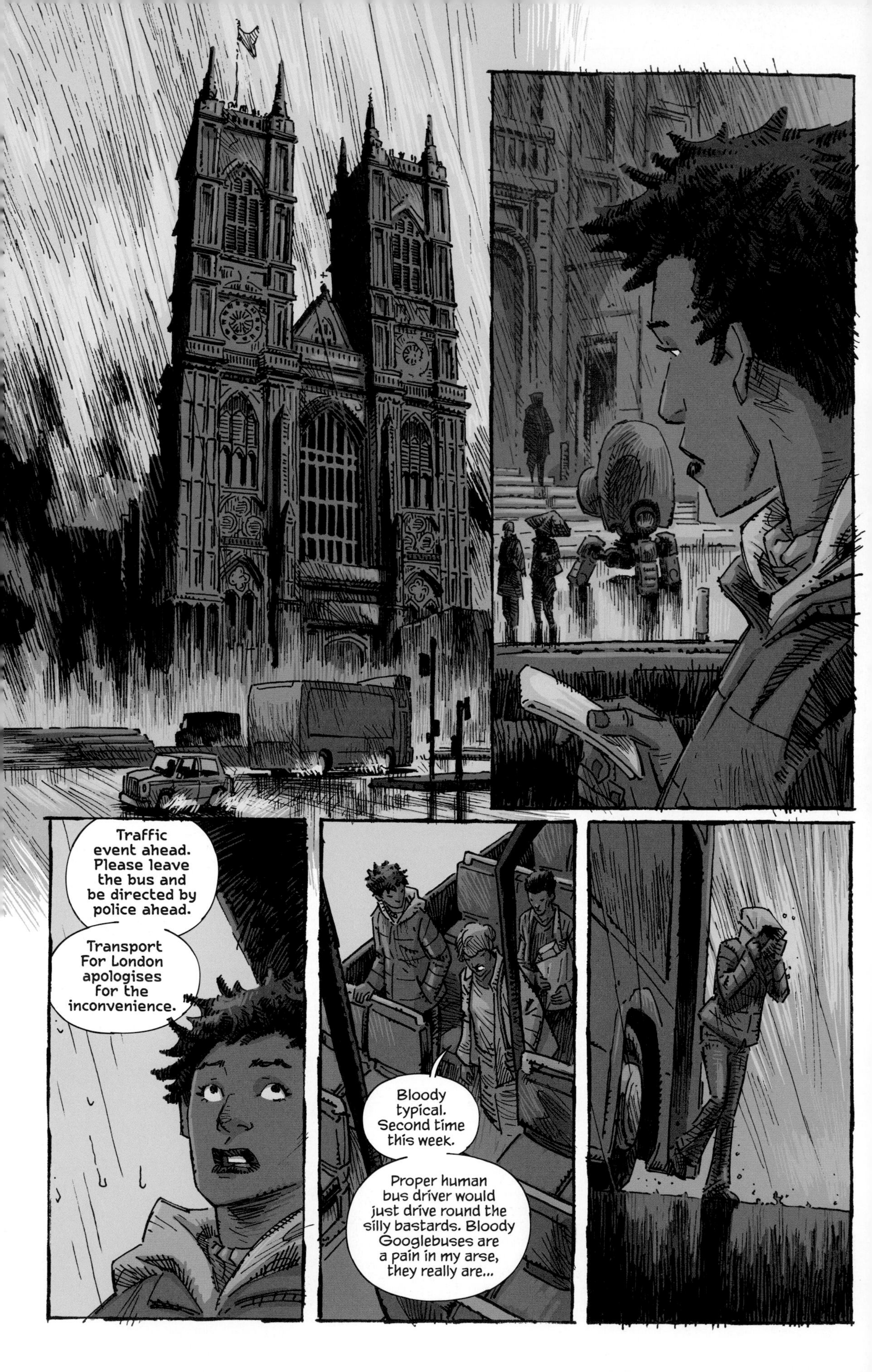
Traffic event ahead. Please leave the bus and be directed by police ahead.
Transport For London apologises for the inconvenience.
Bloody typical. Second time this week.
Proper human bus driver would just drive round the silly bastards. Bloody Googlebuses are a pain in my arse, they really are...

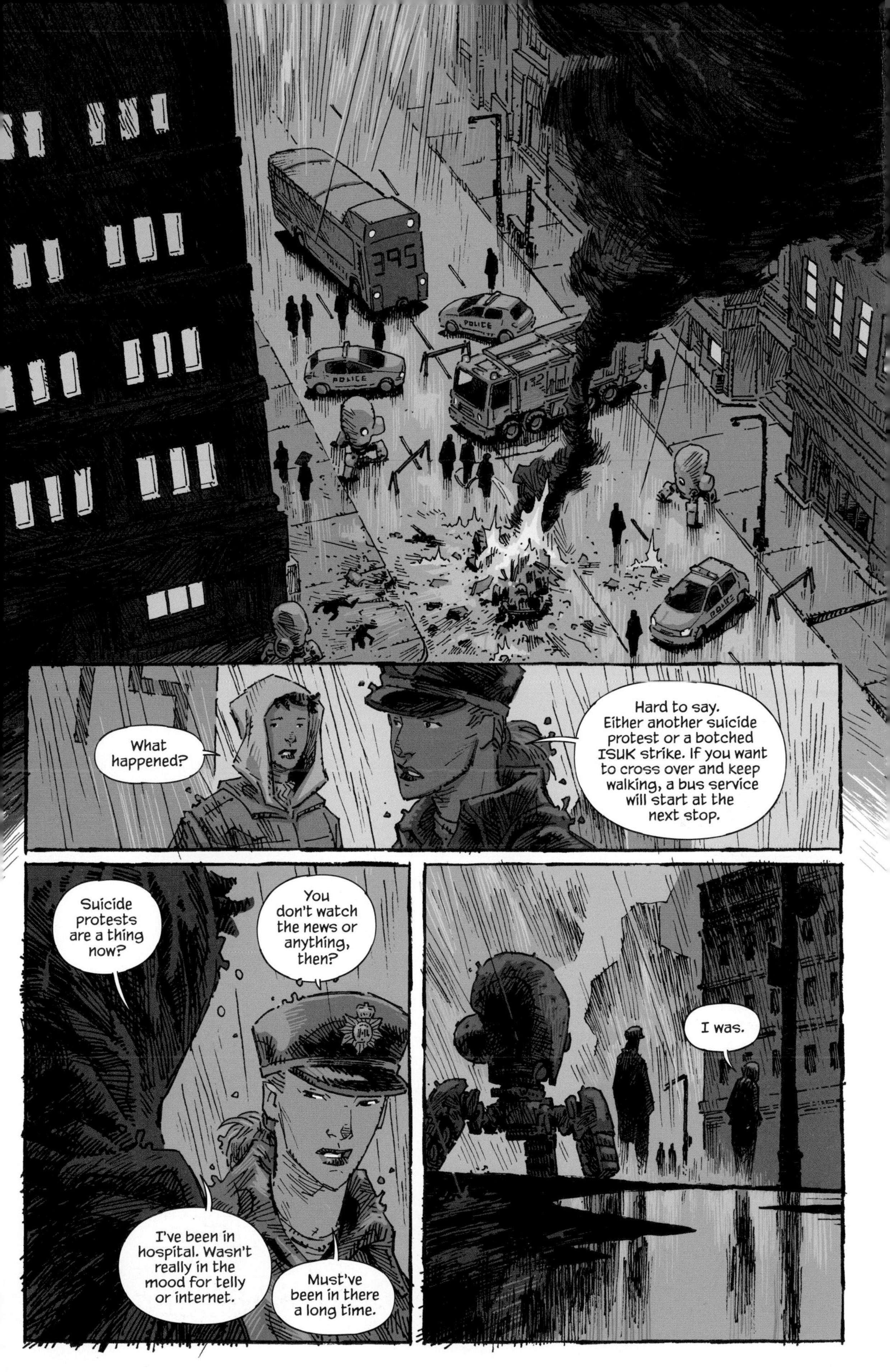

POLICE
What happened?
Hard to say. Either another suicide protest or a botched ISUK strike. If you want to cross over and keep walking, a bus service will start at the next stop.
Suicide protests are a thing now?
You don't watch the news or anything, then?
I've been in hospital. Wasn't really in the mood for telly or internet.
Must've been in there a long time.
I was.

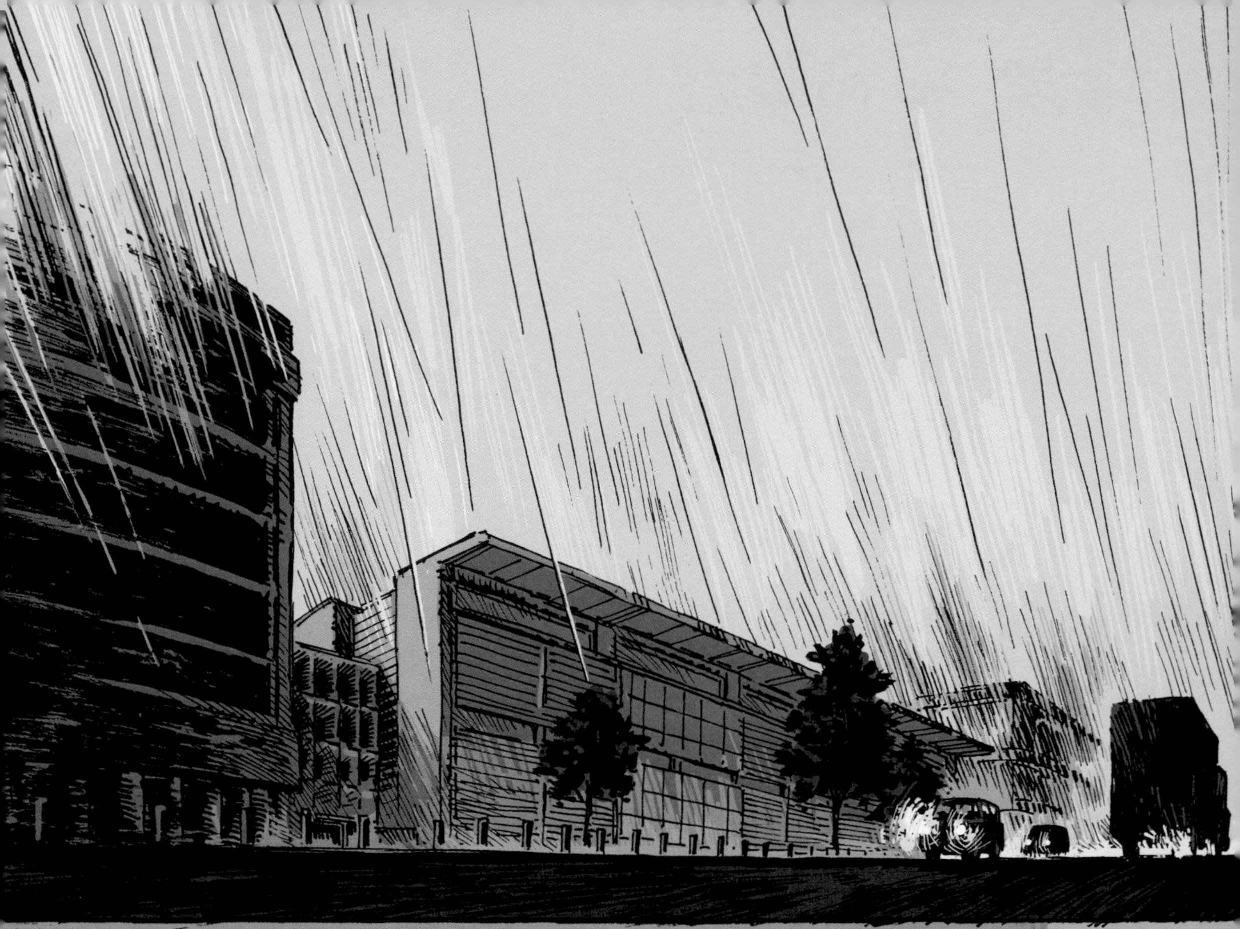

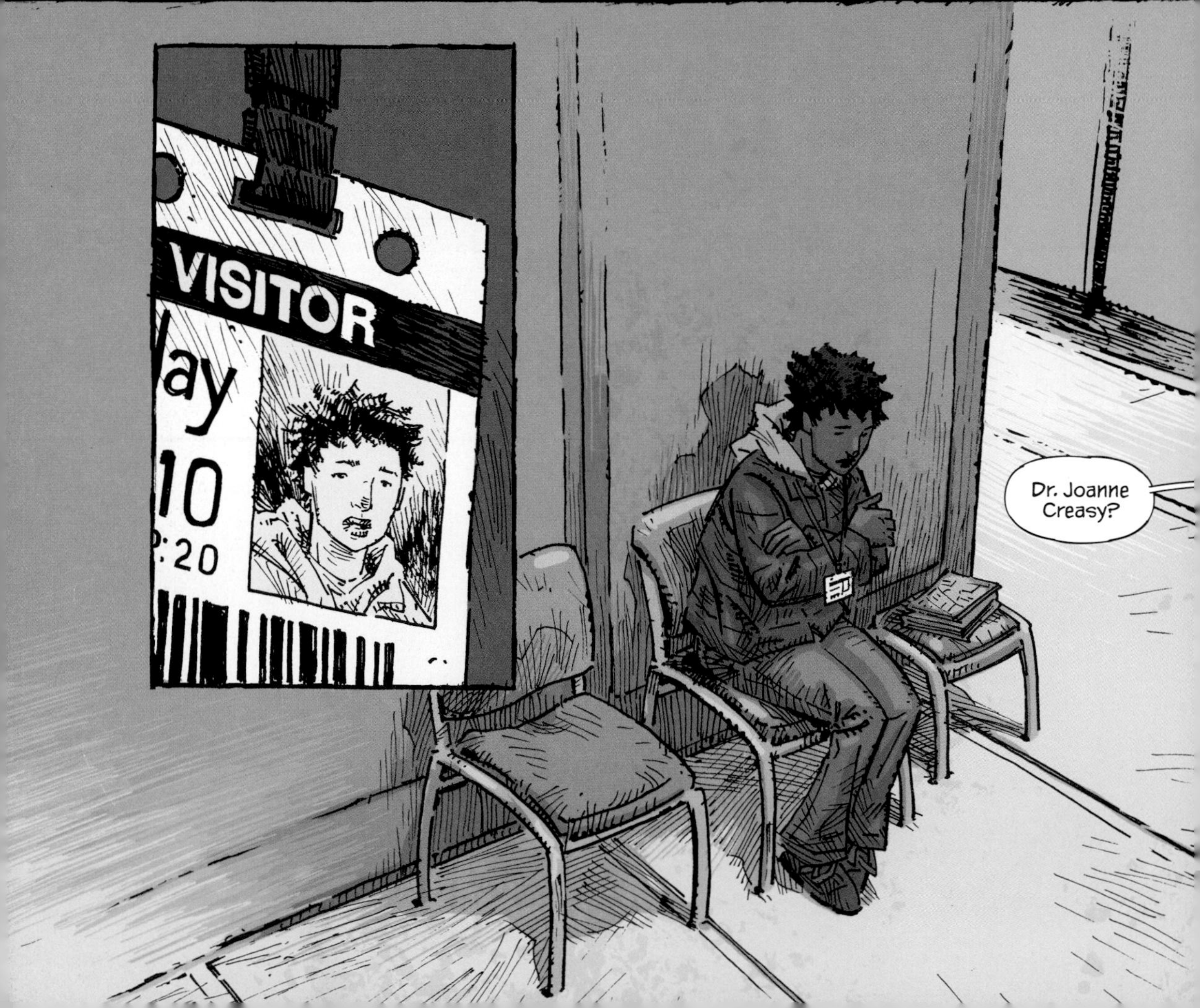
VISITOR
Dr. Joanne Creasy?

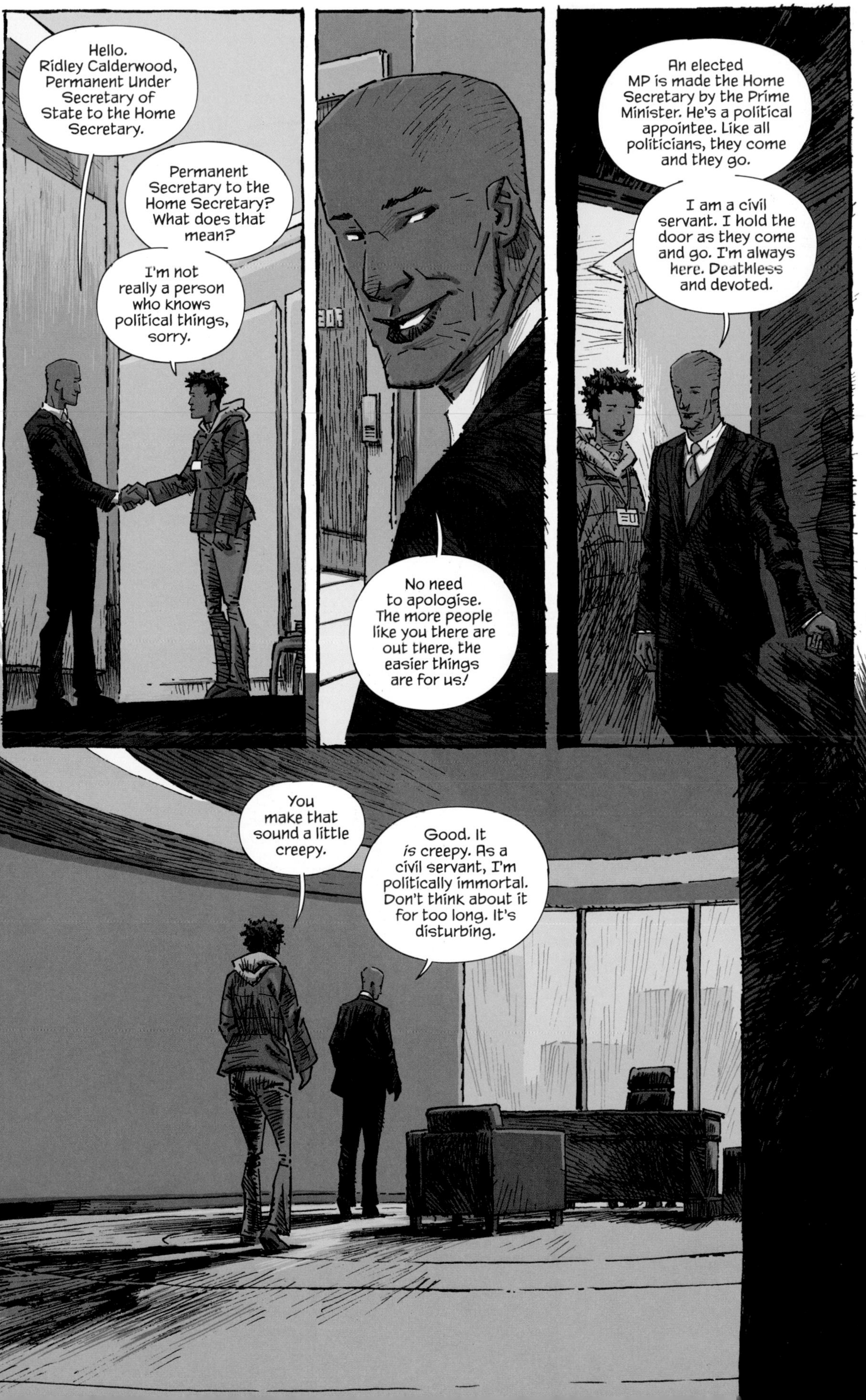
Hello. Ridley Calderwood, Permanent Under Secretary of State to the Home Secretary.
Permanent Secretary to the Home Secretary? What does that mean?
I'm not really a person who knows political things, sorry.
No need to apologise. The more people like you there are out there, the easier things are for us!
An elected MP is made the Home Secretary by the Prime Minister. He's a political appointee. Like all politicians, they come and they go.
I am a civil servant. I hold the door as they come and go. I'm always here. Deathless and devoted.
You make that sound a little creepy.
Good. It *is* creepy. As a civil servant, I'm politically immortal. Don't think about it for too long. It's disturbing.

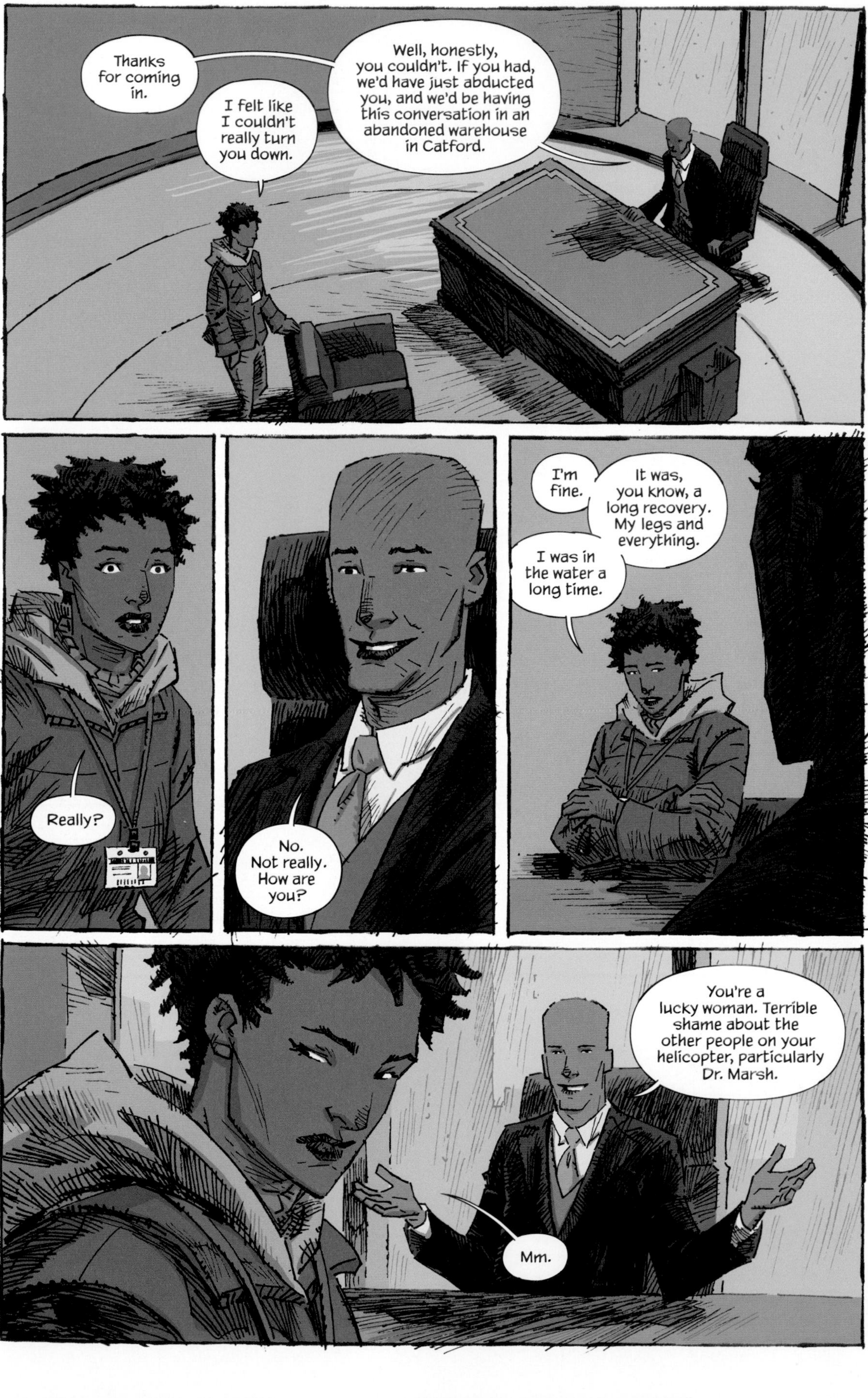
Thanks for coming in.
I felt like I couldn't really turn you down.
Well, honestly, you couldn't. If you had, we'd have just abducted you, and we'd be having this conversation in an abandoned warehouse in Catford.
Really?
No. Not really. How are you?
I'm fine.
It was, you know, a long recovery. My legs and everything.
I was in the water a long time.
You're a lucky woman. Terrible shame about the other people on your helicopter, particularly Dr. Marsh.
Mm.

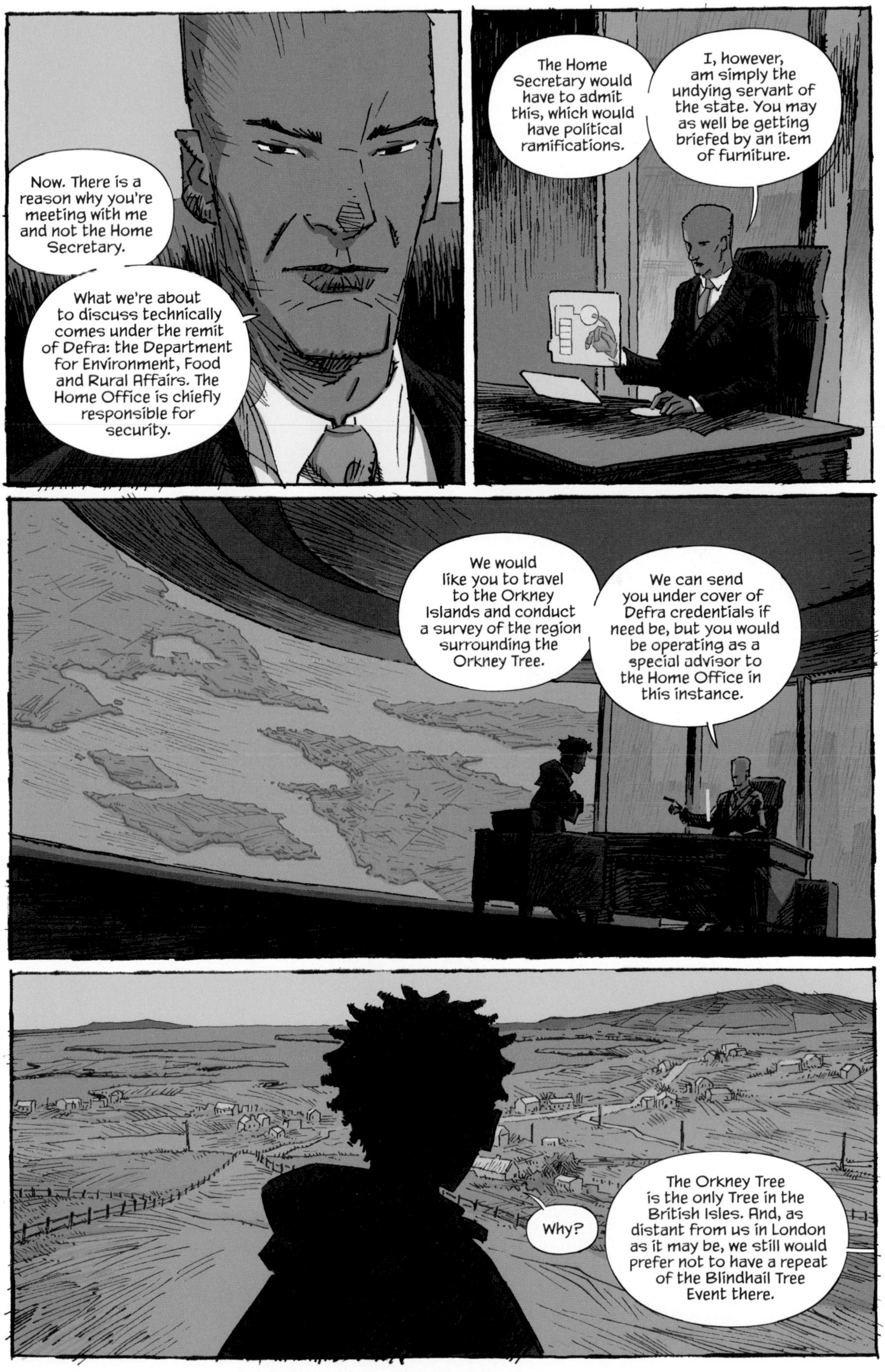
Now. There is a reason why you're meeting with me and not the Home Secretary.
What we're about to discuss technically comes under the remit of Defra: the Department for Environment, Food and Rural Affairs. The Home Office is chiefly responsible for security.
The Home Secretary would have to admit this, which would have political ramifications.
I, however, am simply the undying servant of the state. You may as well be getting briefed by an item of furniture.
We would like you to travel to the Orkney Islands and conduct a survey of the region surrounding the Orkney Tree.
We can send you under cover of Defra credentials if need be, but you would be operating as a special advisor to the Home Office in this instance.
Why?
The Orkney Tree is the only Tree in the British Isles. And, as distant from us in London as it may be, we still would prefer not to have a repeat of the Blindhail Tree Event there.

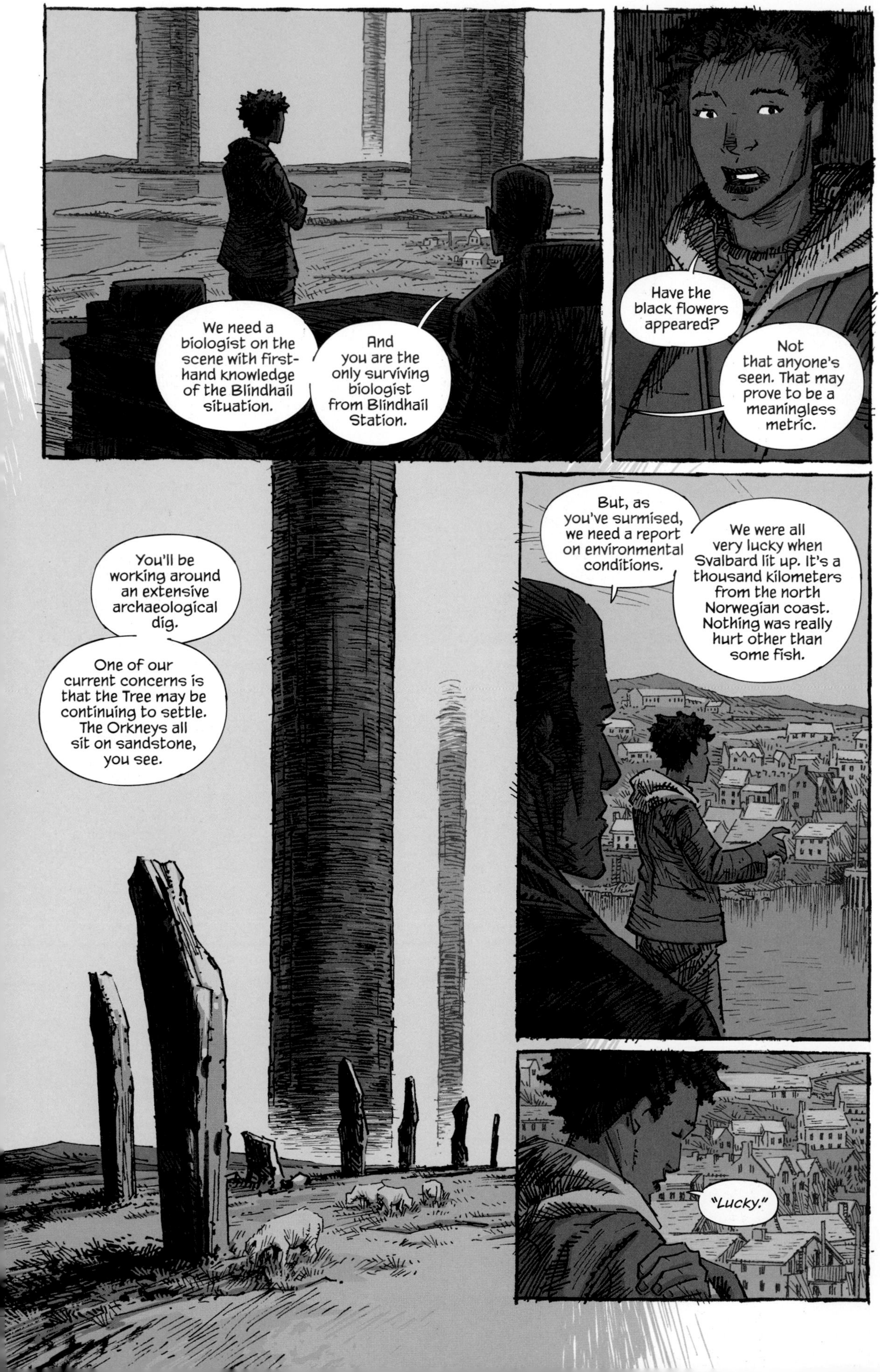
We need a biologist on the scene with first-hand knowledge of the Blindhail situation.
And you are the only surviving biologist from Blindhail Station.
Have the black flowers appeared?
Not that anyone's seen. That may prove to be a meaningless metric.
You'll be working around an extensive archaeological dig.
One of our current concerns is that the Tree may be continuing to settle. The Orkneys all sit on sandstone, you see.
But, as you've surmised, we need a report on environmental conditions.
We were all very lucky when Svalbard lit up. It's a thousand kilometers from the north Norwegian coast. Nothing was really hurt other than some fish.
"Lucky."

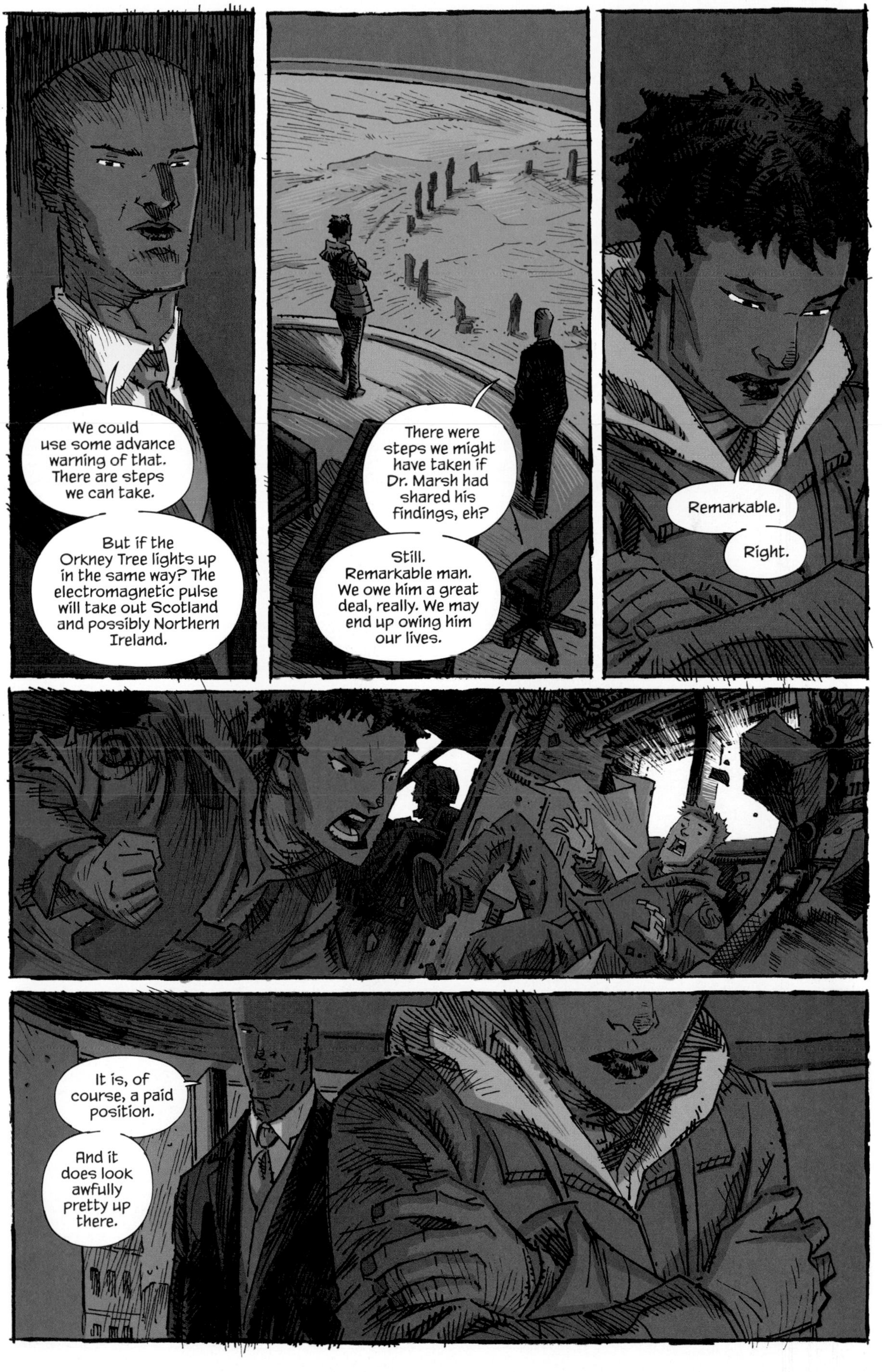
We could use some advance warning of that. There are steps we can take.
But if the Orkney Tree lights up in the same way? The electromagnetic pulse will take out Scotland and possibly Northern Ireland.
There were steps we might have taken if Dr. Marsh had shared his findings, eh?
Still. Remarkable man. We owe him a great deal, really. We may end up owing him our lives.
Remarkable.
Right.
It is, of course, a paid position.
And it does look awfully pretty up there.

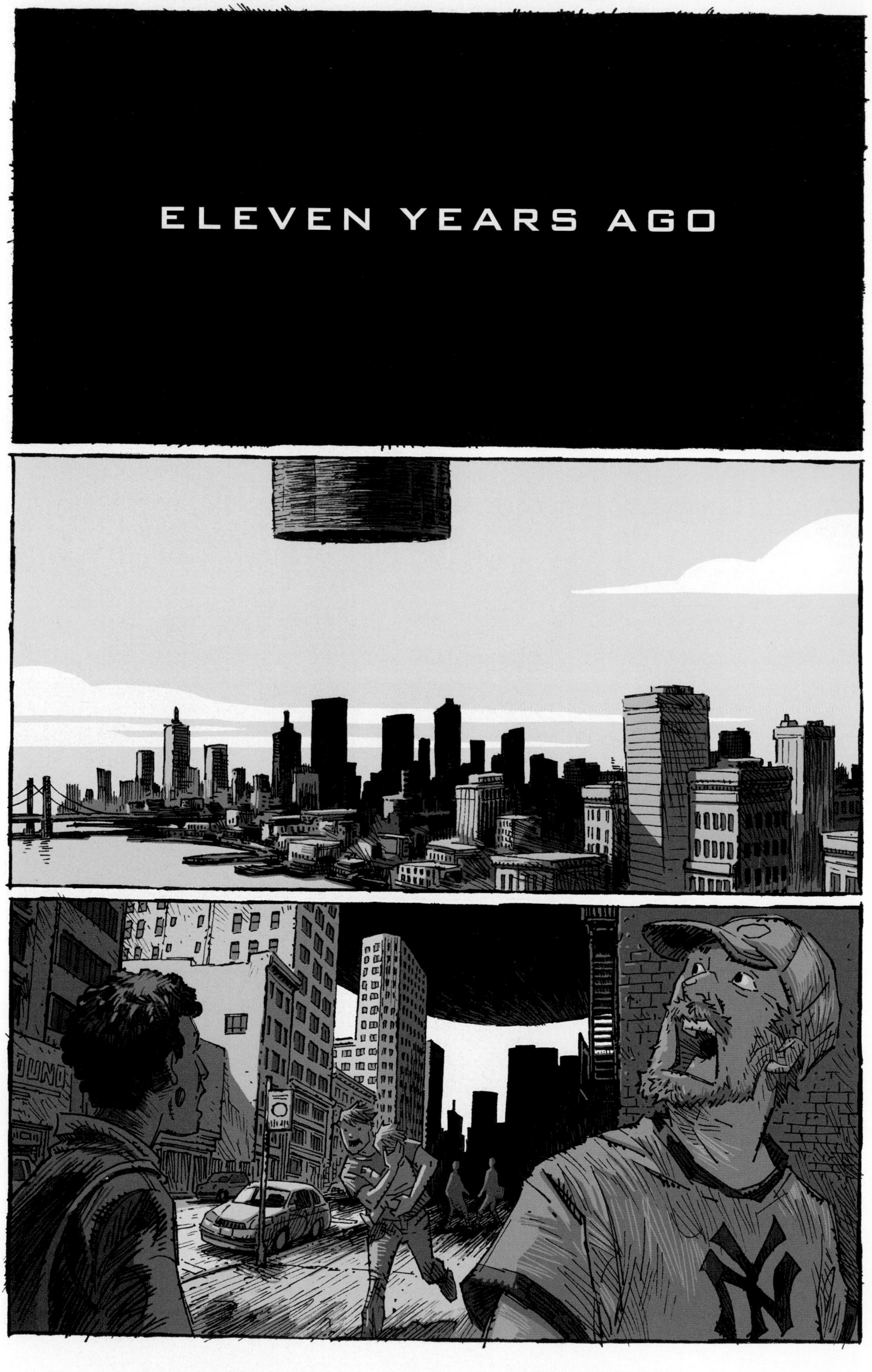
ELEVEN YEARS AGO

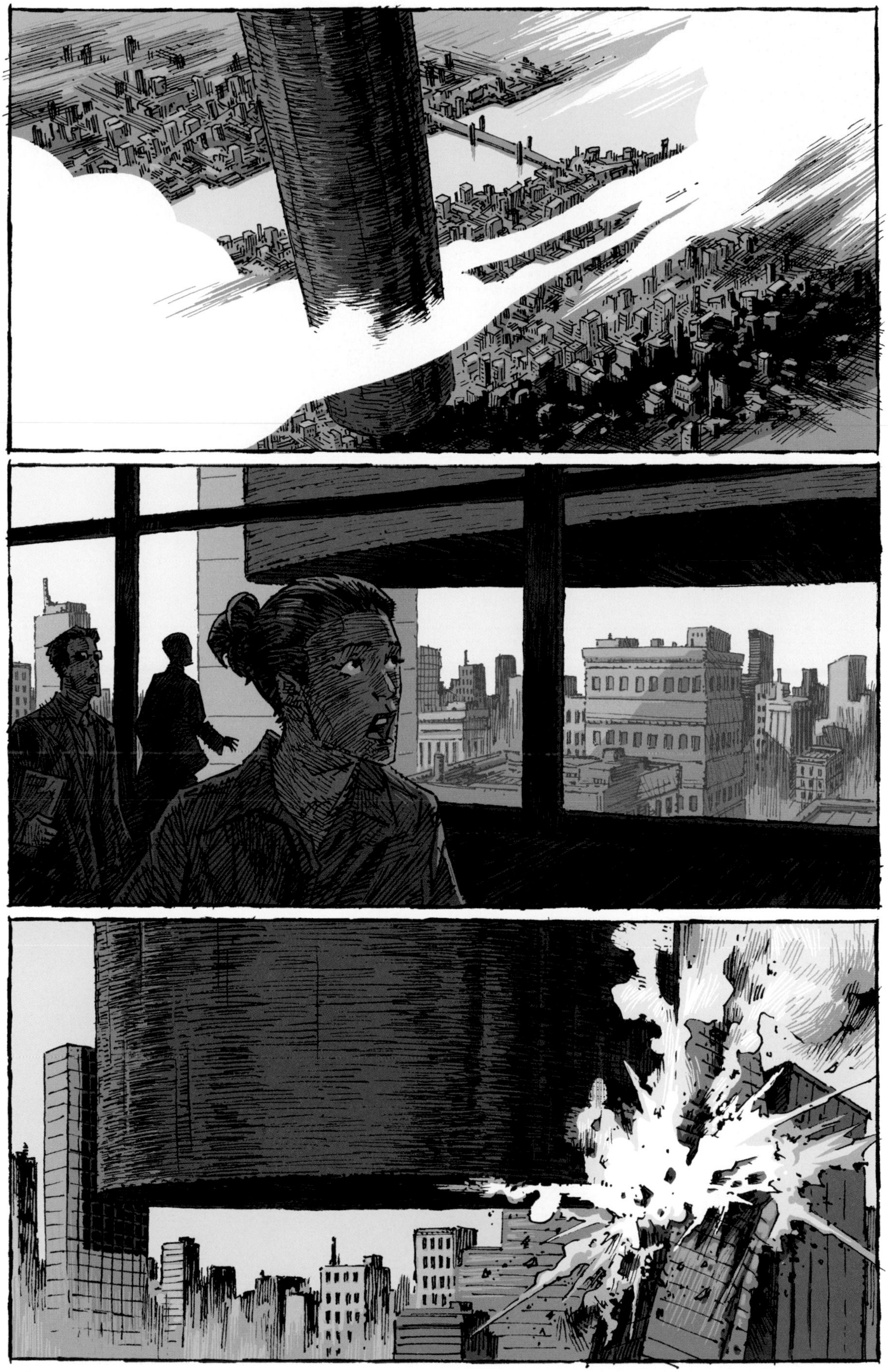

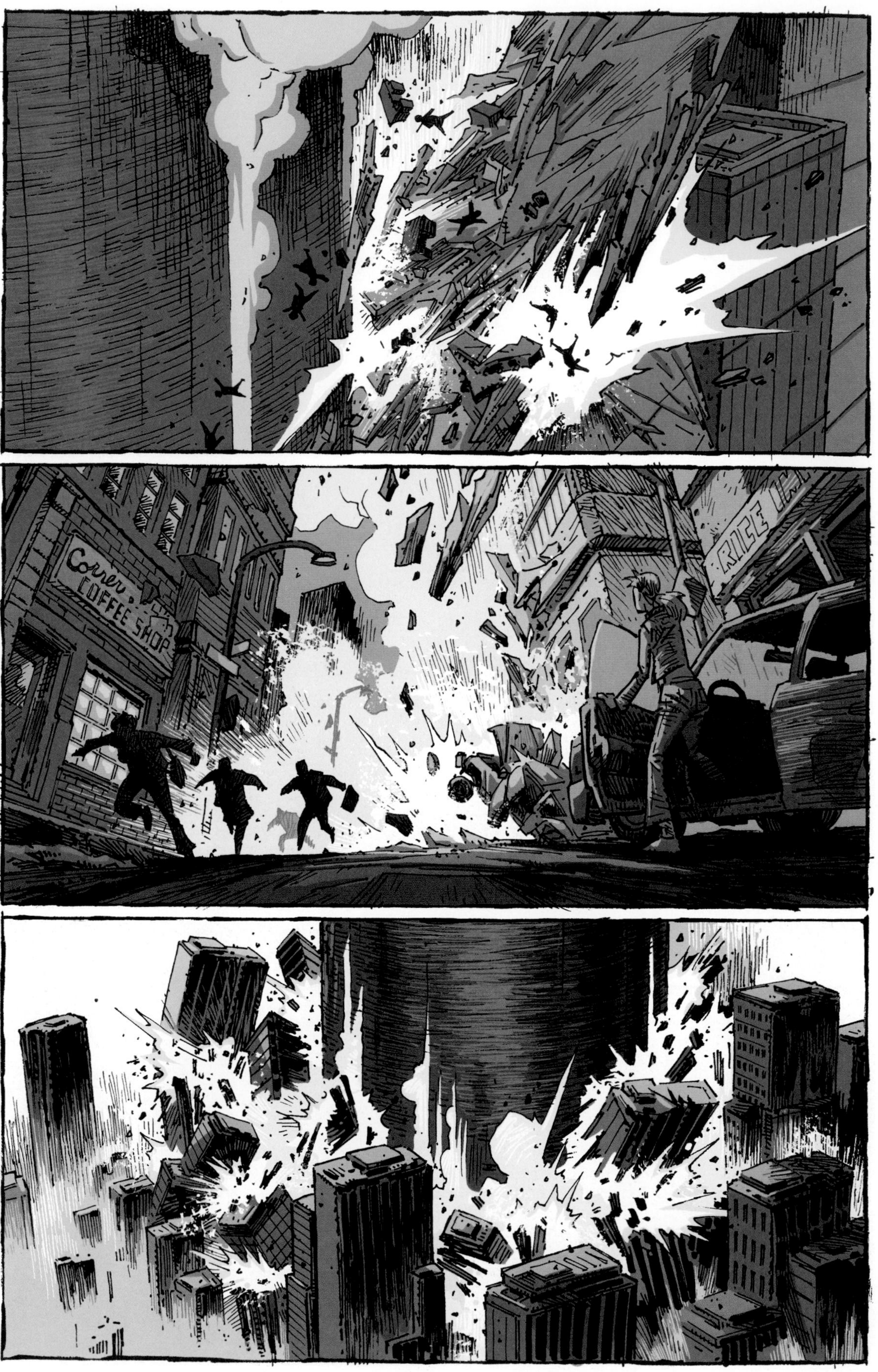
Corner
COFFEE SHOP

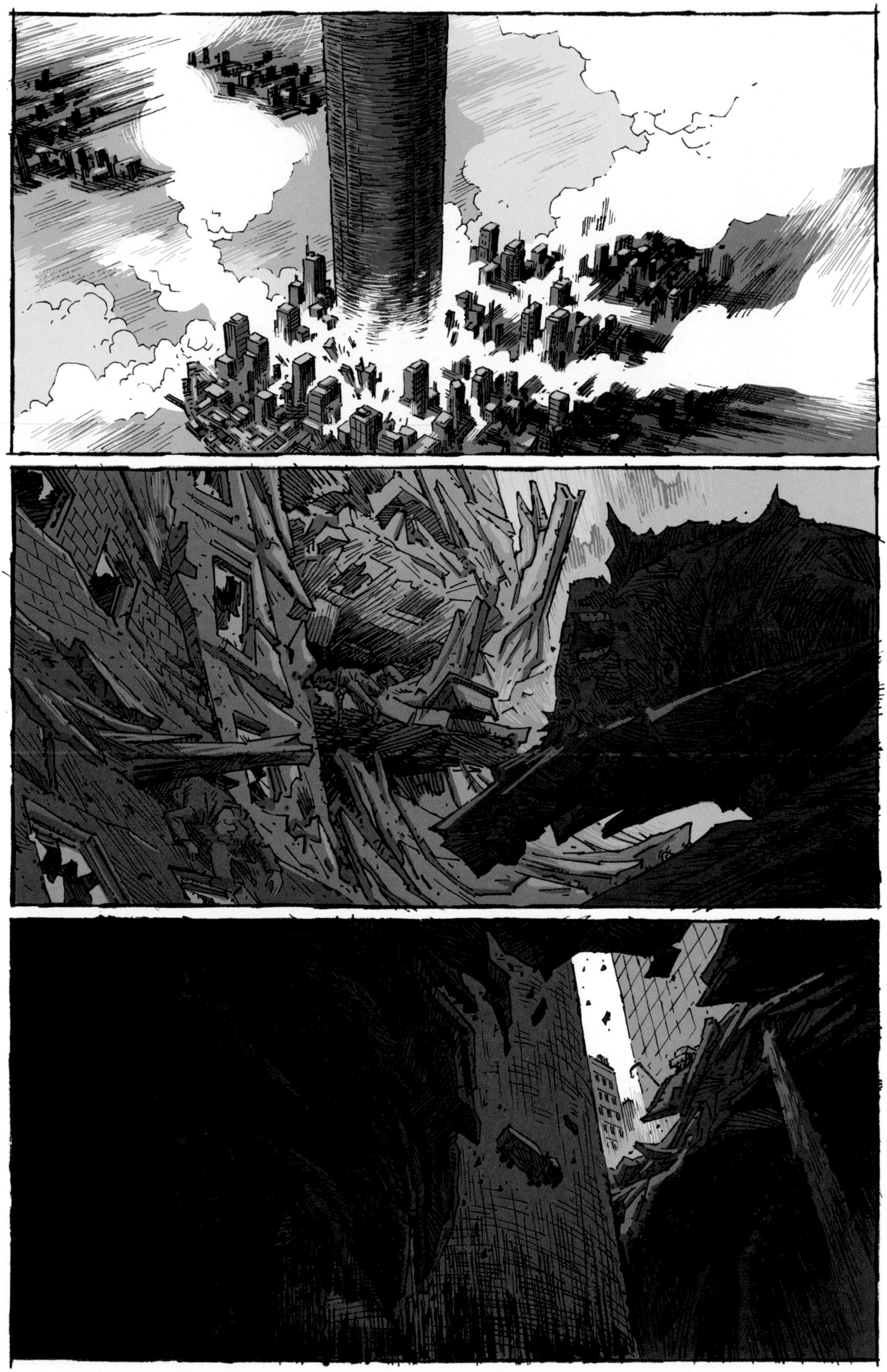

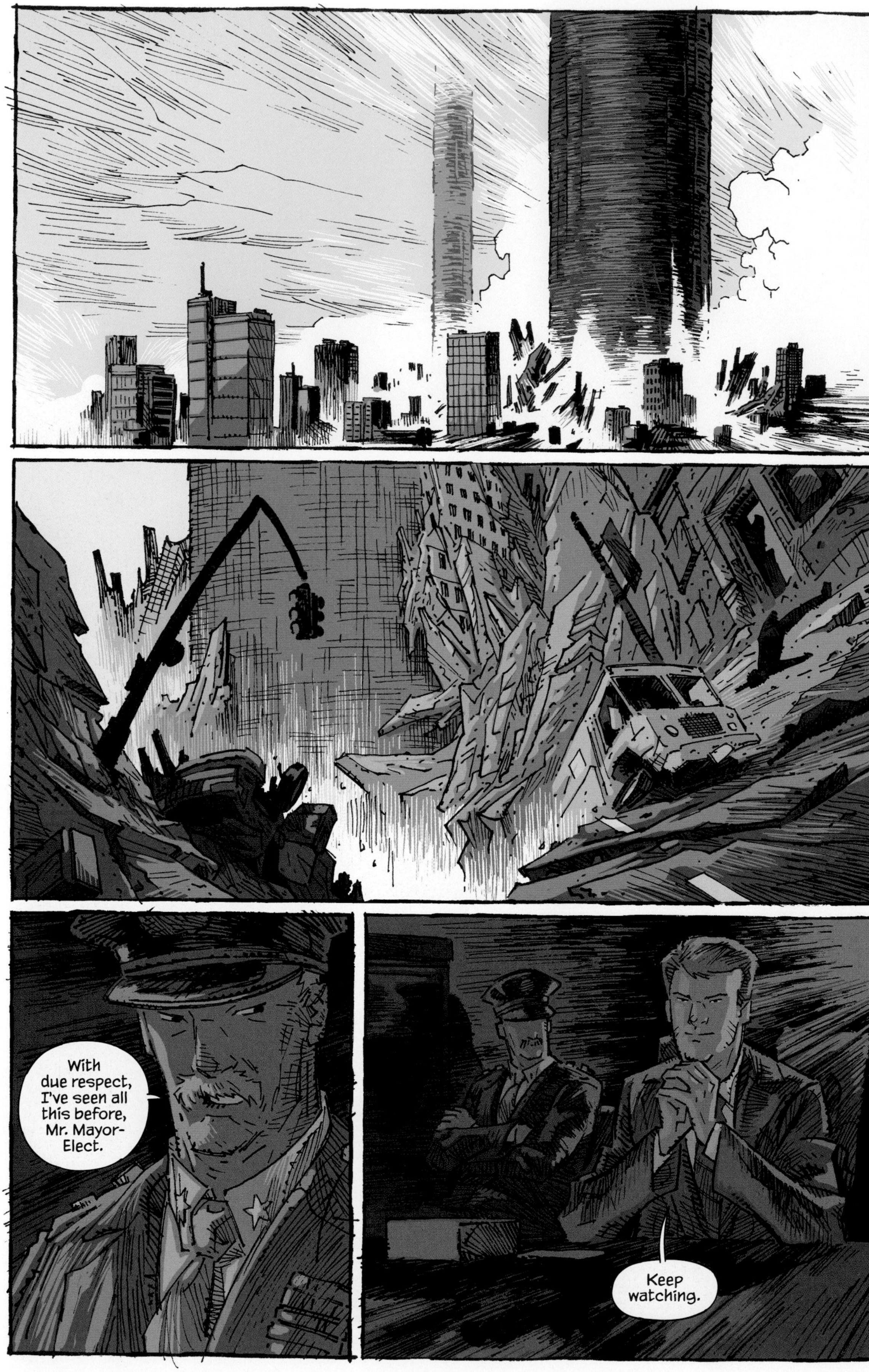
With due respect, I've seen all this before, Mr. Mayor-Elect.
Keep watching.

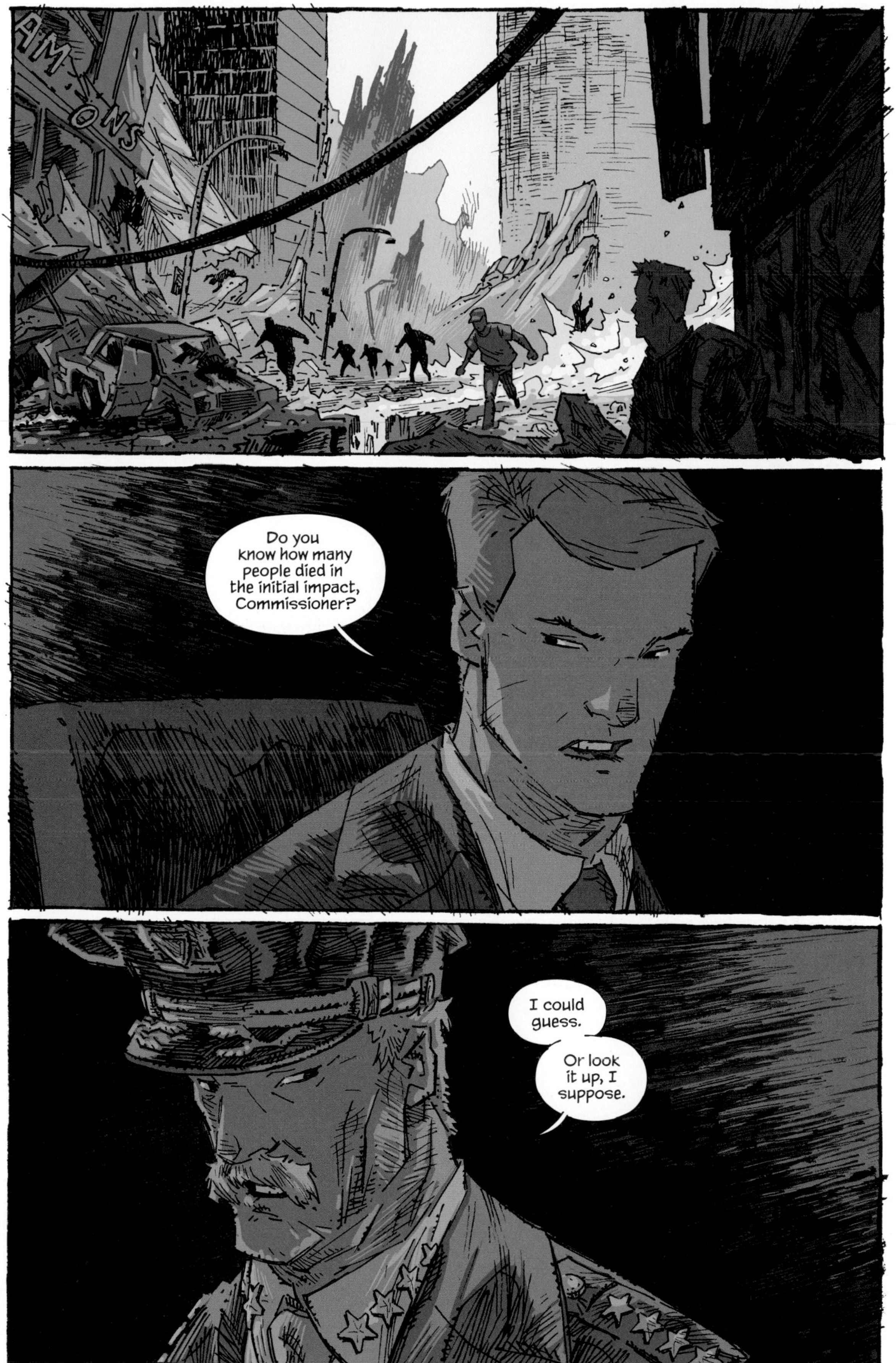
Do you know how many people died in the initial impact, Commissioner?
I could guess.
Or look it up, I suppose.

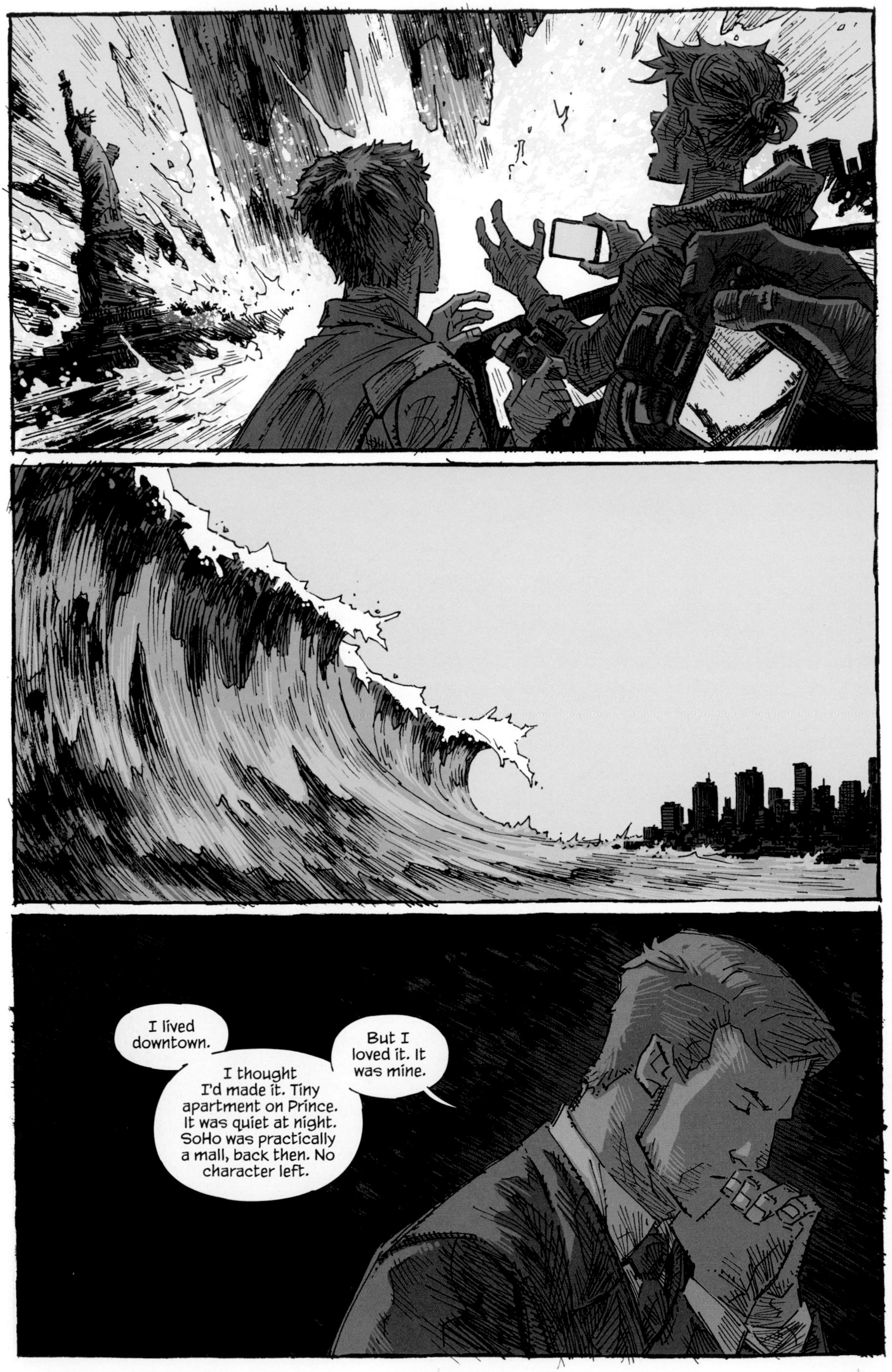
I lived downtown.
I thought I'd made it. Tiny apartment on Prince. It was quiet at night. SoHo was practically a mall, back then. No character left.
But I loved it. It was mine.

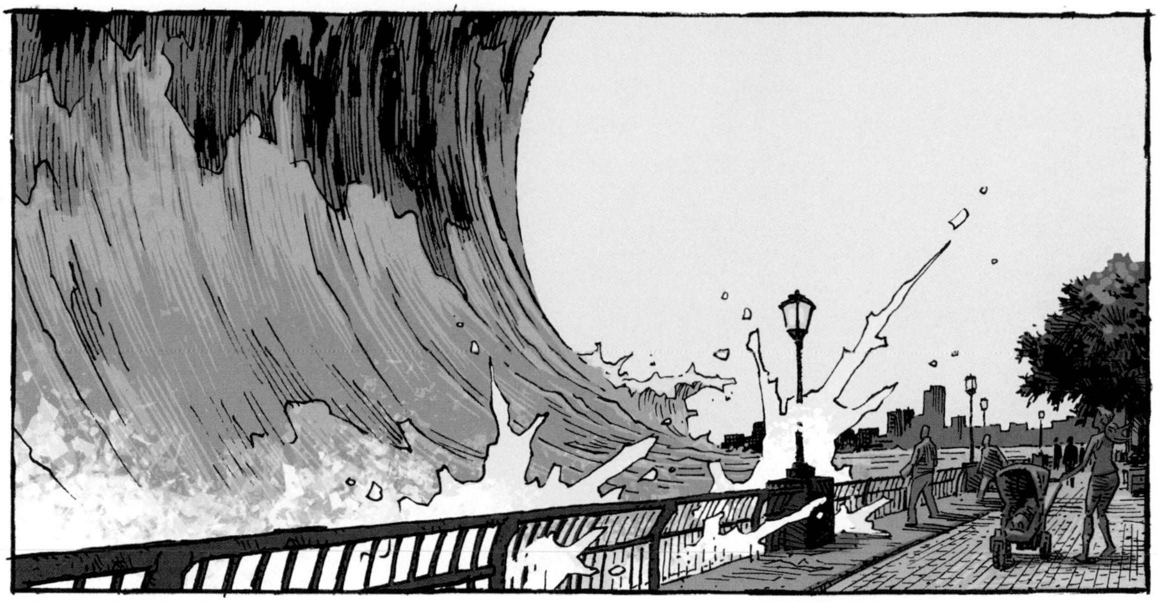

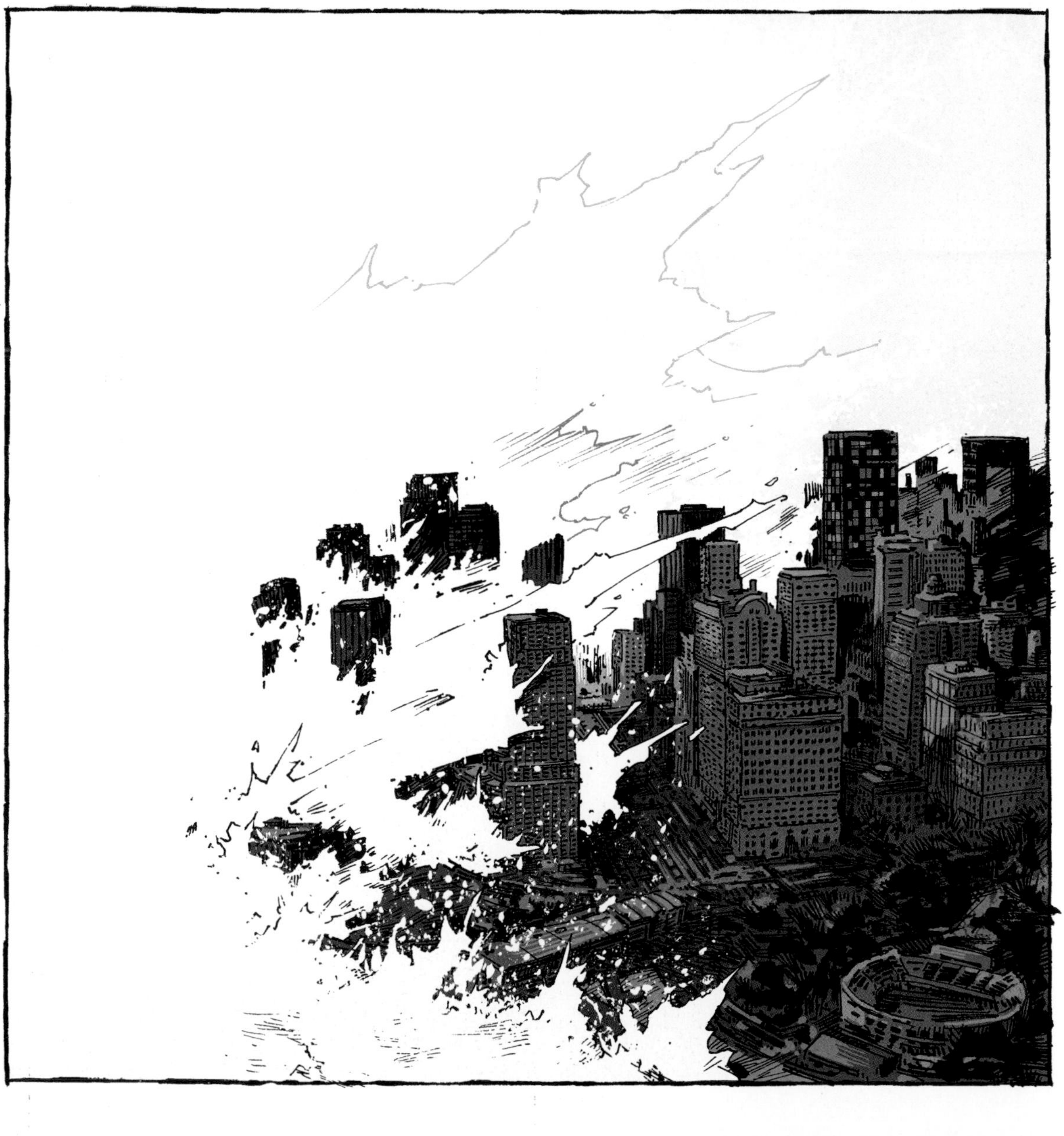

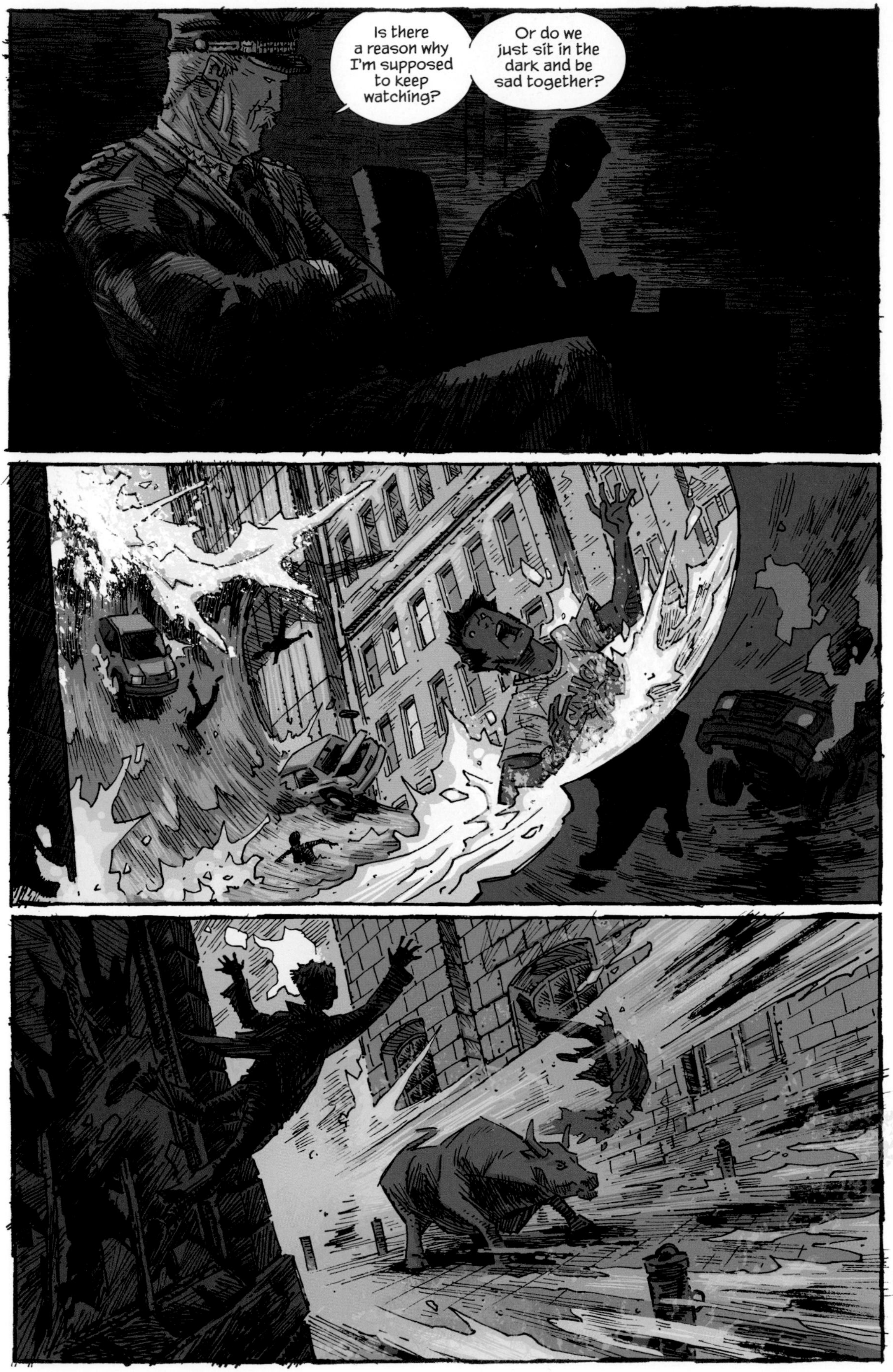
Is there a reason why I'm supposed to keep watching?
Or do we just sit in the dark and be sad together?

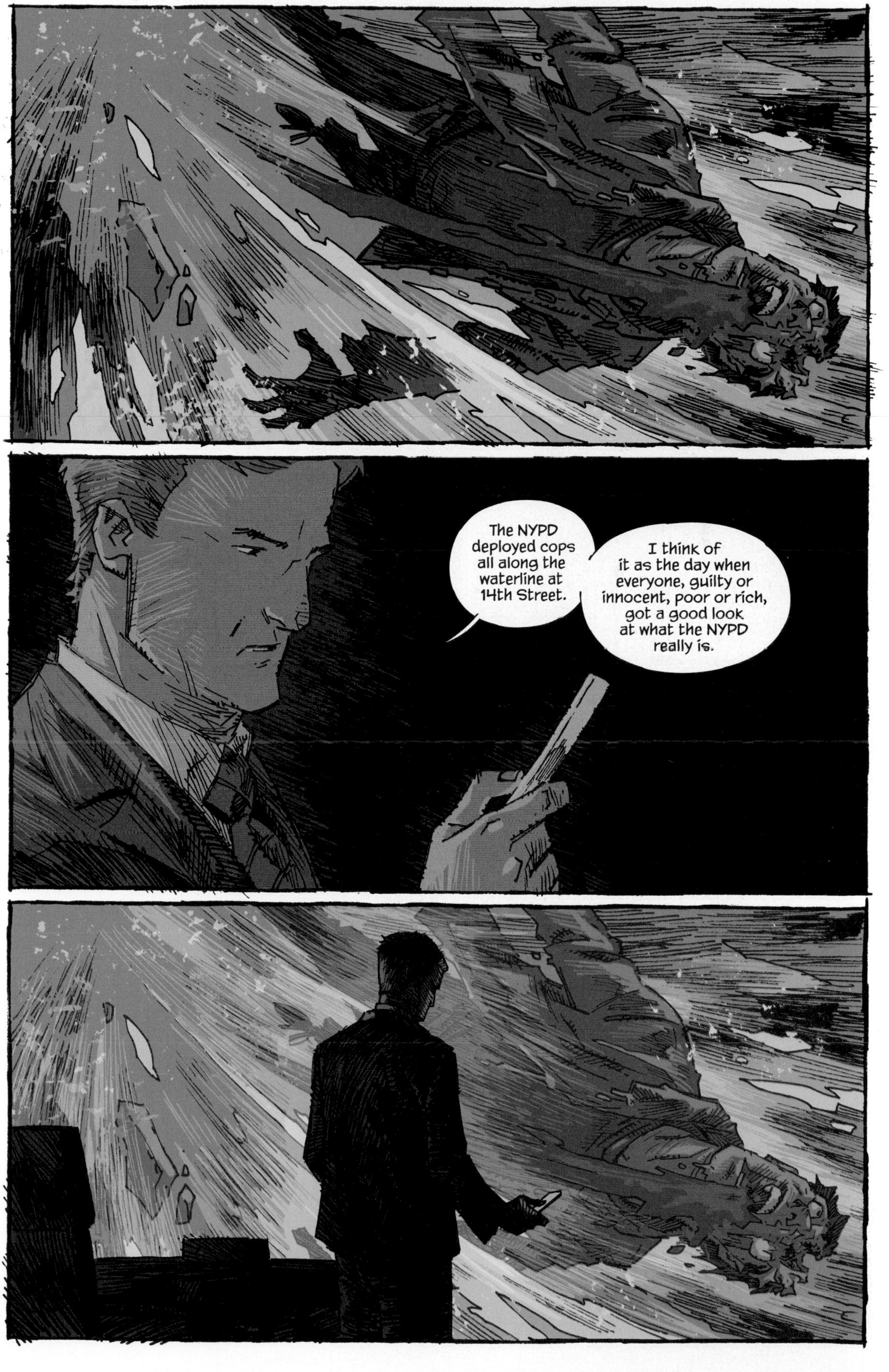
The NYPD deployed cops all along the waterline at 14th Street.
I think of it as the day when everyone, guilty or innocent, poor or rich, got a good look at what the NYPD really is.

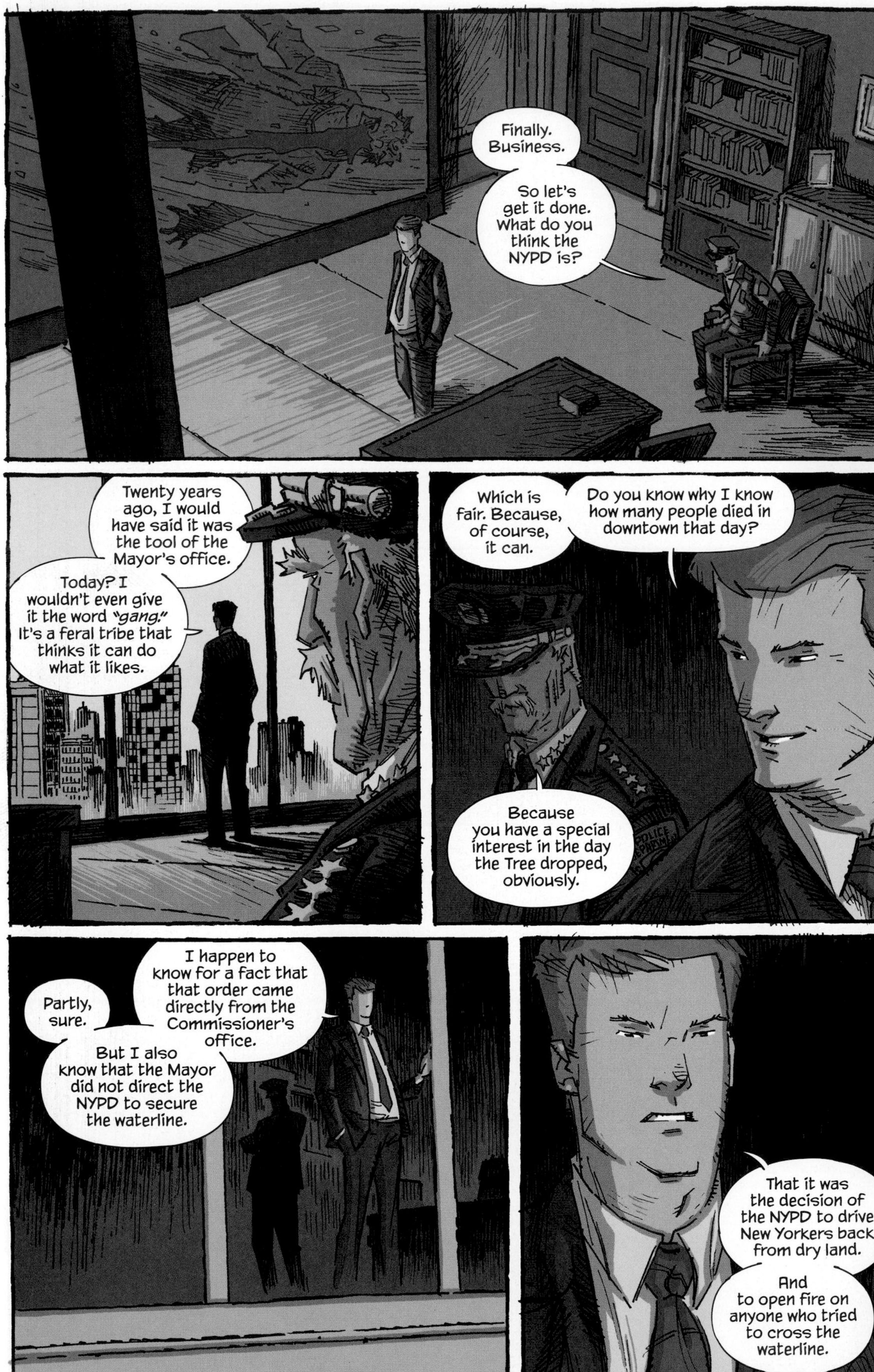
Finally. Business.
So let's get it done. What do you think the NYPD is?
Twenty years ago, I would have said it was the tool of the Mayor's office.
Today? I wouldn't even give it the word "gang." It's a feral tribe that thinks it can do what it likes.
Which is fair. Because, of course, it can.
Do you know why I know how many people died in downtown that day?
Because you have a special interest in the day the Tree dropped, obviously.
Partly, sure.
I happen to know for a fact that that order came directly from the Commissioner's office.
But I also know that the Mayor did not direct the NYPD to secure the waterline.
That it was the decision of the NYPD to drive New Yorkers back from dry land.
And to open fire on anyone who tried to cross the waterline.

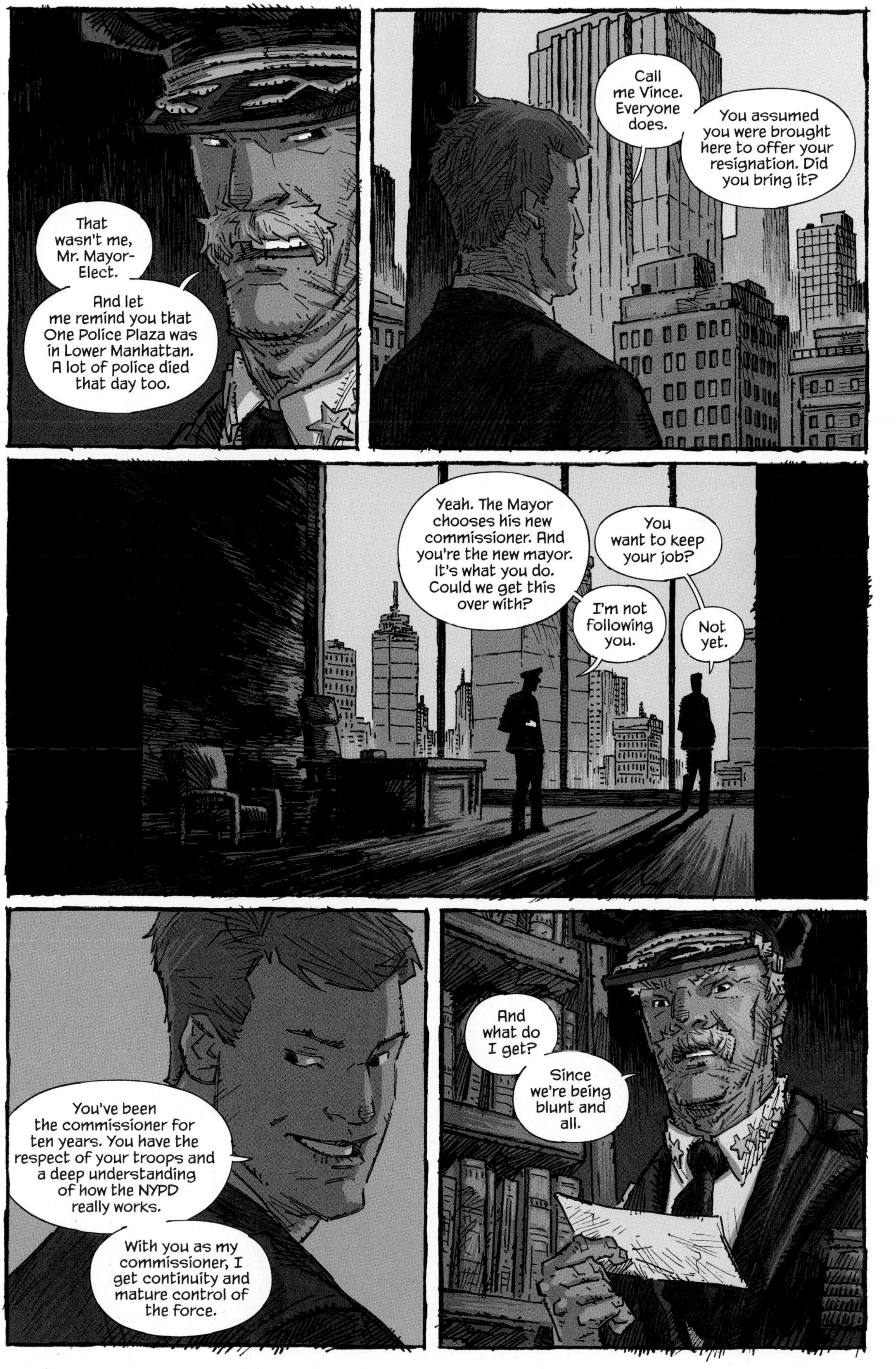
That wasn't me, Mr. Mayor-Elect.
And let me remind you that One Police Plaza was in Lower Manhattan. A lot of police died that day too.
Call me Vince. Everyone does.
You assumed you were brought here to offer your resignation. Did you bring it?
Yeah. The Mayor chooses his new commissioner. And you're the new mayor. It's what you do. Could we get this over with?
You want to keep your job?
I'm not following you.
Not yet.
You've been the commissioner for ten years. You have the respect of your troops and a deep understanding of how the NYPD really works.
With you as my commissioner, I get continuity and mature control of the force.
And what do I get?
Since we're being blunt and all.

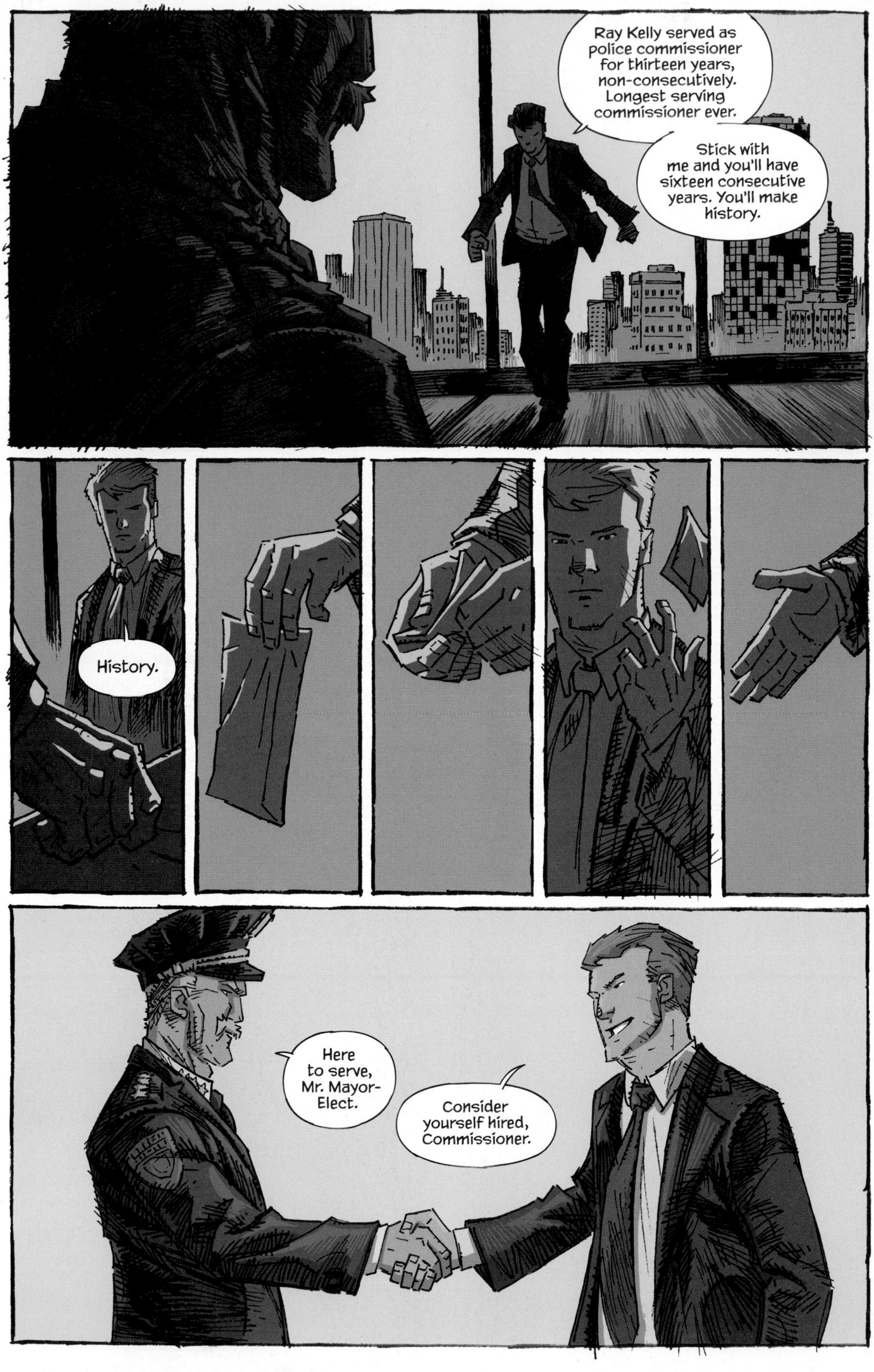
Ray Kelly served as police commissioner for thirteen years, non-consecutively. Longest serving commissioner ever.
Stick with me and you'll have sixteen consecutive years. You'll make history.
History.
Here to serve, Mr. Mayor-Elect.
Consider yourself hired, Commissioner.

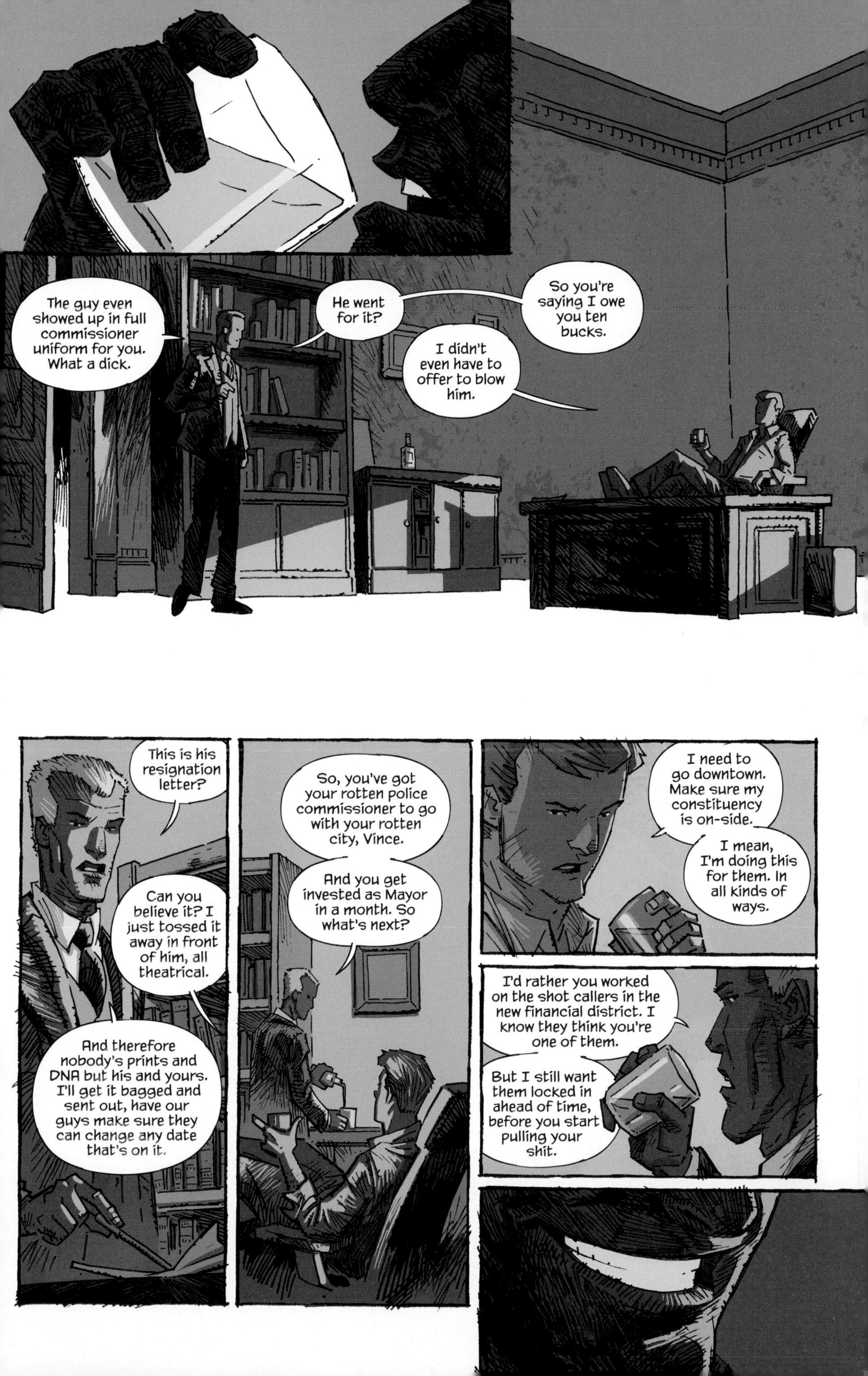
The guy even showed up in full commissioner uniform for you. What a dick.
He went for it?
So you're saying I owe you ten bucks.
I didn't even have to offer to blow him.
This is his resignation letter?
Can you believe it? I just tossed it away in front of him, all theatrical.
And therefore nobody's prints and DNA but his and yours. I'll get it bagged and sent out, have our guys make sure they can change any date that's on it.
So, you've got your rotten police commissioner to go with your rotten city, Vince.
And you get invested as Mayor in a month. So what's next?
I need to go downtown. Make sure my constituency is on-side.
I mean, I'm doing this for them. In all kinds of ways.
I'd rather you worked on the shot callers in the new financial district. I know they think you're one of them.
But I still want them locked in ahead of time, before you start pulling your shit.

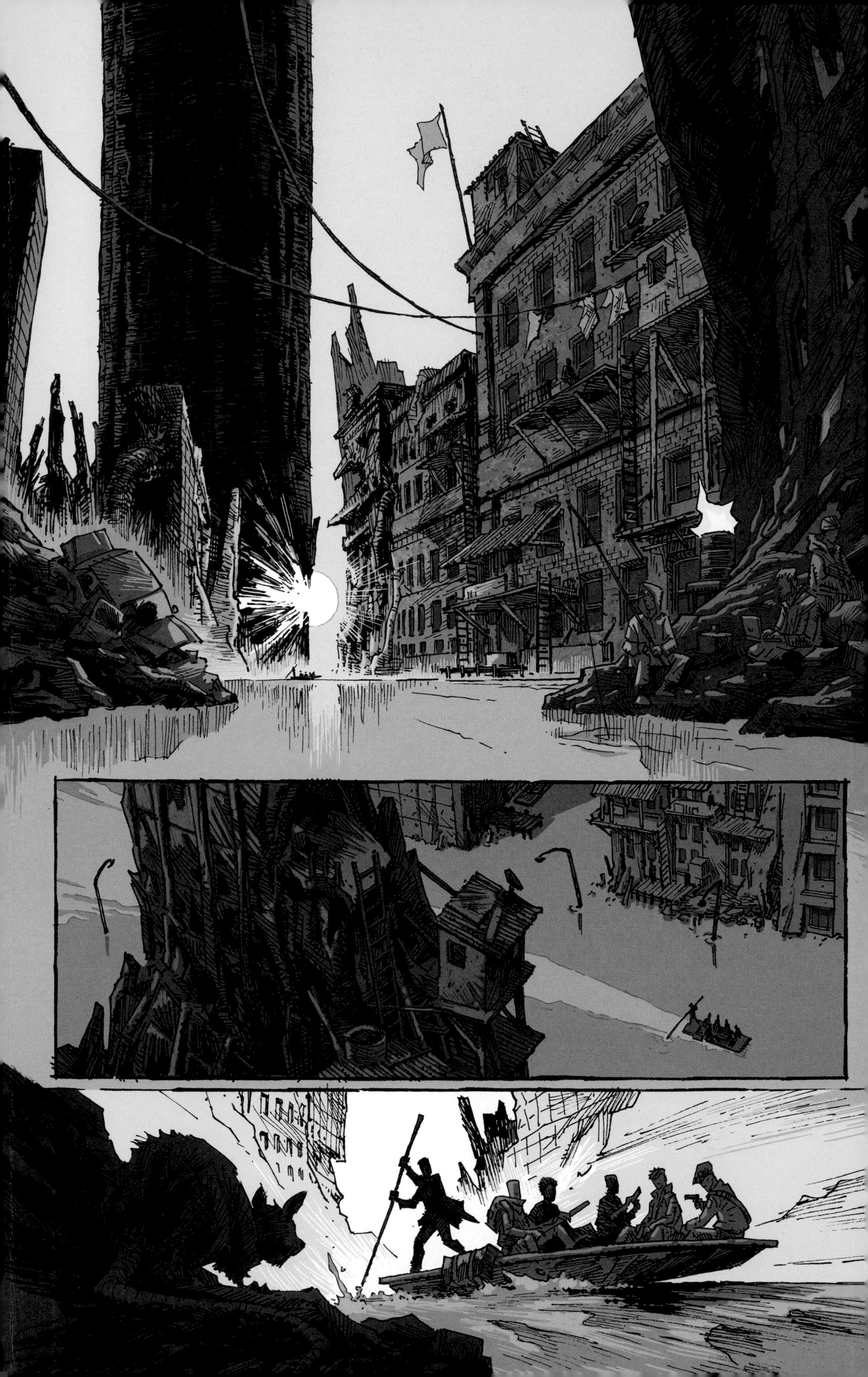

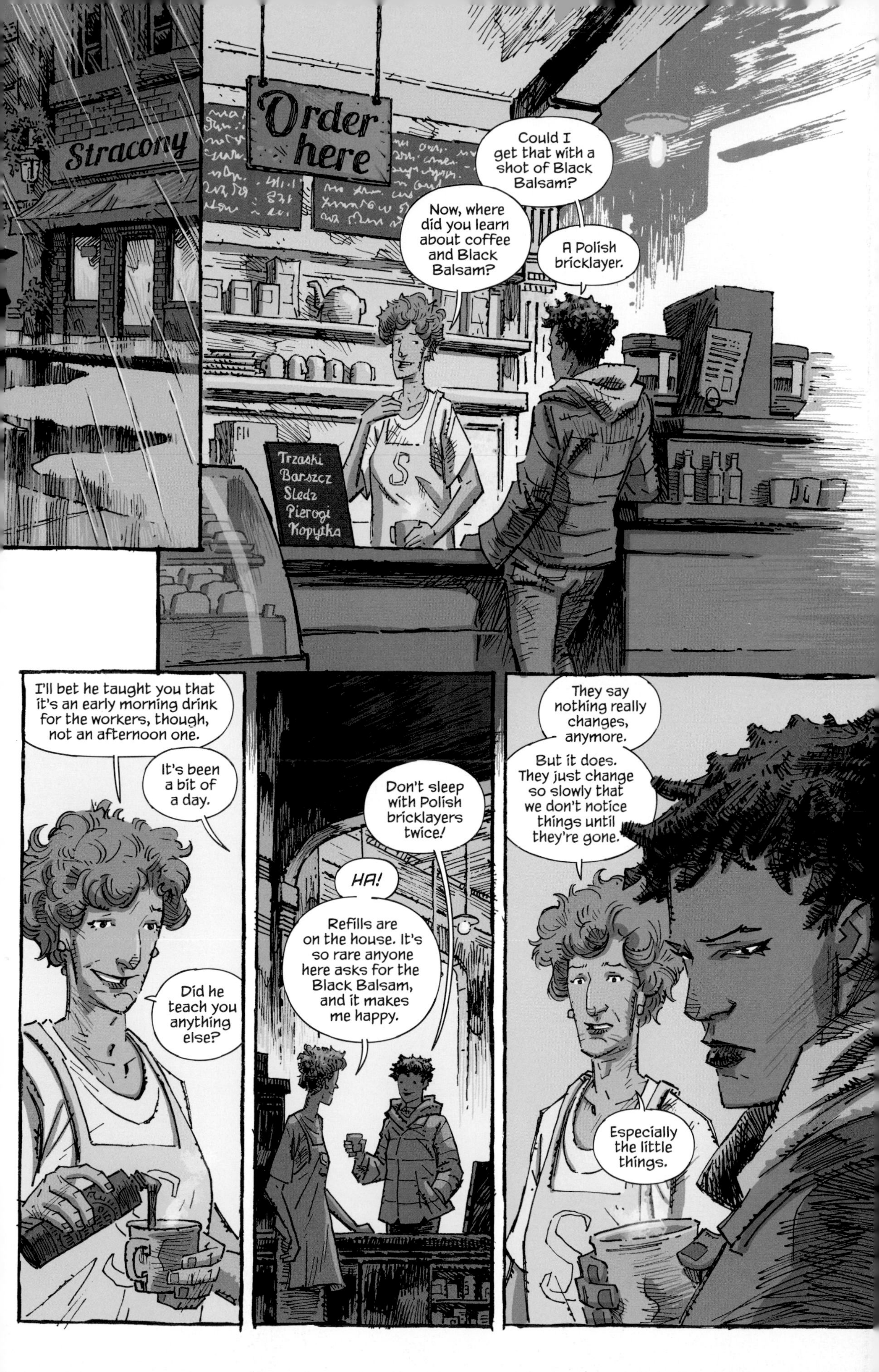
Stracony
Order here
Trzaski
Barszcz
Sledz
Pierogi
Kopytka
Could I get that with a shot of Black Balsam?
Now, where did you learn about coffee and Black Balsam?
A Polish bricklayer.
I'll bet he taught you that it's an early morning drink for the workers, though, not an afternoon one.
It's been a bit of a day.
Did he teach you anything else?
Don't sleep with Polish bricklayers twice!
HA!
Refills are on the house. It's so rare anyone here asks for the Black Balsam, and it makes me happy.
They say nothing really changes, anymore.
But it does. They just change so slowly that we don't notice things until they're gone.
Especially the little things.

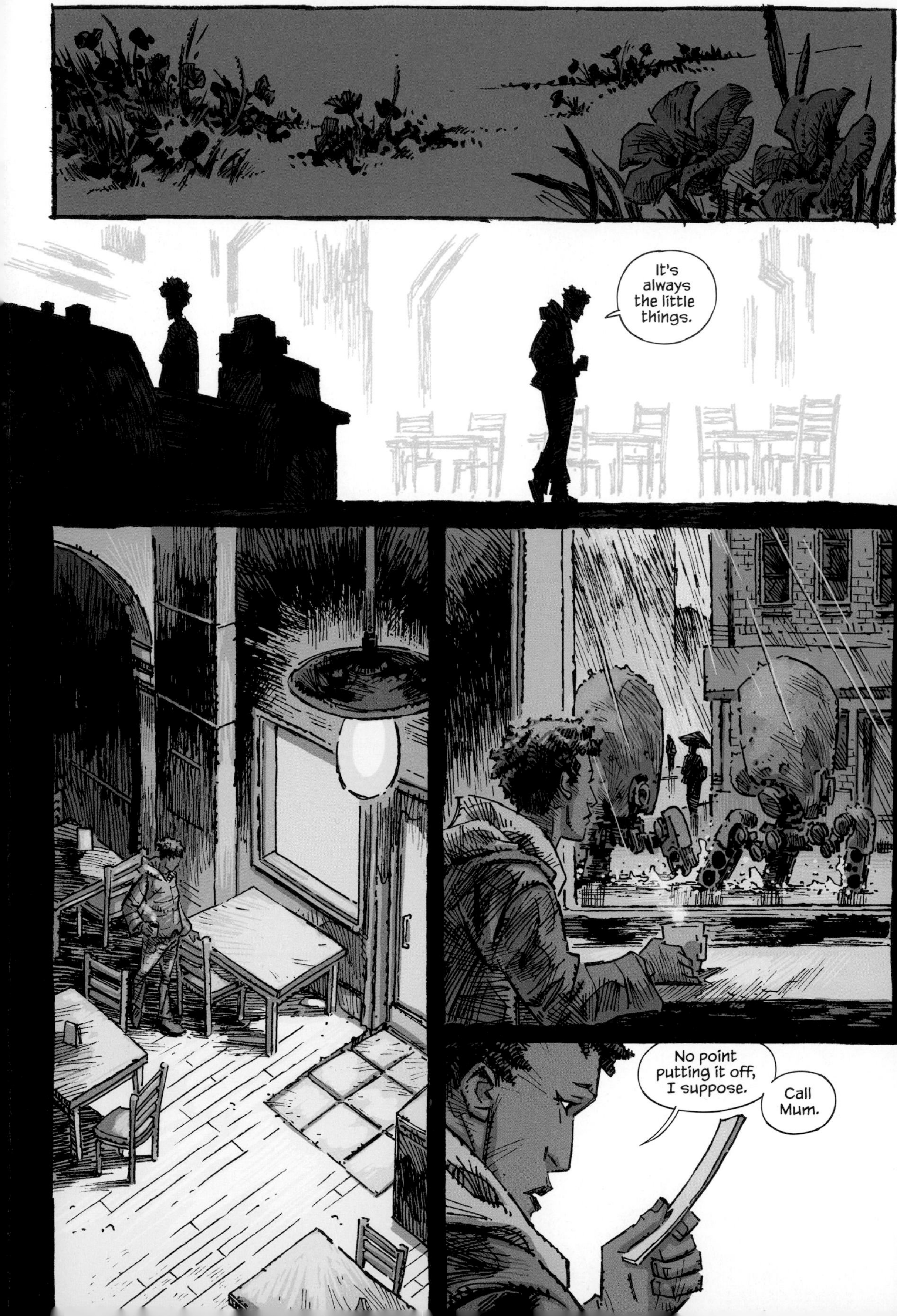
It's always the little things.
No point putting it off, I suppose.
Call Mum.

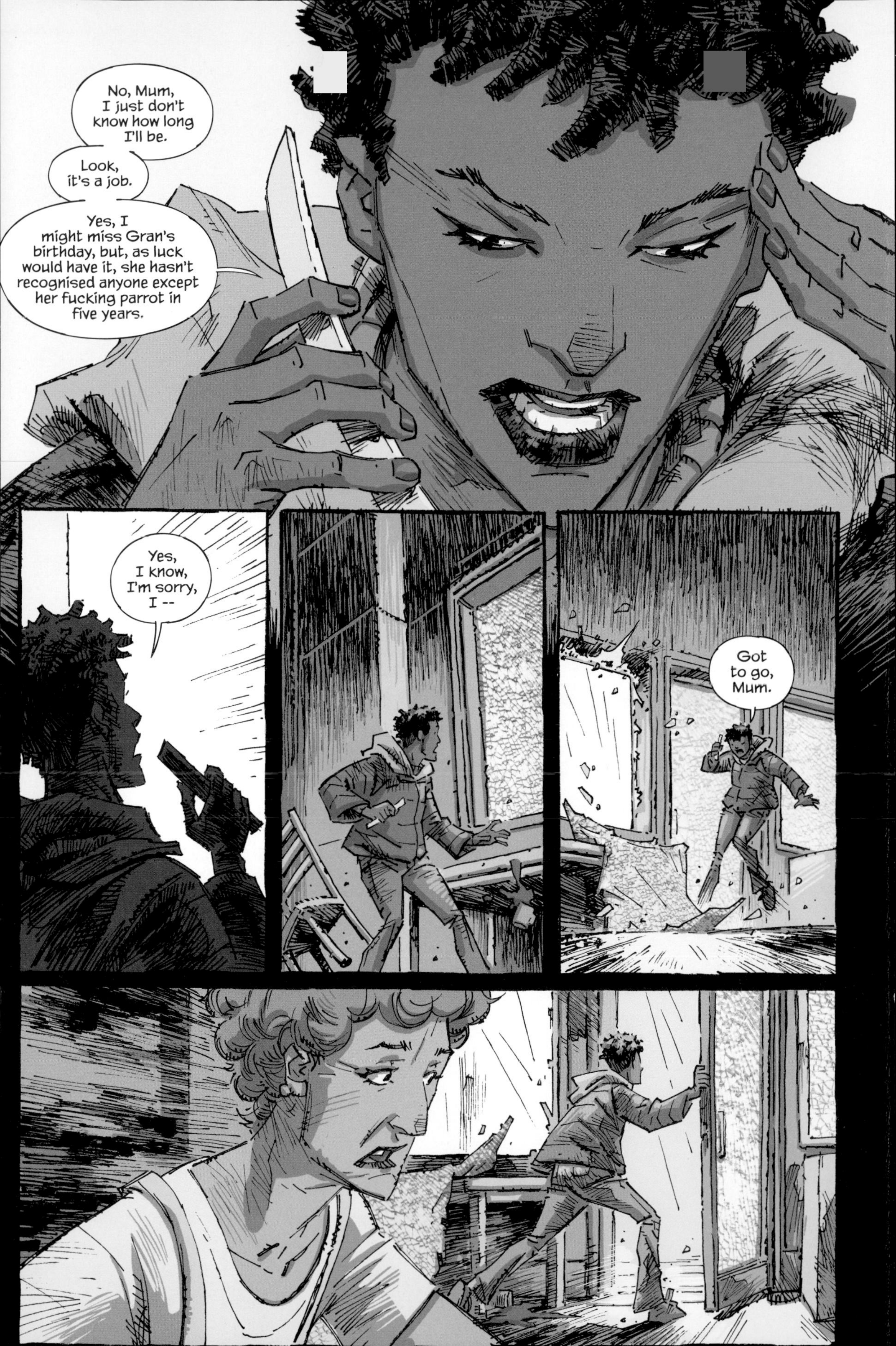
No, Mum, I just don't know how long I'll be.
Look, it's a job.
Yes, I might miss Gran's birthday, but, as luck would have it, she hasn't recognised anyone except her fucking parrot in five years.
Yes, I know, I'm sorry, I --
Got to go, Mum.

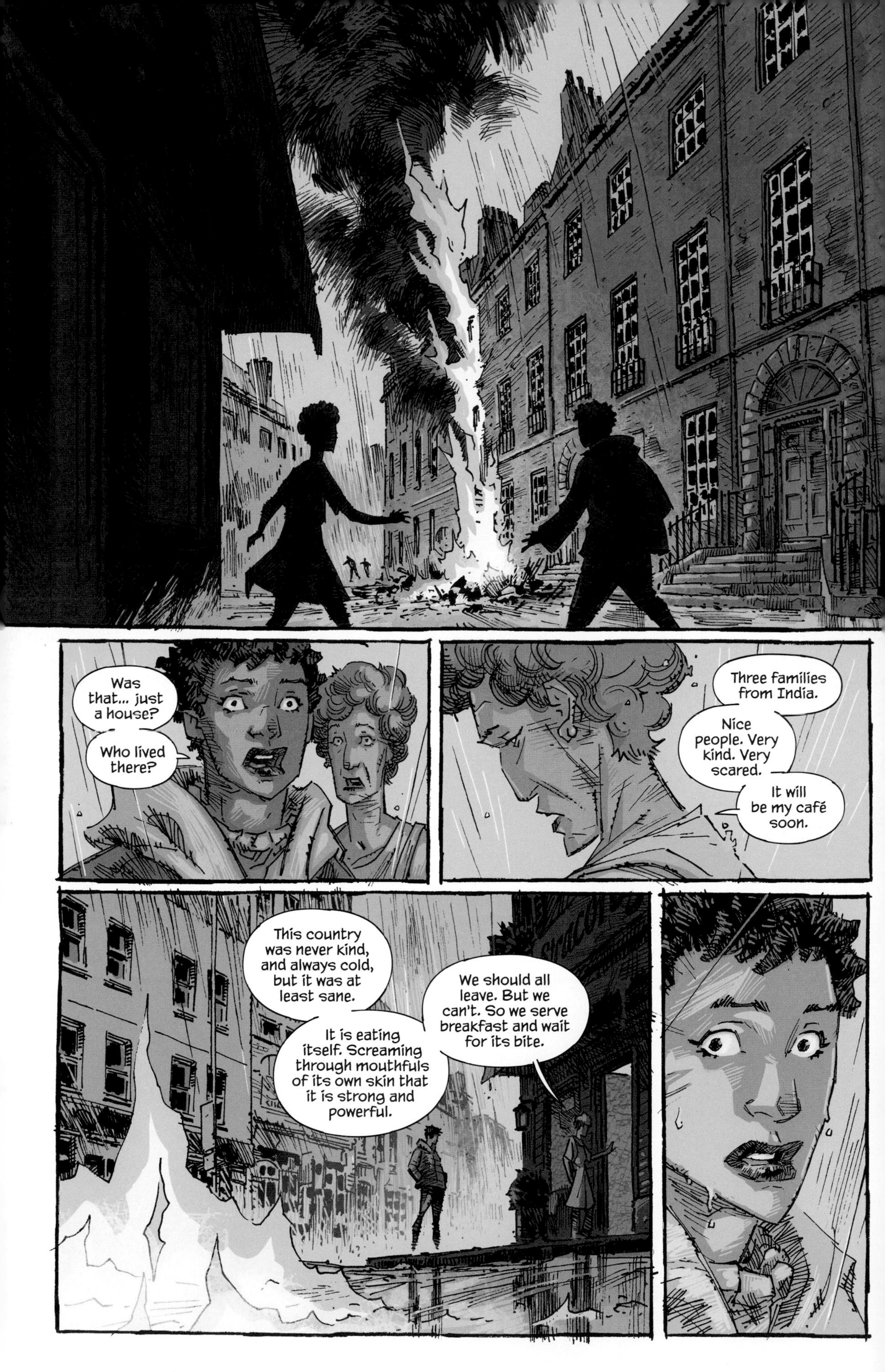
Was that... just a house?
Who lived there?
Three families from India.
Nice people. Very kind. Very scared.
It will be my café soon.
This country was never kind, and always cold, but it was at least sane.
It is eating itself. Screaming through mouthfuls of its own skin that it is strong and powerful.
We should all leave. But we can't. So we serve breakfast and wait for its bite.

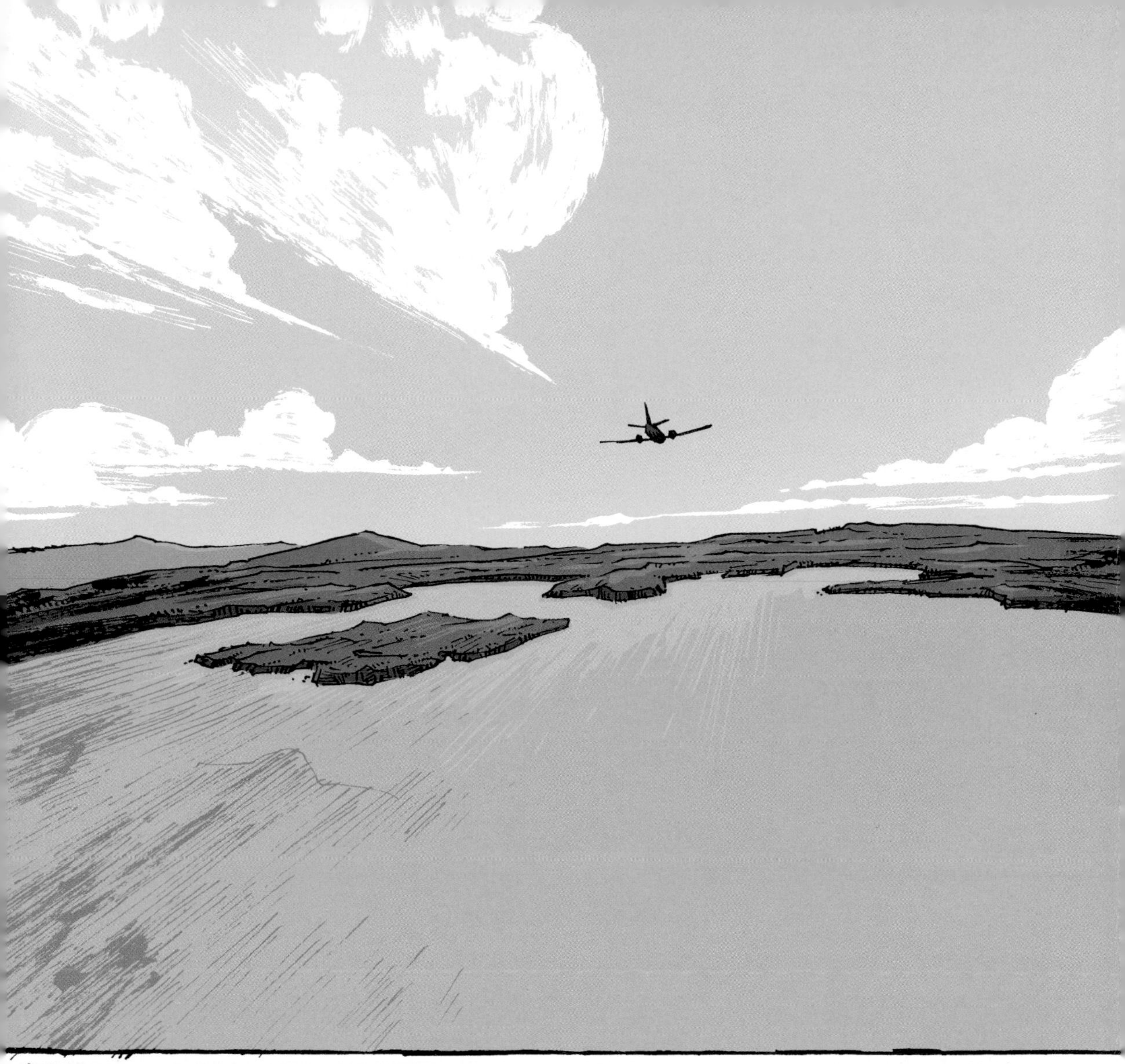

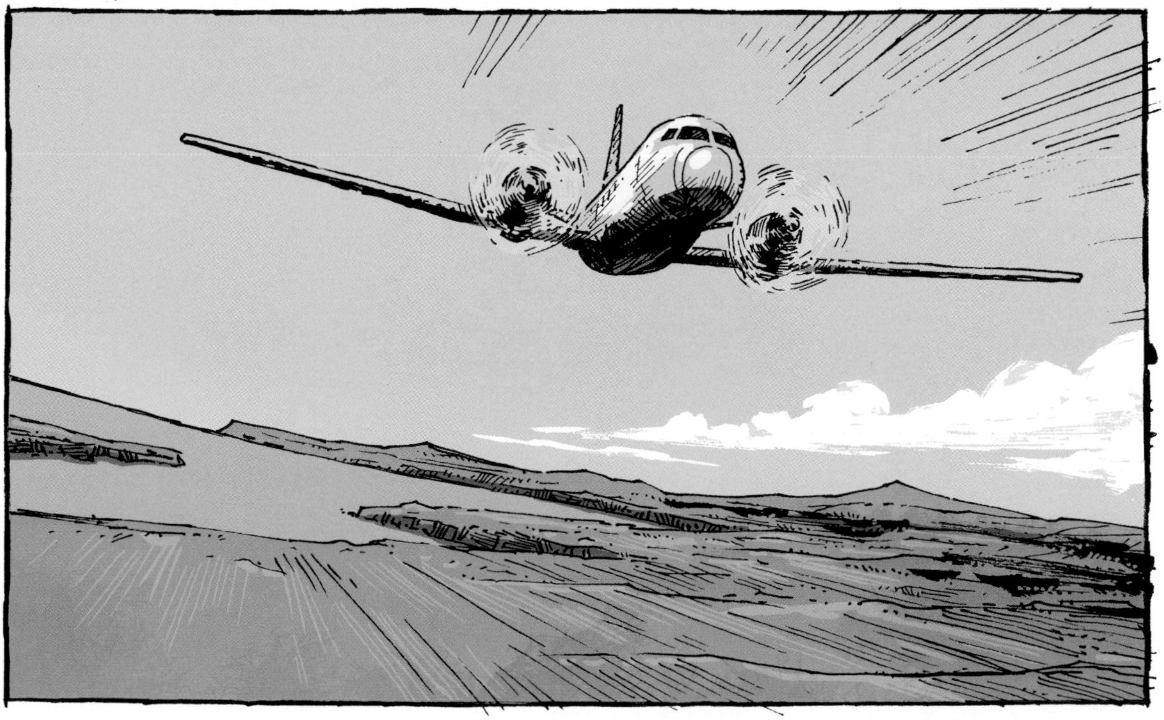

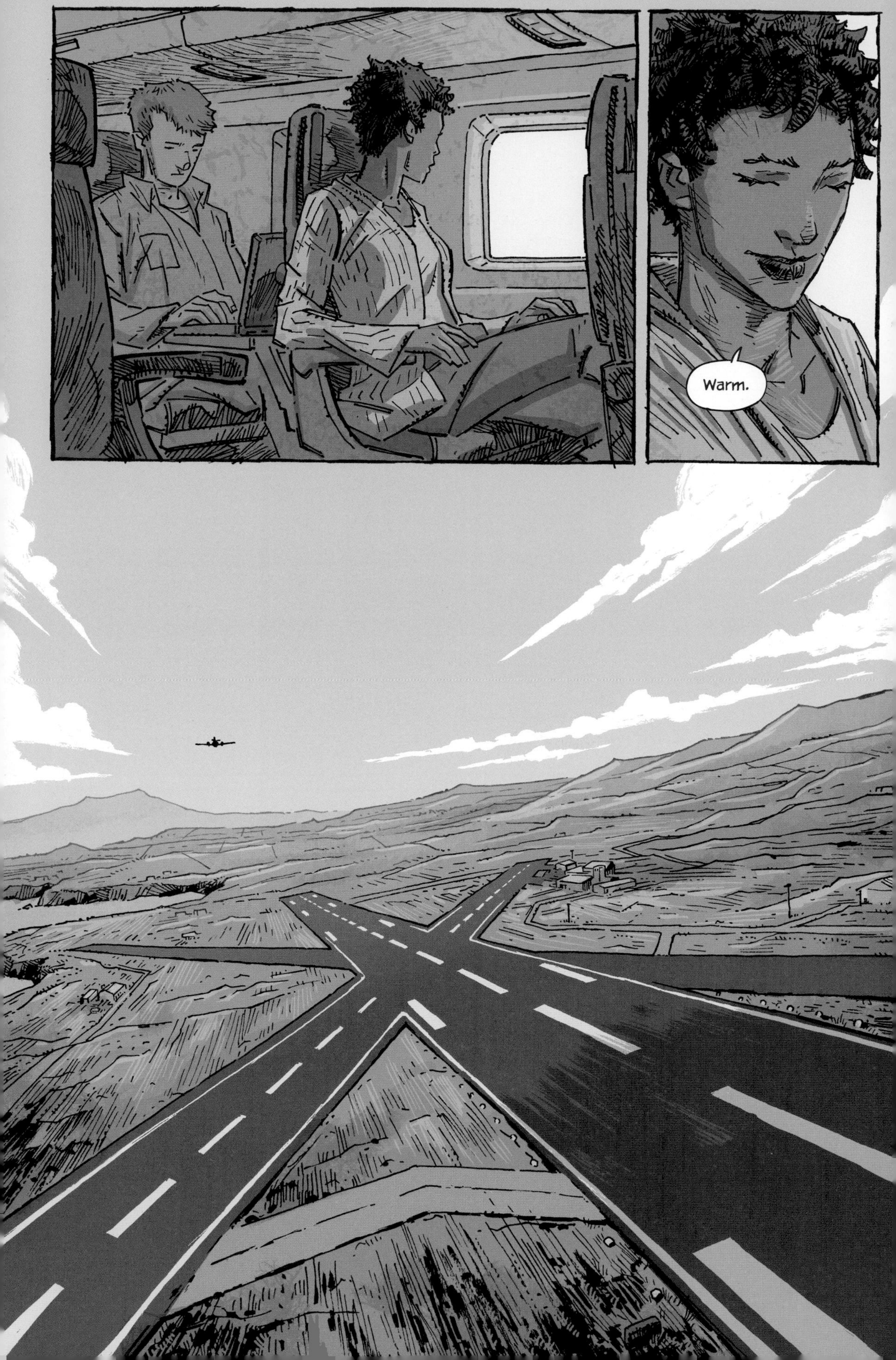
Warm.

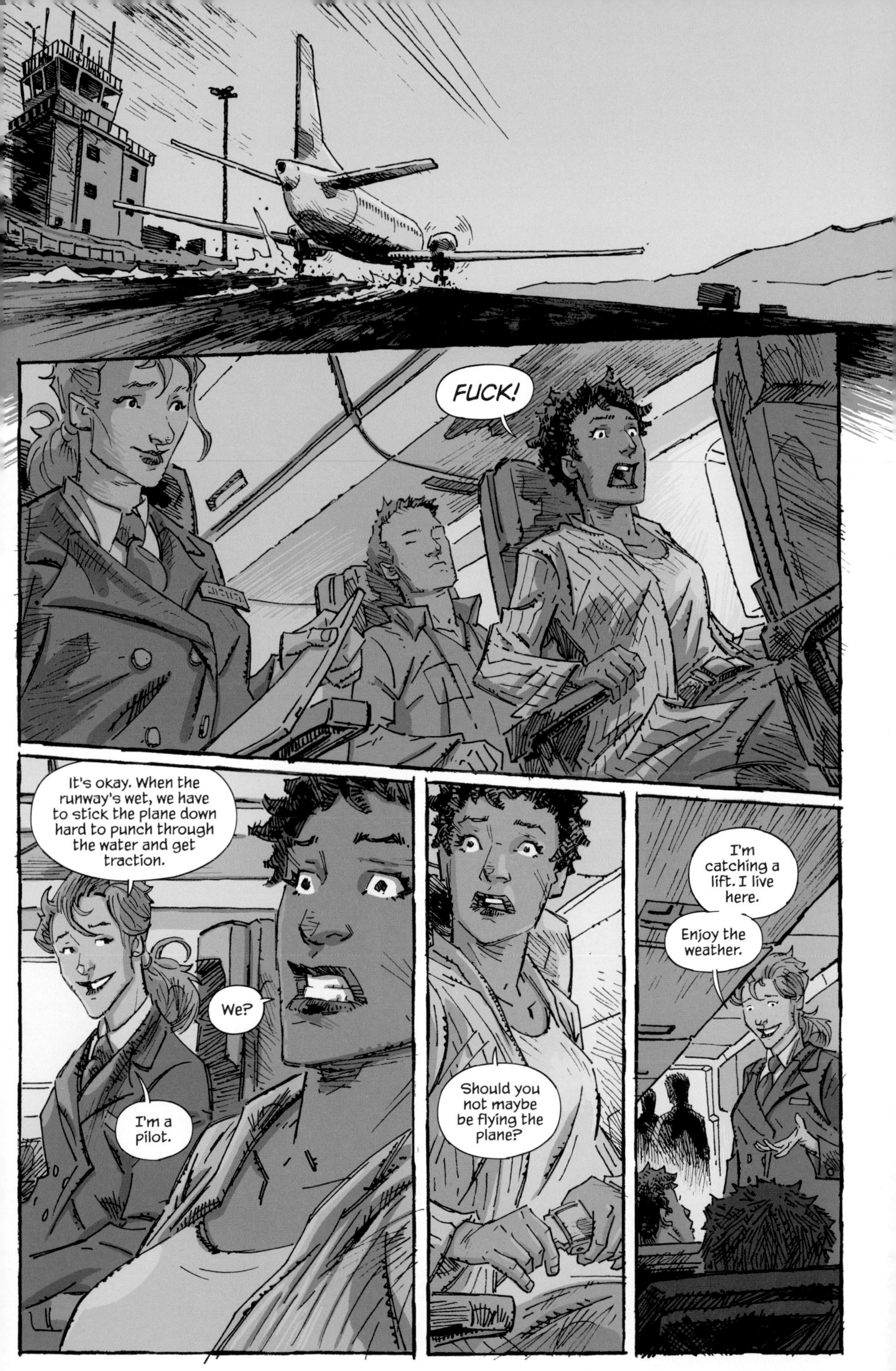
FUCK!
It's okay. When the runway's wet, we have to stick the plane down hard to punch through the water and get traction.
We?
I'm a pilot.
Should you not maybe be flying the plane?
I'm catching a lift. I live here.
Enjoy the weather.

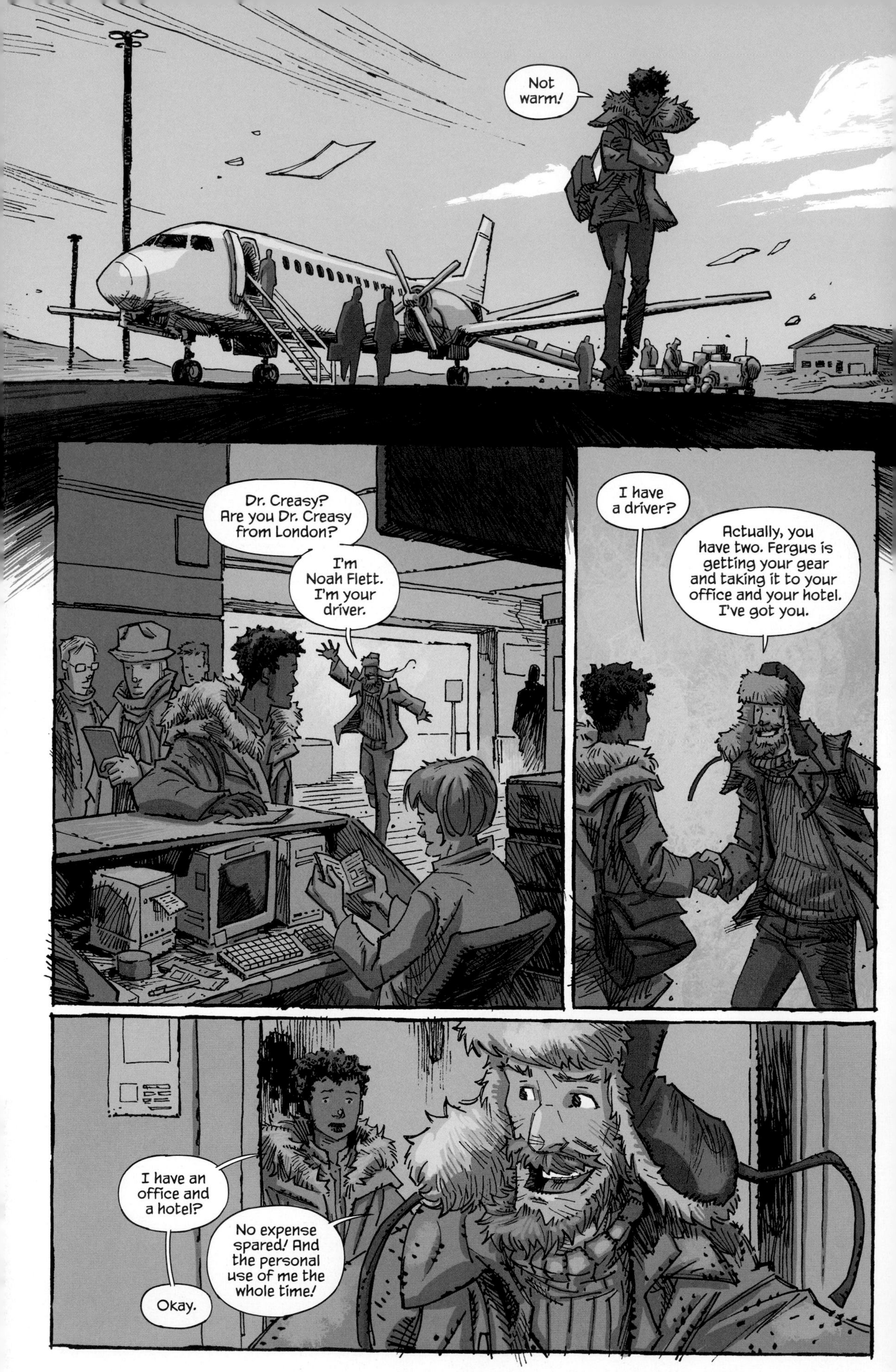

Not warm!
Dr. Creasy? Are you Dr. Creasy from London?
I'm Noah Flett. I'm your driver.
I have a driver?
Actually, you have two. Fergus is getting your gear and taking it to your office and your hotel. I've got you.
I have an office and a hotel?
No expense spared! And the personal use of me the whole time!
Okay.

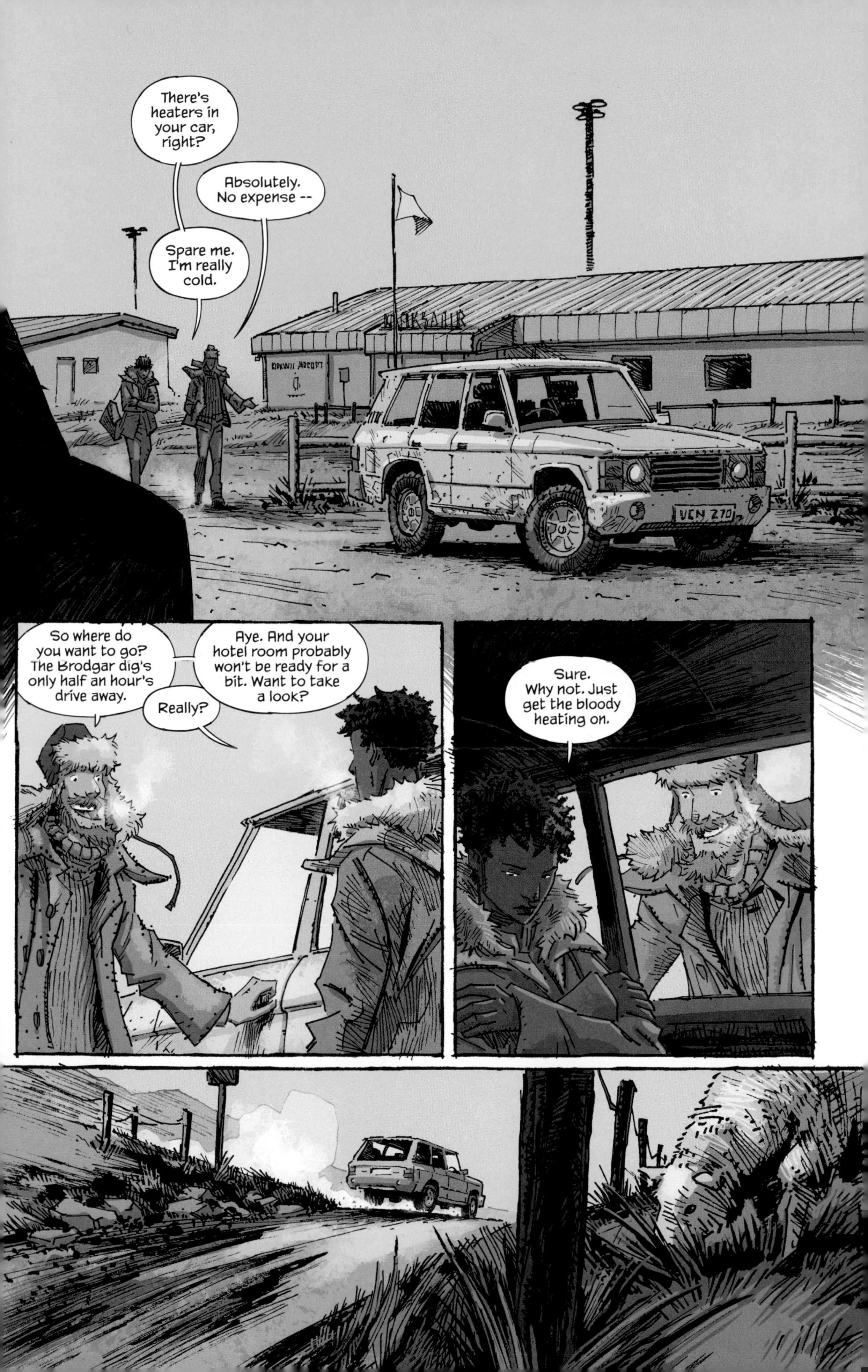
There's heaters in your car, right?
Absolutely. No expense --
Spare me. I'm really cold.
VCN 270
So where do you want to go? The Brodgar dig's only half an hour's drive away.
Really?
Aye. And your hotel room probably won't be ready for a bit. Want to take a look?
Sure. Why not. Just get the bloody heating on.

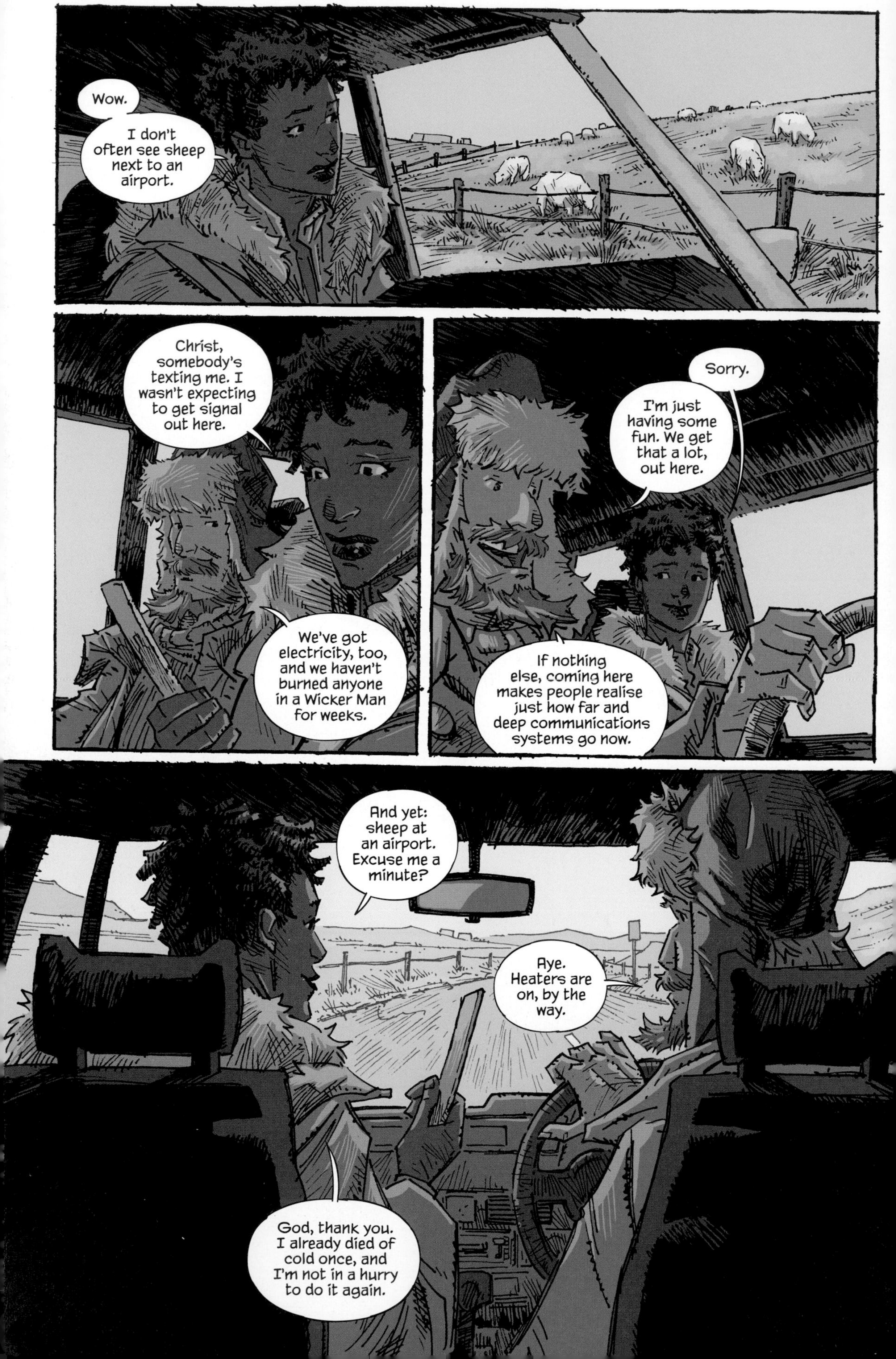
Wow.
I don't often see sheep next to an airport.
Christ, somebody's texting me. I wasn't expecting to get signal out here.
We've got electricity, too, and we haven't burned anyone in a Wicker Man for weeks.
Sorry.
I'm just having some fun. We get that a lot, out here.
If nothing else, coming here makes people realise just how far and deep communications systems go now.
And yet: sheep at an airport. Excuse me a minute?
Aye. Heaters are on, by the way.
God, thank you. I already died of cold once, and I'm not in a hurry to do it again.

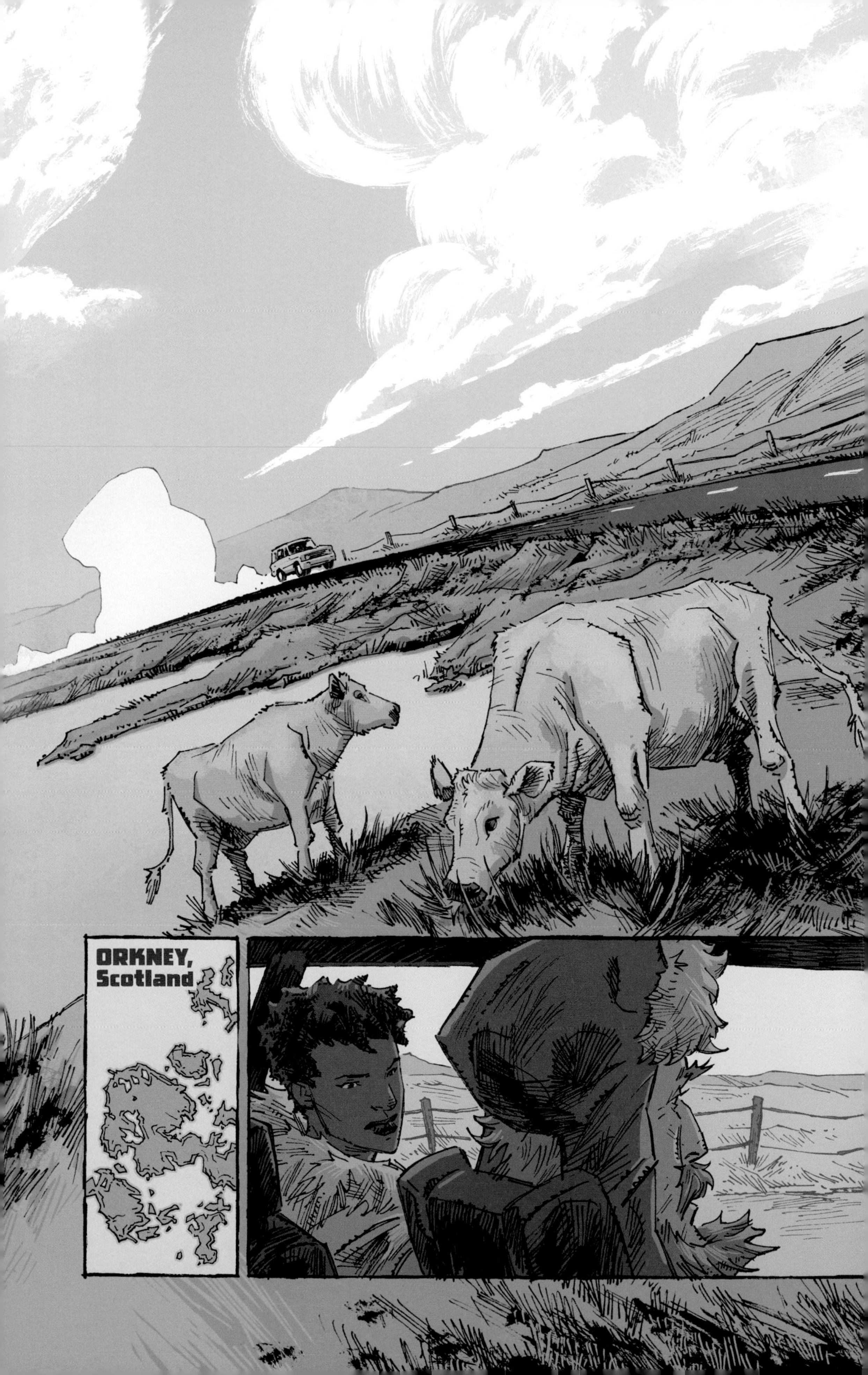
ORKNEY, Scotland

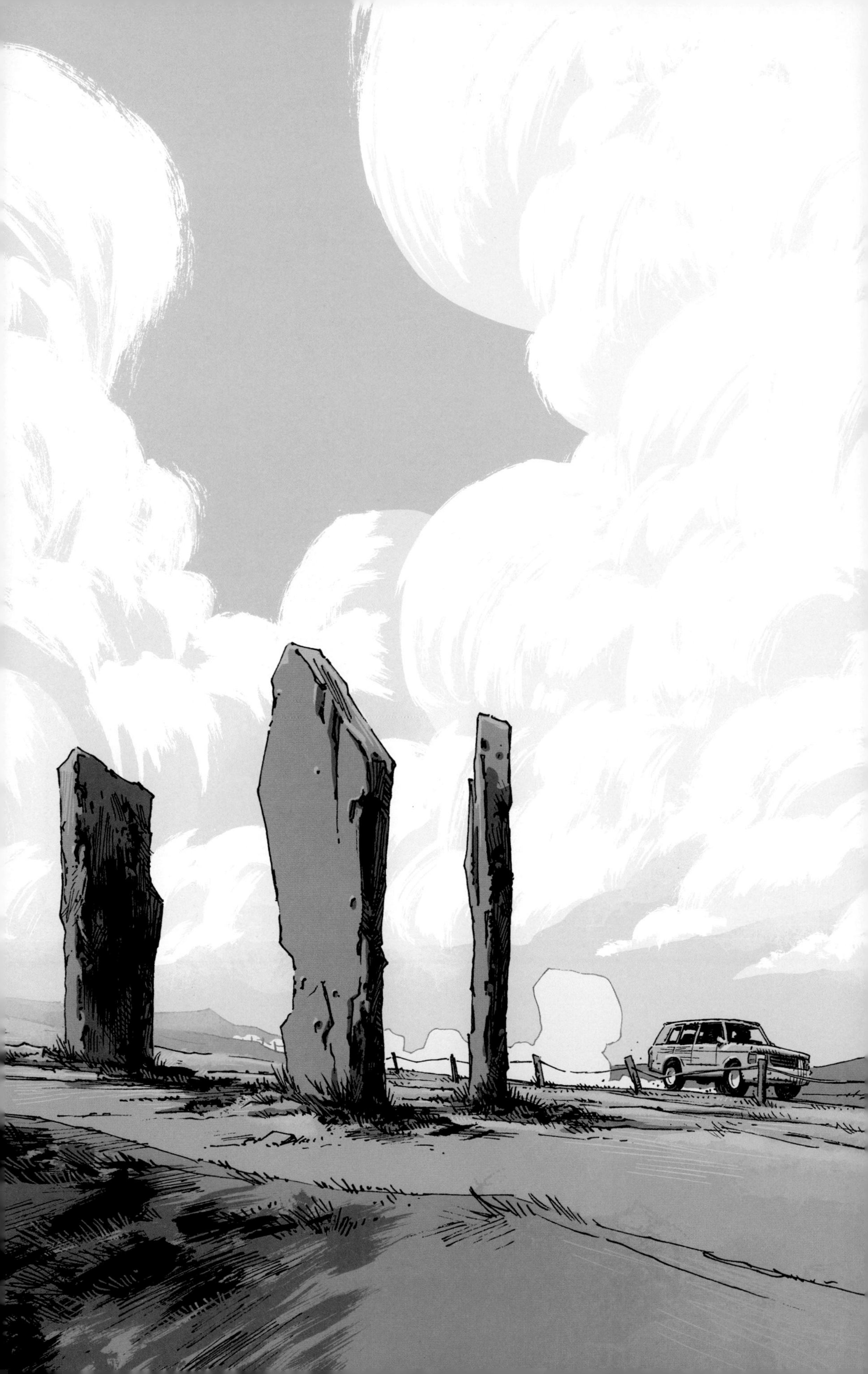

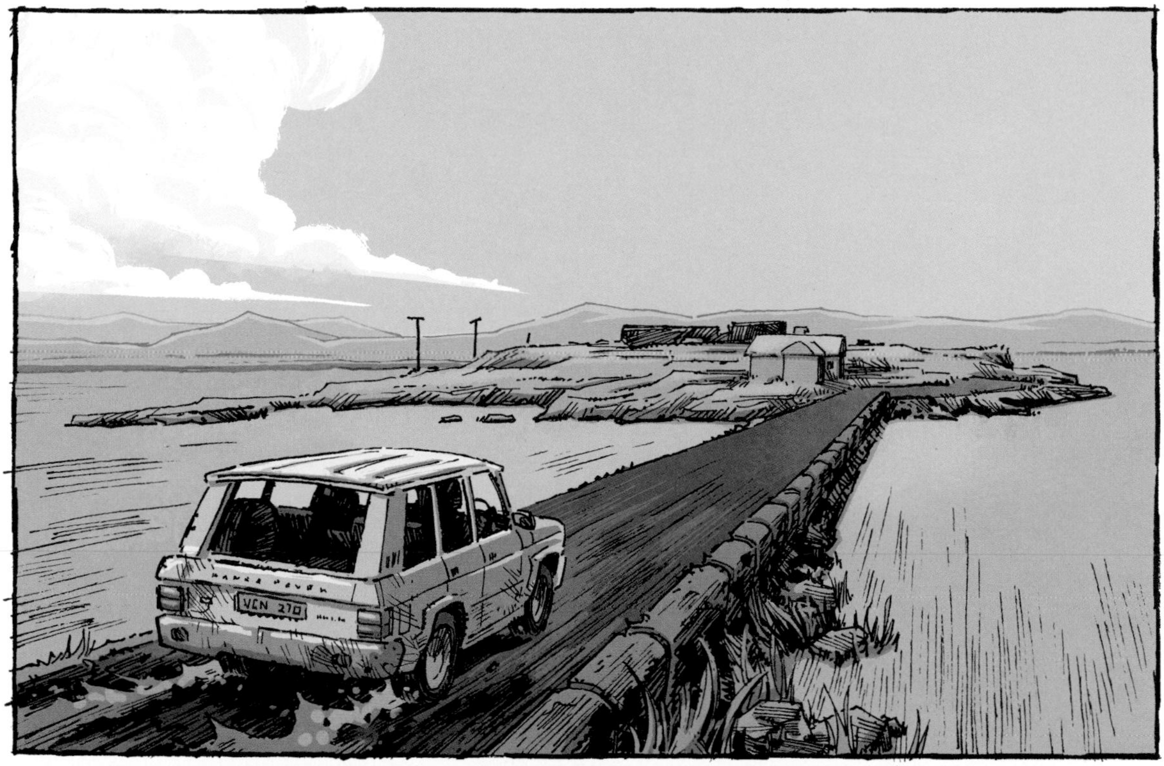
VCN 270

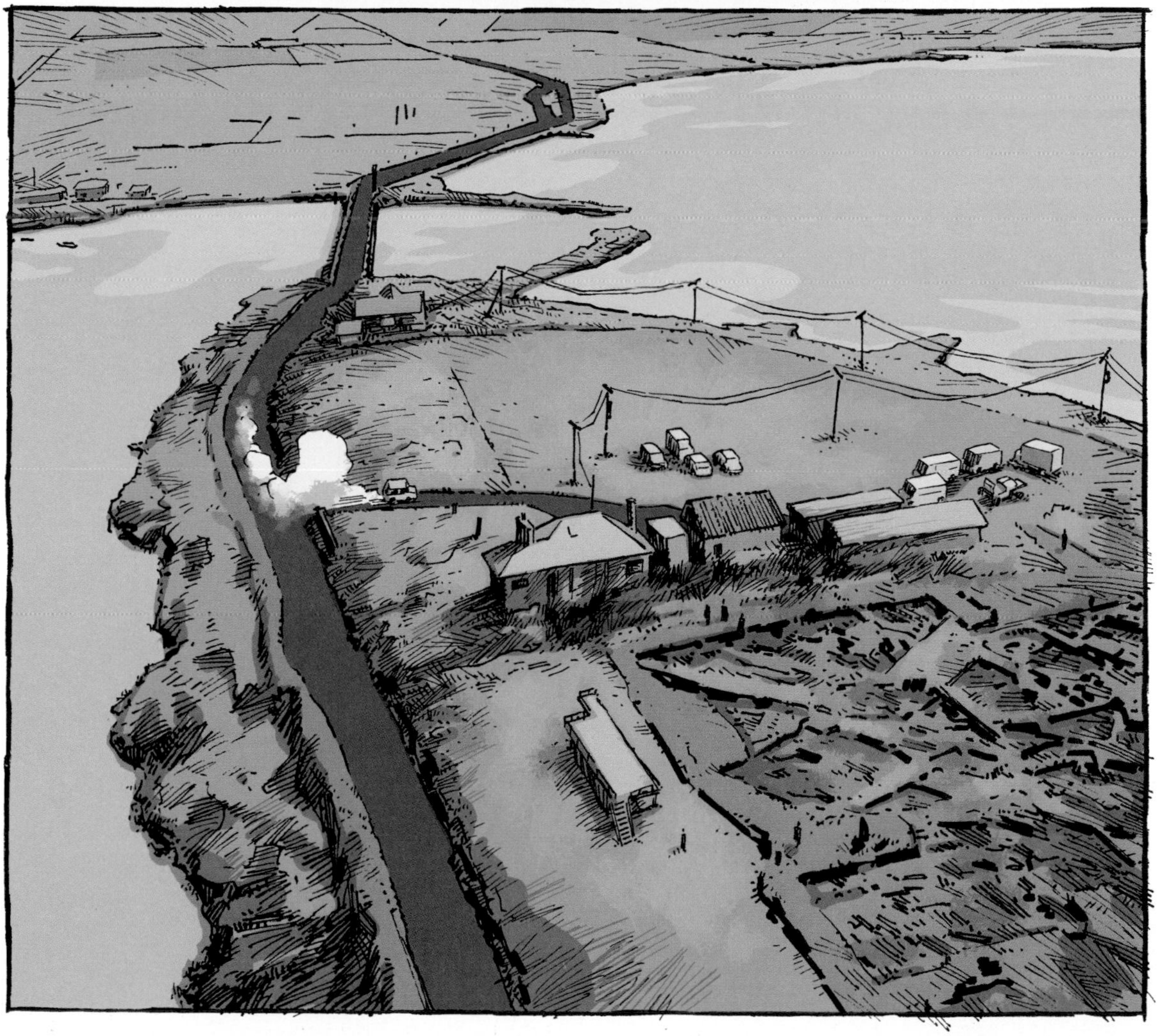

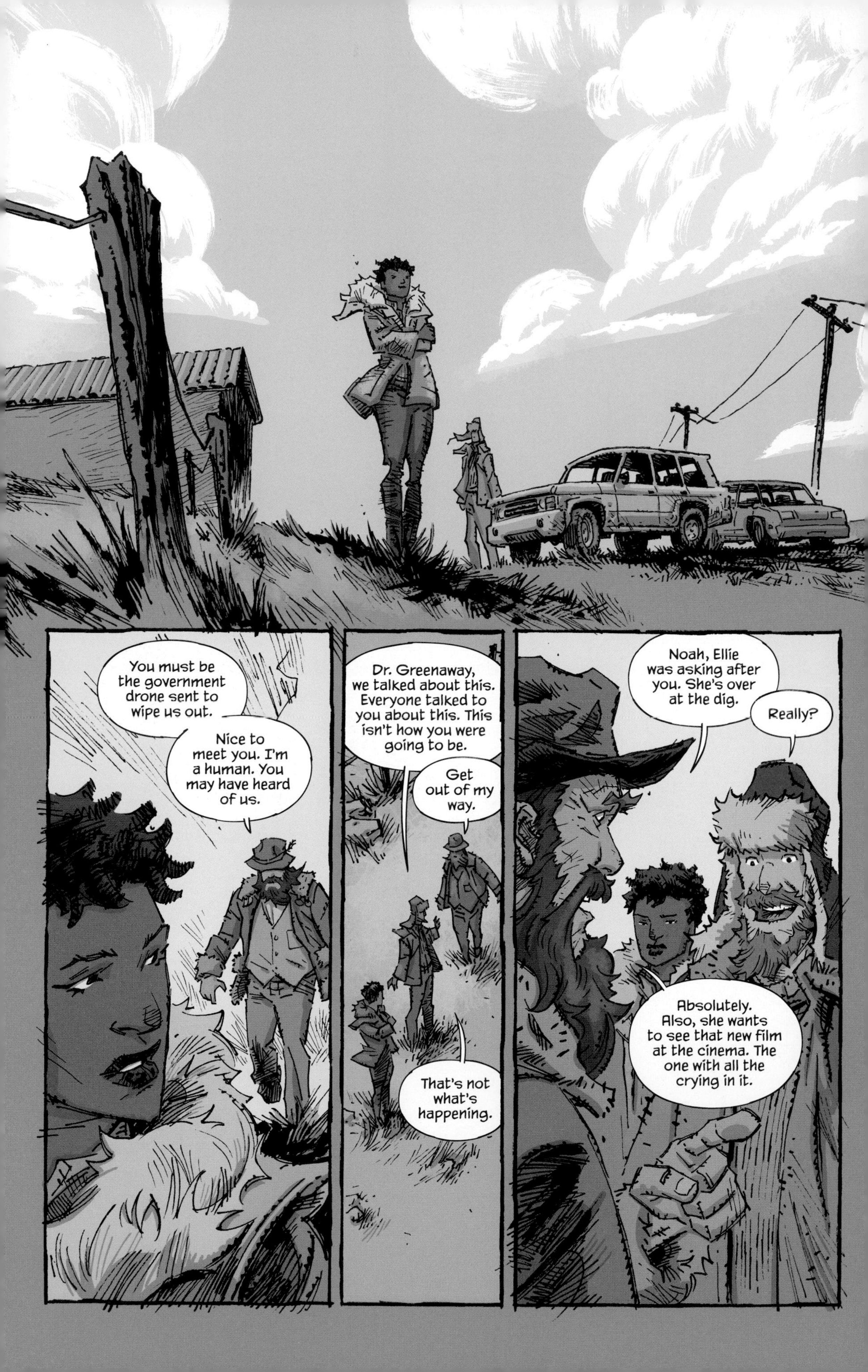

You must be the government drone sent to wipe us out.
Nice to meet you. I'm a human. You may have heard of us.
Dr. Greenaway, we talked about this. Everyone talked to you about this. This isn't how you were going to be.
Get out of my way.
That's not what's happening.
Noah, Ellie was asking after you. She's over at the dig.
Really?
Absolutely. Also, she wants to see that new film at the cinema. The one with all the crying in it.

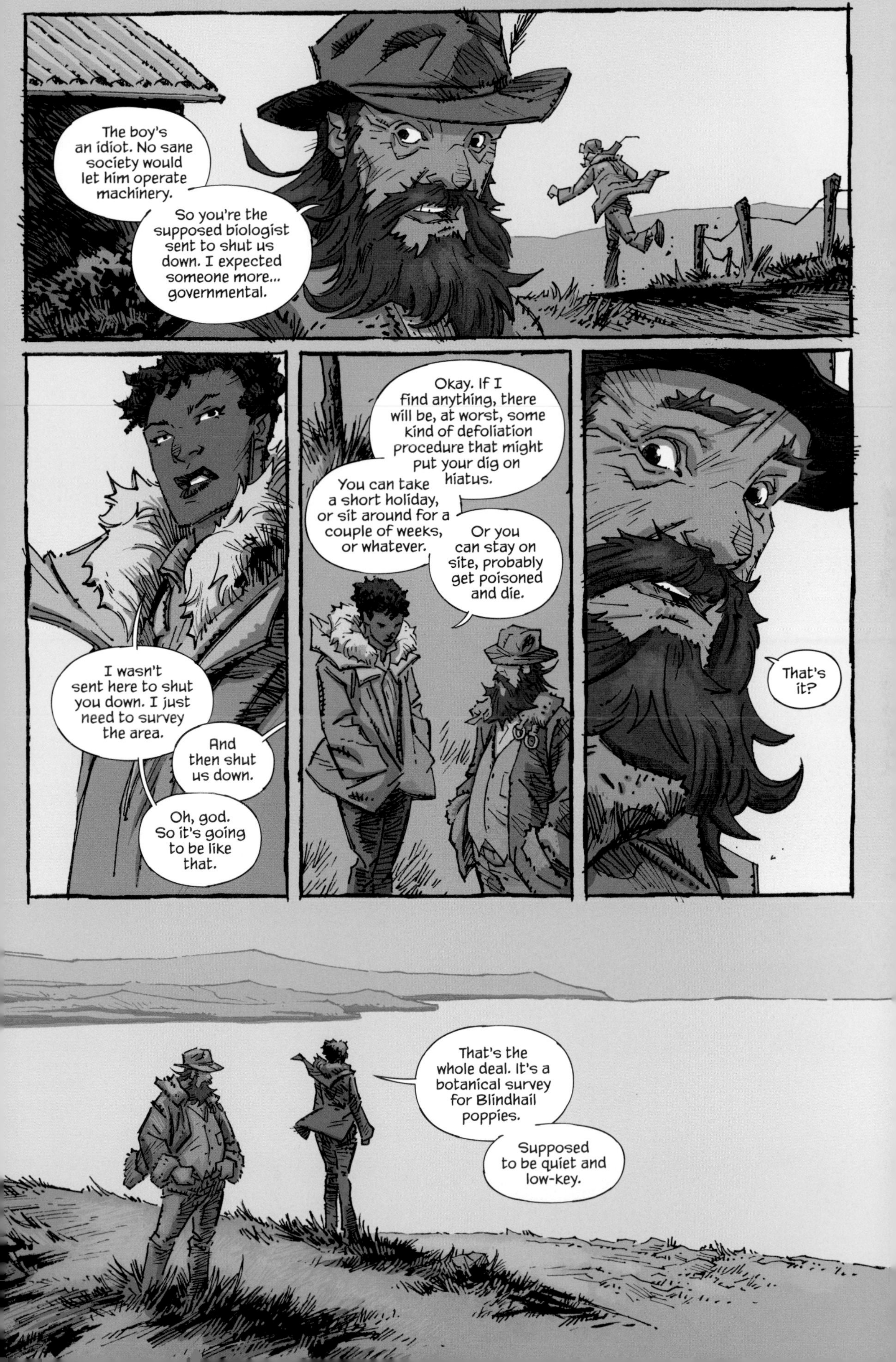
The boy's an idiot. No sane society would let him operate machinery.
So you're the supposed biologist sent to shut us down. I expected someone more... governmental.
I wasn't sent here to shut you down. I just need to survey the area.
And then shut us down.
Oh, god. So it's going to be like that.
Okay. If I find anything, there will be, at worst, some kind of defoliation procedure that might put your dig on hiatus.
You can take a short holiday, or sit around for a couple of weeks, or whatever.
Or you can stay on site, probably get poisoned and die.
That's it?
That's the whole deal. It's a botanical survey for Blindhail poppies.
Supposed to be quiet and low-key.

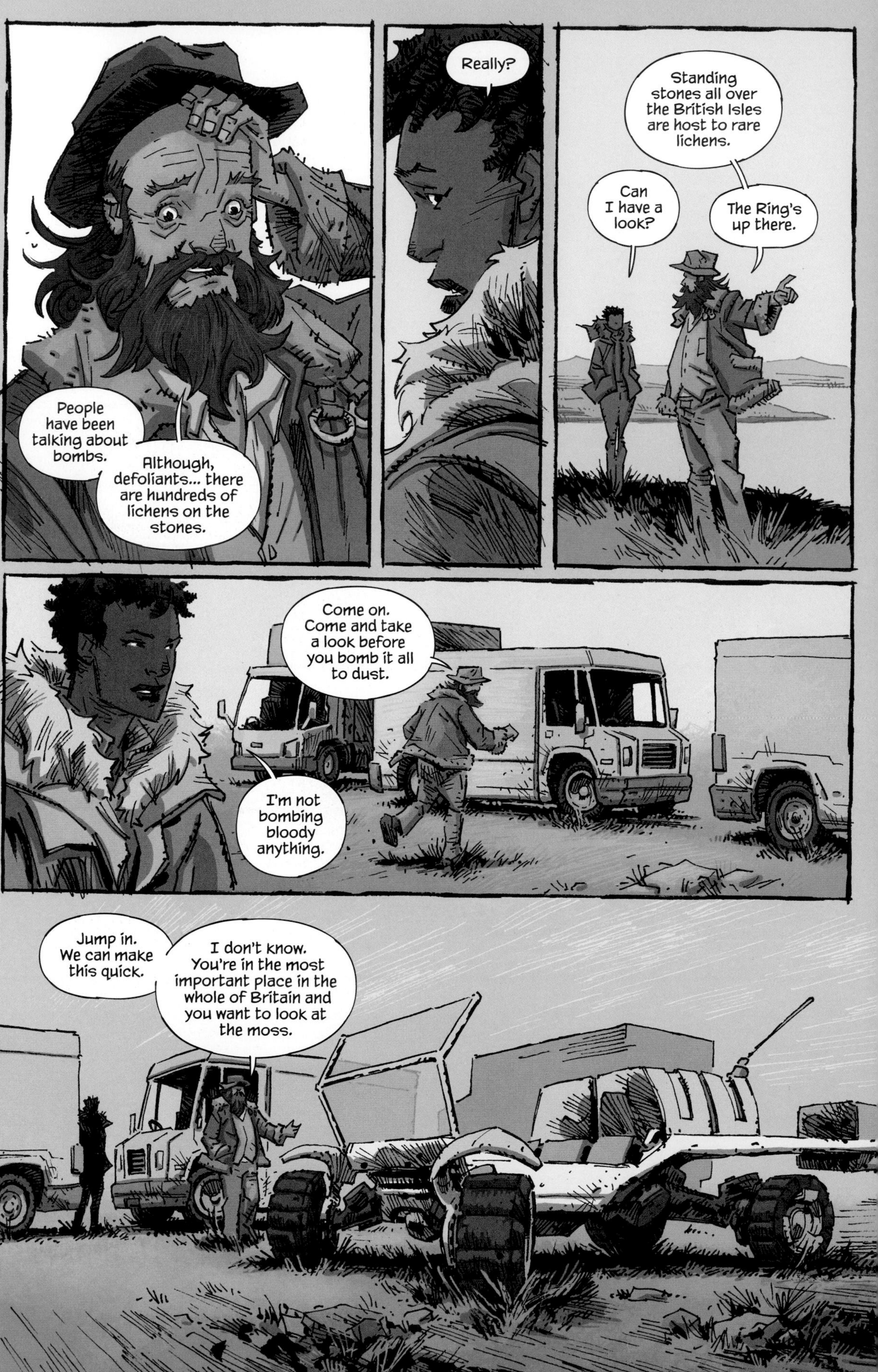
People have been talking about bombs.
Although, defoliants... there are hundreds of lichens on the stones.
Really?
Standing stones all over the British Isles are host to rare lichens.
Can I have a look?
The Ring's up there.
Come on. Come and take a look before you bomb it all to dust.
I'm not bombing bloody anything.
Jump in. We can make this quick.
I don't know. You're in the most important place in the whole of Britain and you want to look at the moss.

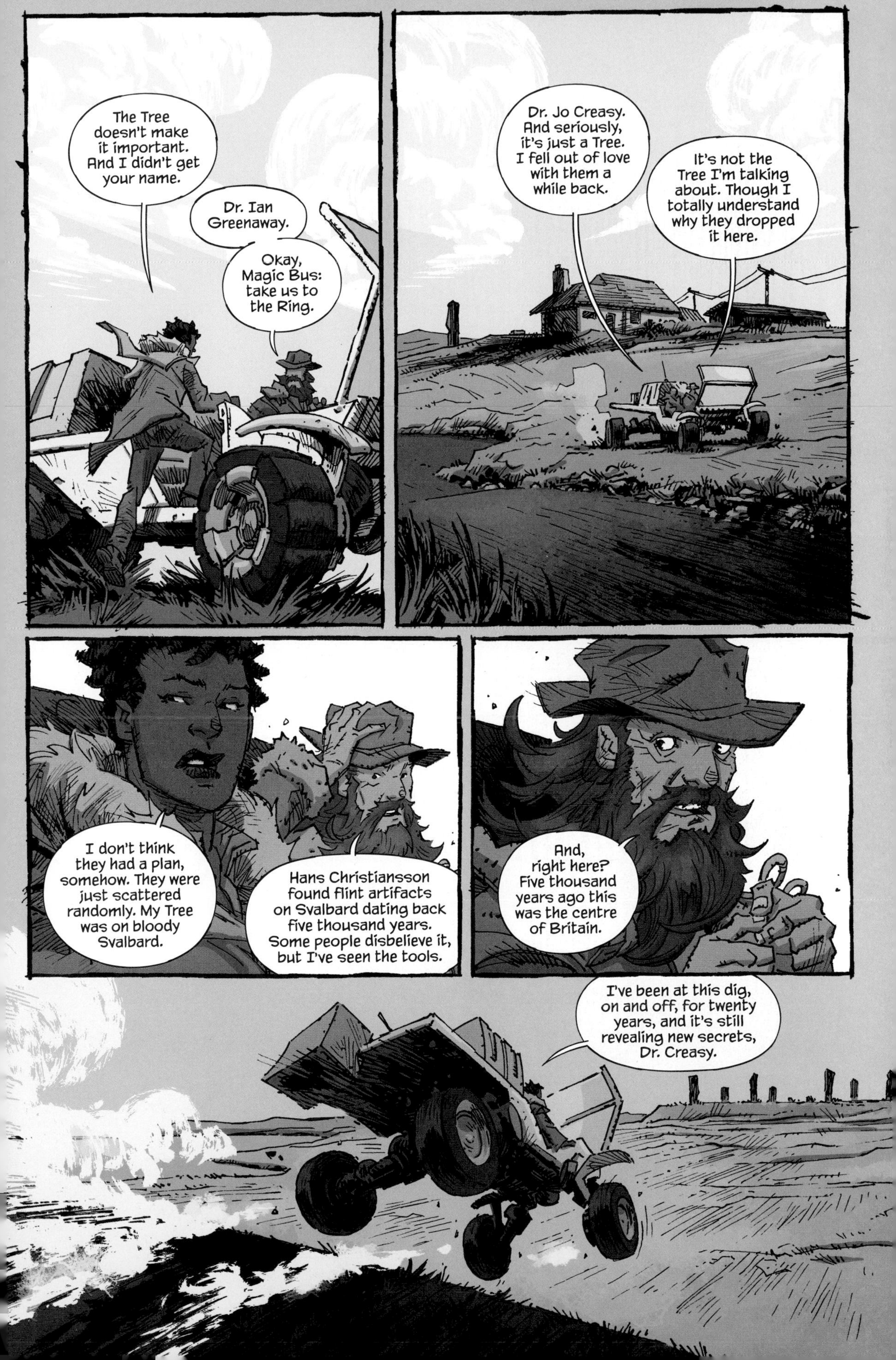

The Tree doesn't make it important. And I didn't get your name.
Dr. Ian Greenaway.
Okay, Magic Bus: take us to the Ring.
Dr. Jo Creasy. And seriously, it's just a Tree. I fell out of love with them a while back.
It's not the Tree I'm talking about. Though I totally understand why they dropped it here.
I don't think they had a plan, somehow. They were just scattered randomly. My Tree was on bloody Svalbard.
Hans Christiansson found flint artifacts on Svalbard dating back five thousand years. Some people disbelieve it, but I've seen the tools.
And, right here? Five thousand years ago this was the centre of Britain.
I've been at this dig, on and off, for twenty years, and it's still revealing new secrets, Dr. Creasy.

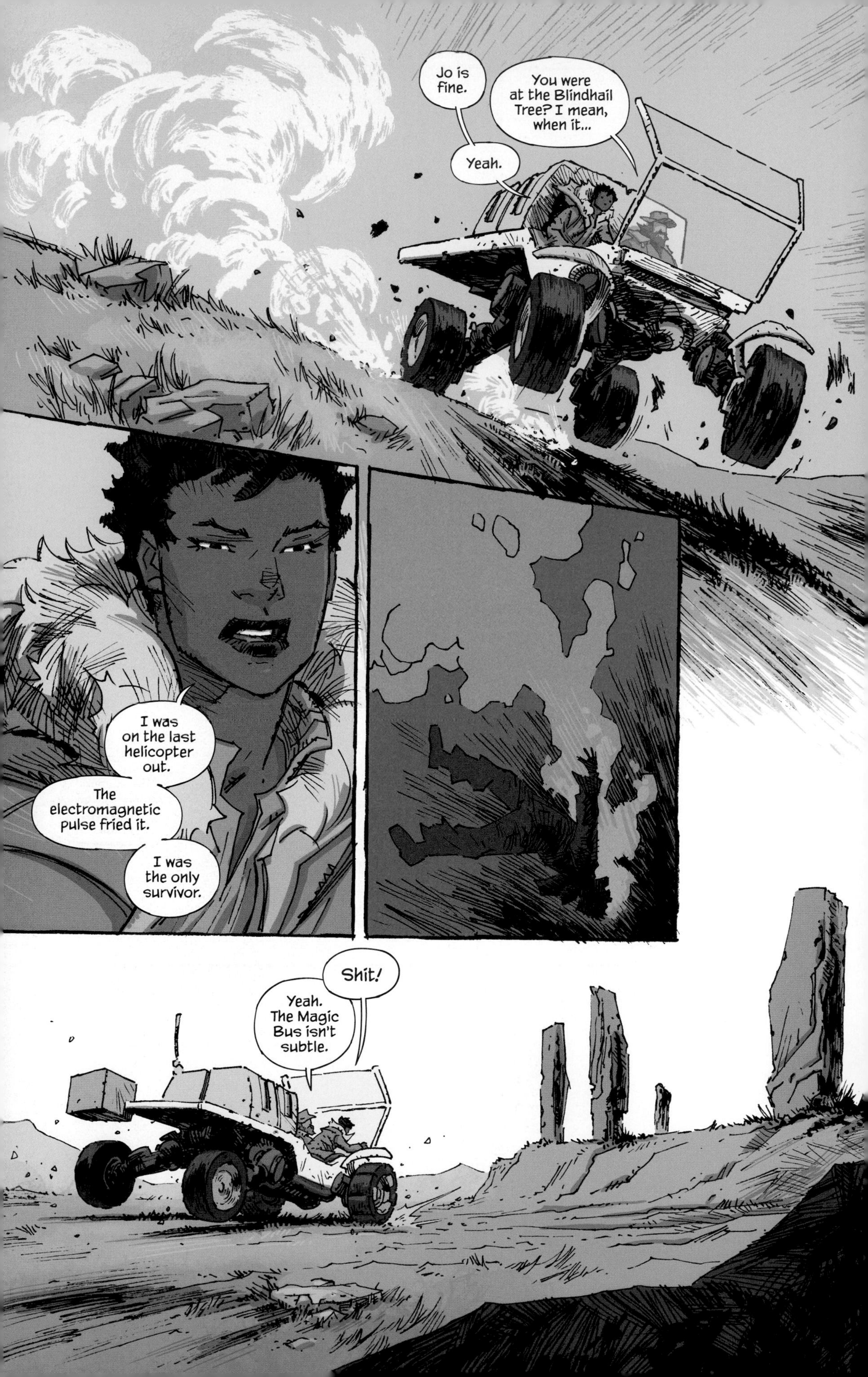
Jo is fine.
You were at the Blindhail Tree? I mean, when it...
Yeah.
I was on the last helicopter out.
The electromagnetic pulse fried it.
I was the only survivor.
Shit!
Yeah. The Magic Bus isn't subtle.

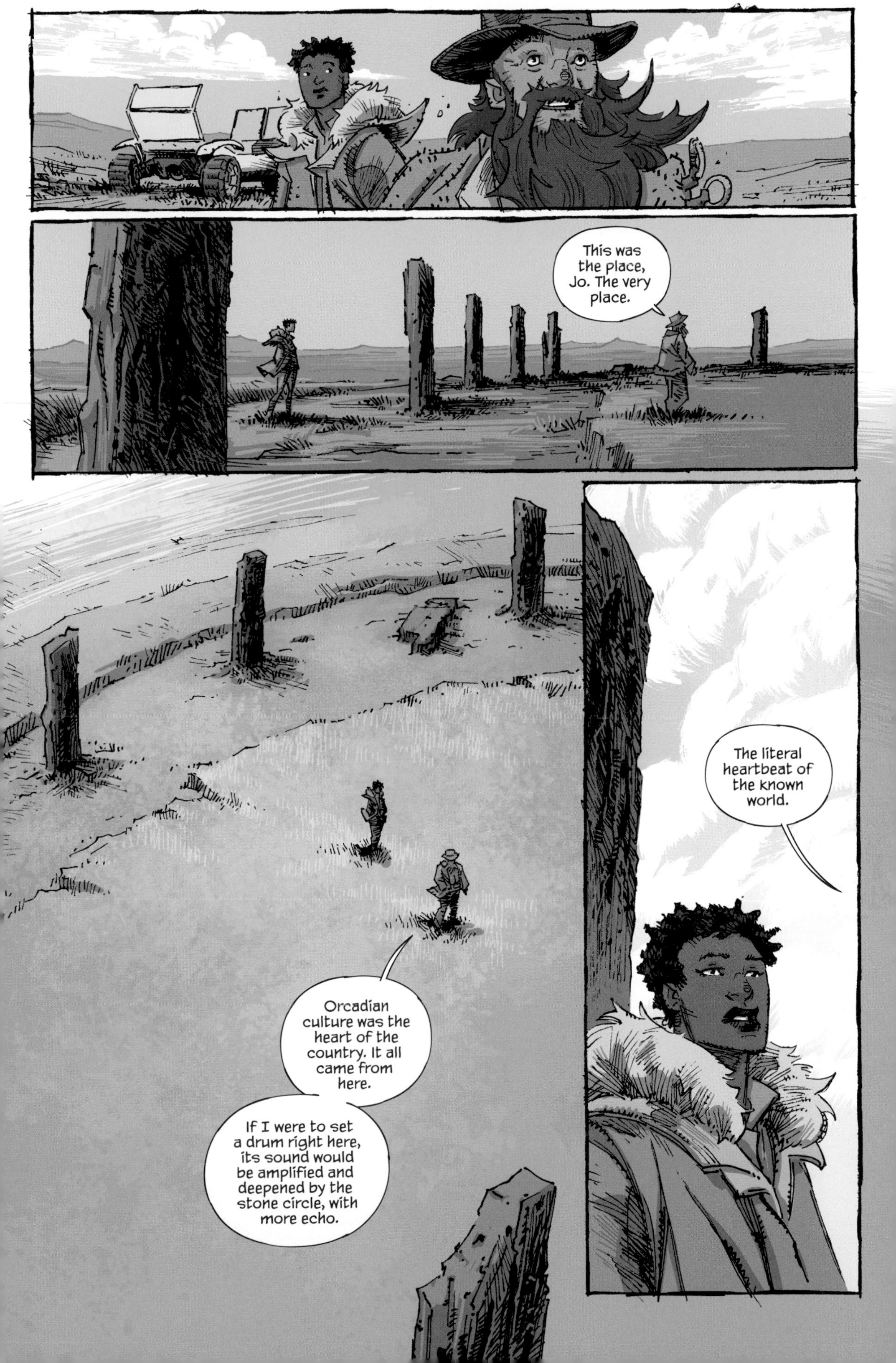
This was the place, Jo. The very place.
Orcadian culture was the heart of the country. It all came from here.
If I were to set a drum right here, its sound would be amplified and deepened by the stone circle, with more echo.
The literal heartbeat of the known world.

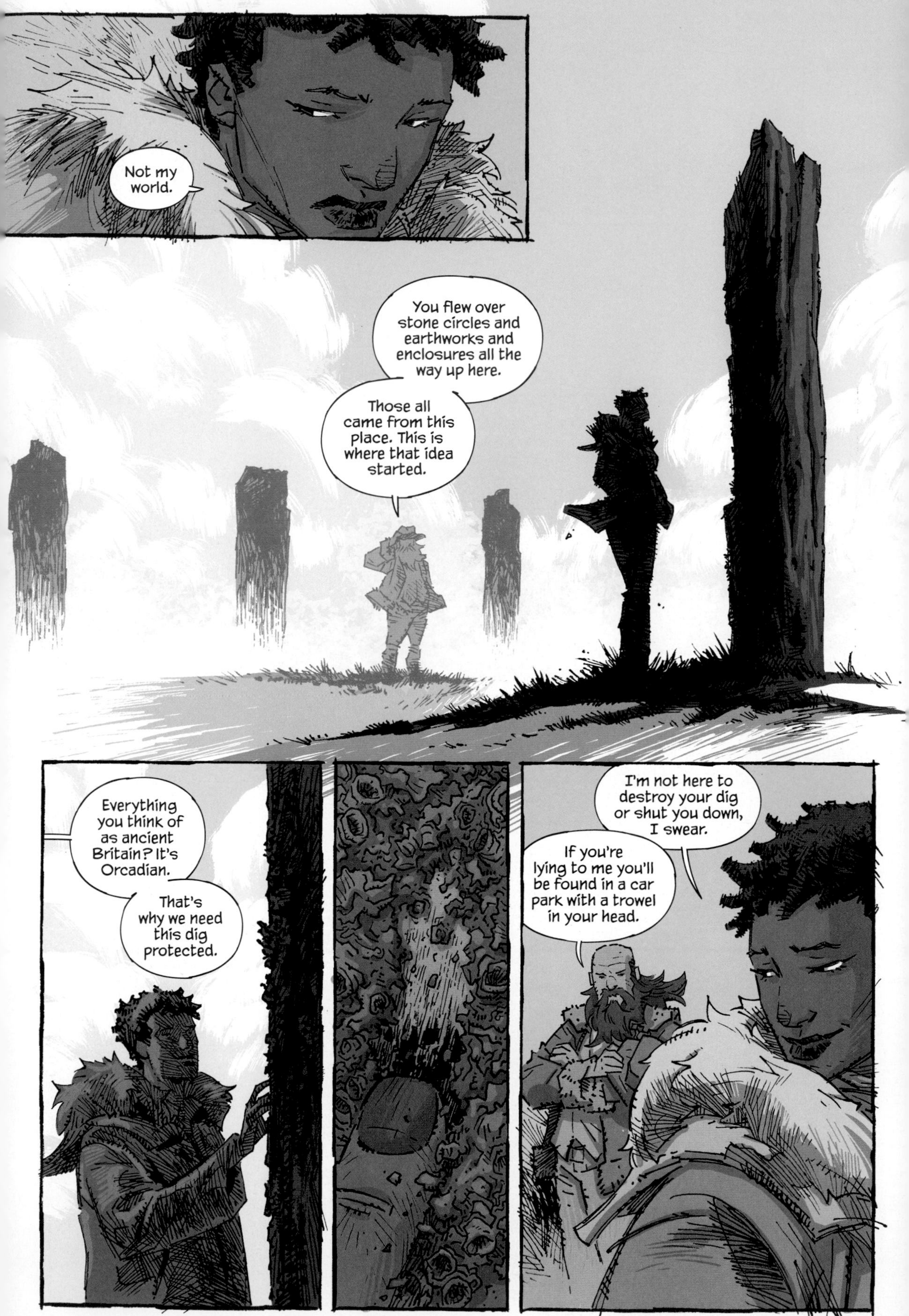
Not my world.
You flew over stone circles and earthworks and enclosures all the way up here.
Those all came from this place. This is where that idea started.
Everything you think of as ancient Britain? It's Orcadian.
That's why we need this dig protected.
I'm not here to destroy your dig or shut you down, I swear.
If you're lying to me you'll be found in a car park with a trowel in your head.

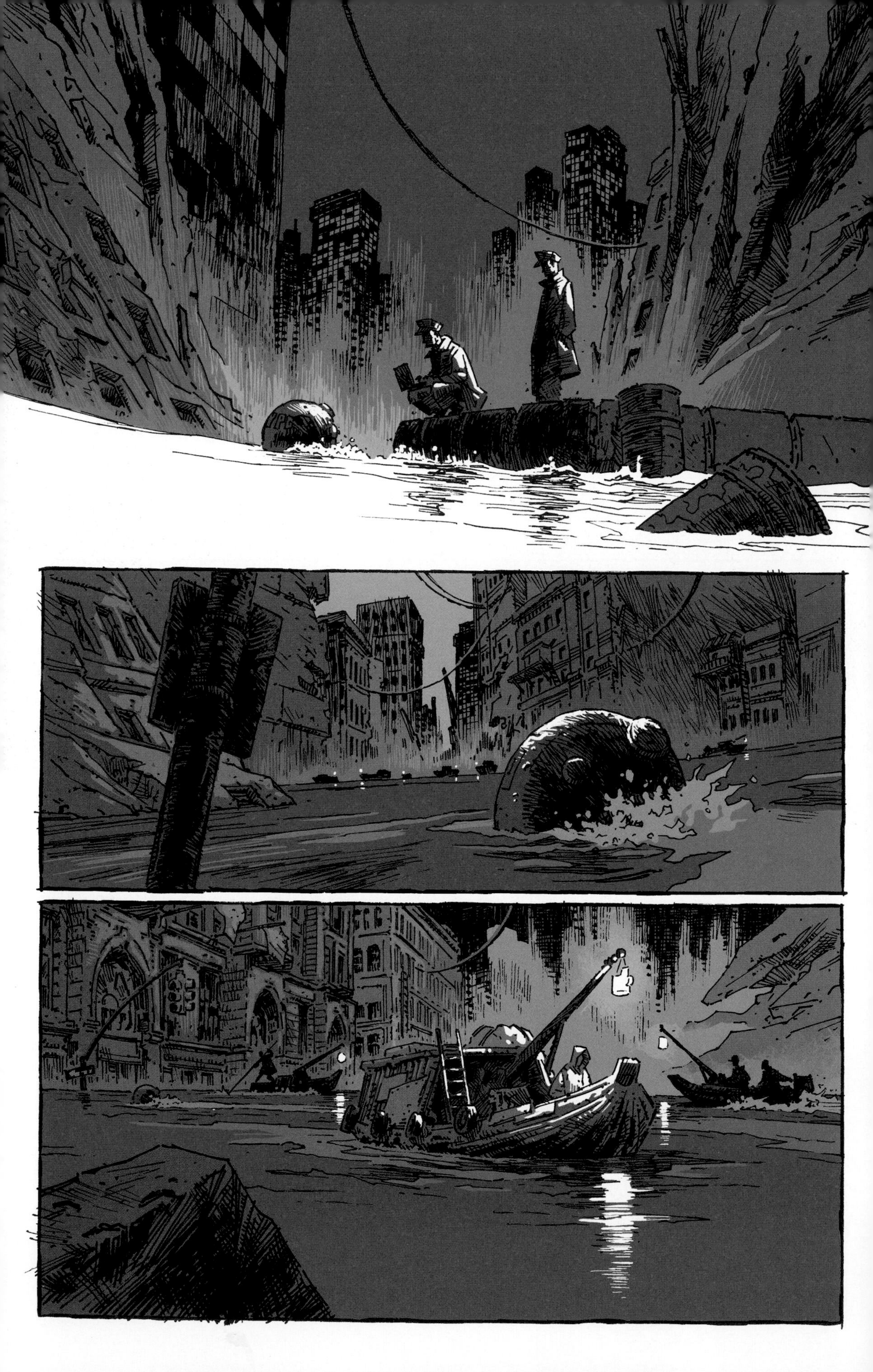

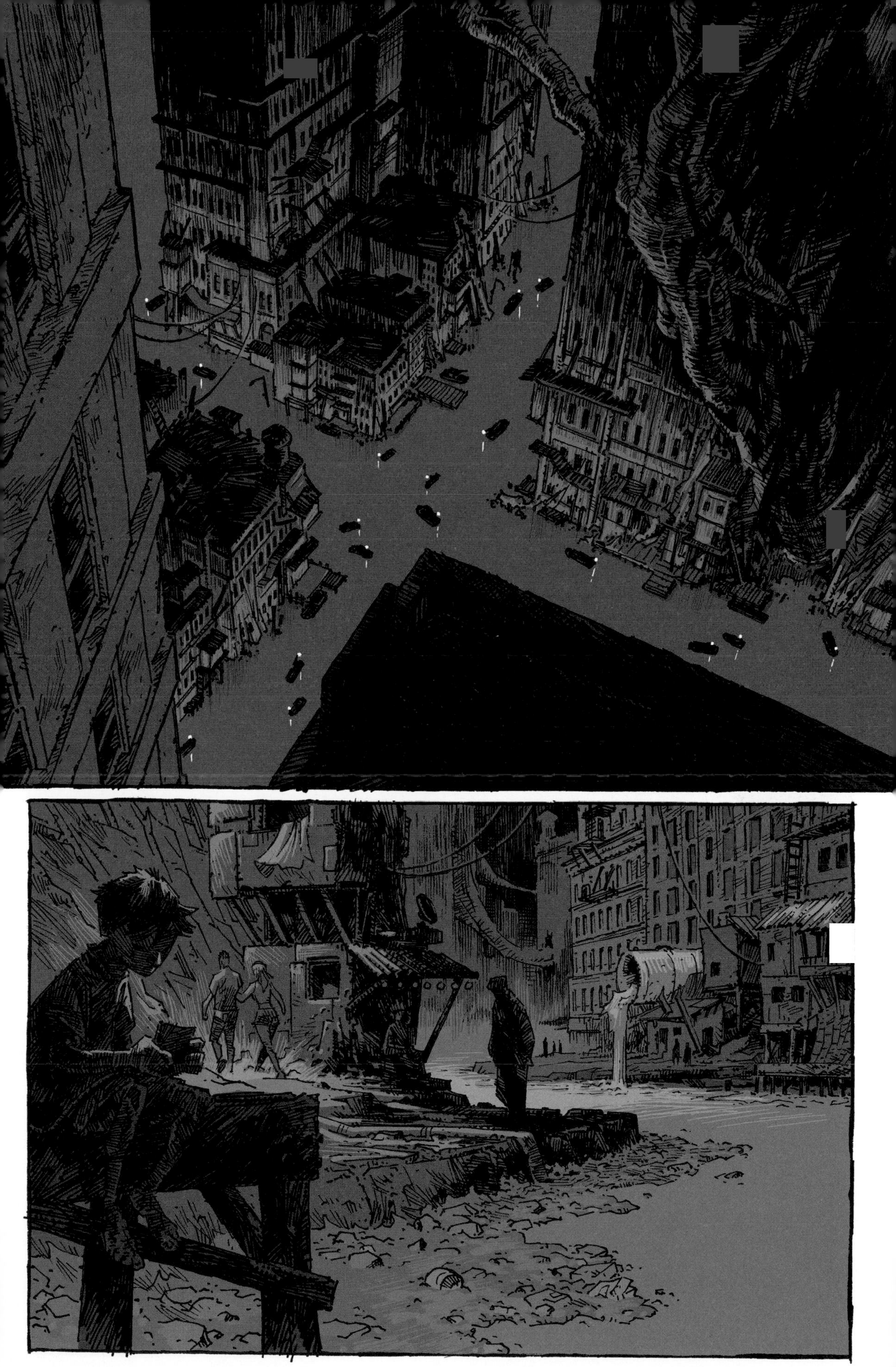

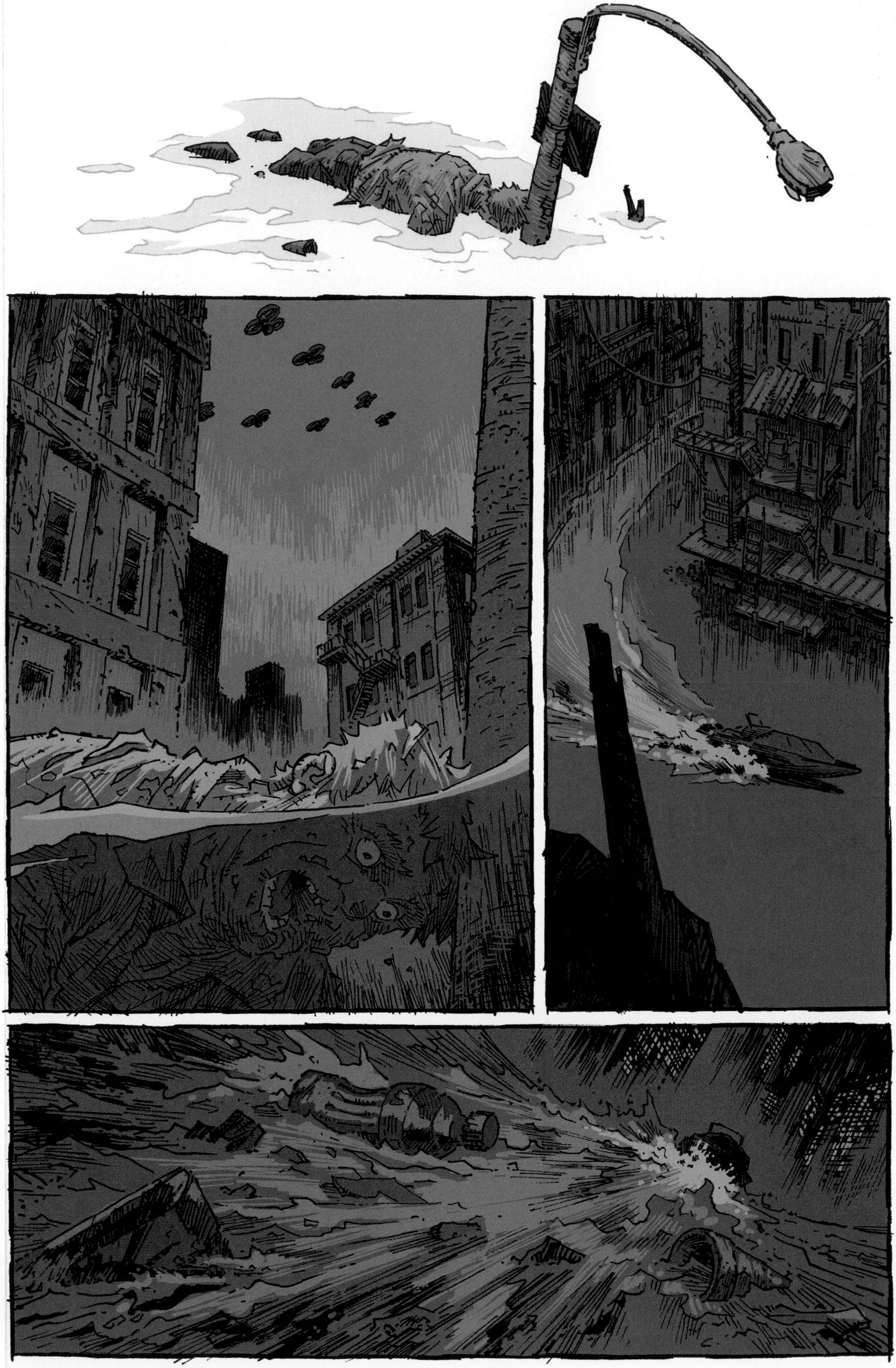

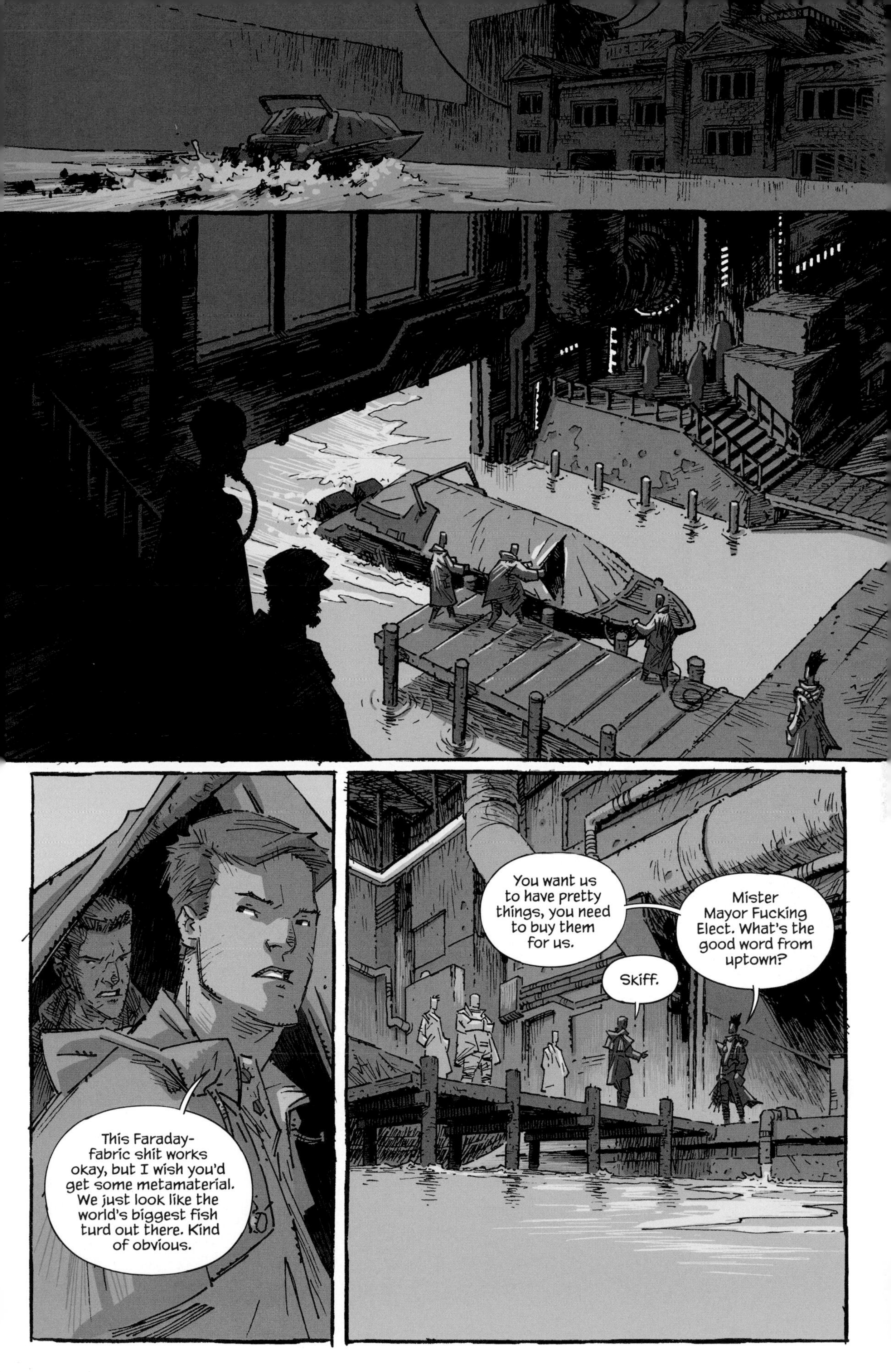
This Faraday-fabric shit works okay, but I wish you'd get some metamaterial. We just look like the world's biggest fish turd out there. Kind of obvious.
You want us to have pretty things, you need to buy them for us.
Mister Mayor Fucking Elect. What's the good word from uptown?
Skiff.

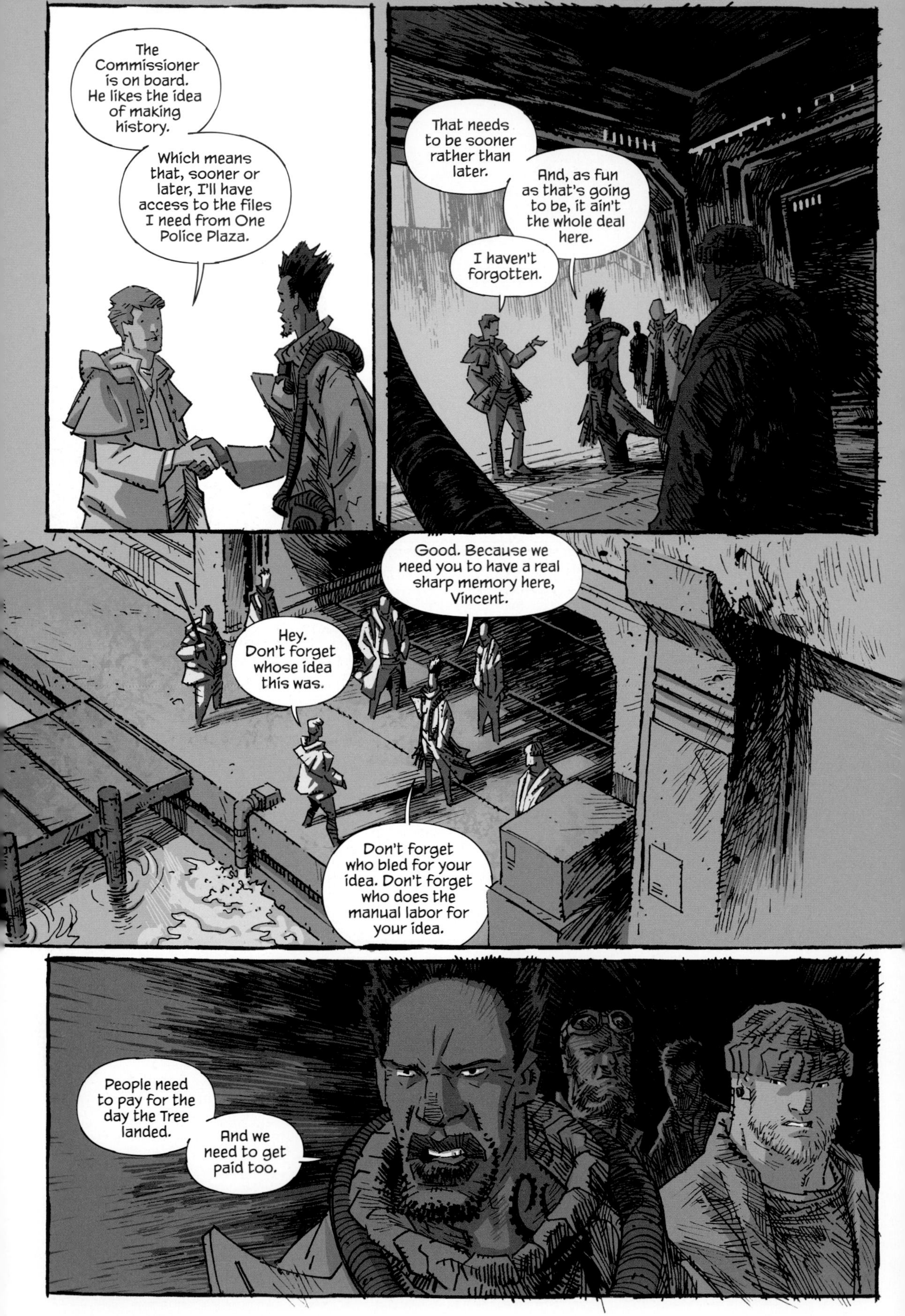

The Commissioner is on board. He likes the idea of making history.
Which means that, sooner or later, I'll have access to the files I need from One Police Plaza.
That needs to be sooner rather than later.
And, as fun as that's going to be, it ain't the whole deal here.
I haven't forgotten.
Good. Because we need you to have a real sharp memory here, Vincent.
Hey. Don't forget whose idea this was.
Don't forget who bled for your idea. Don't forget who does the manual labor for your idea.
People need to pay for the day the Tree landed.
And we need to get paid too.

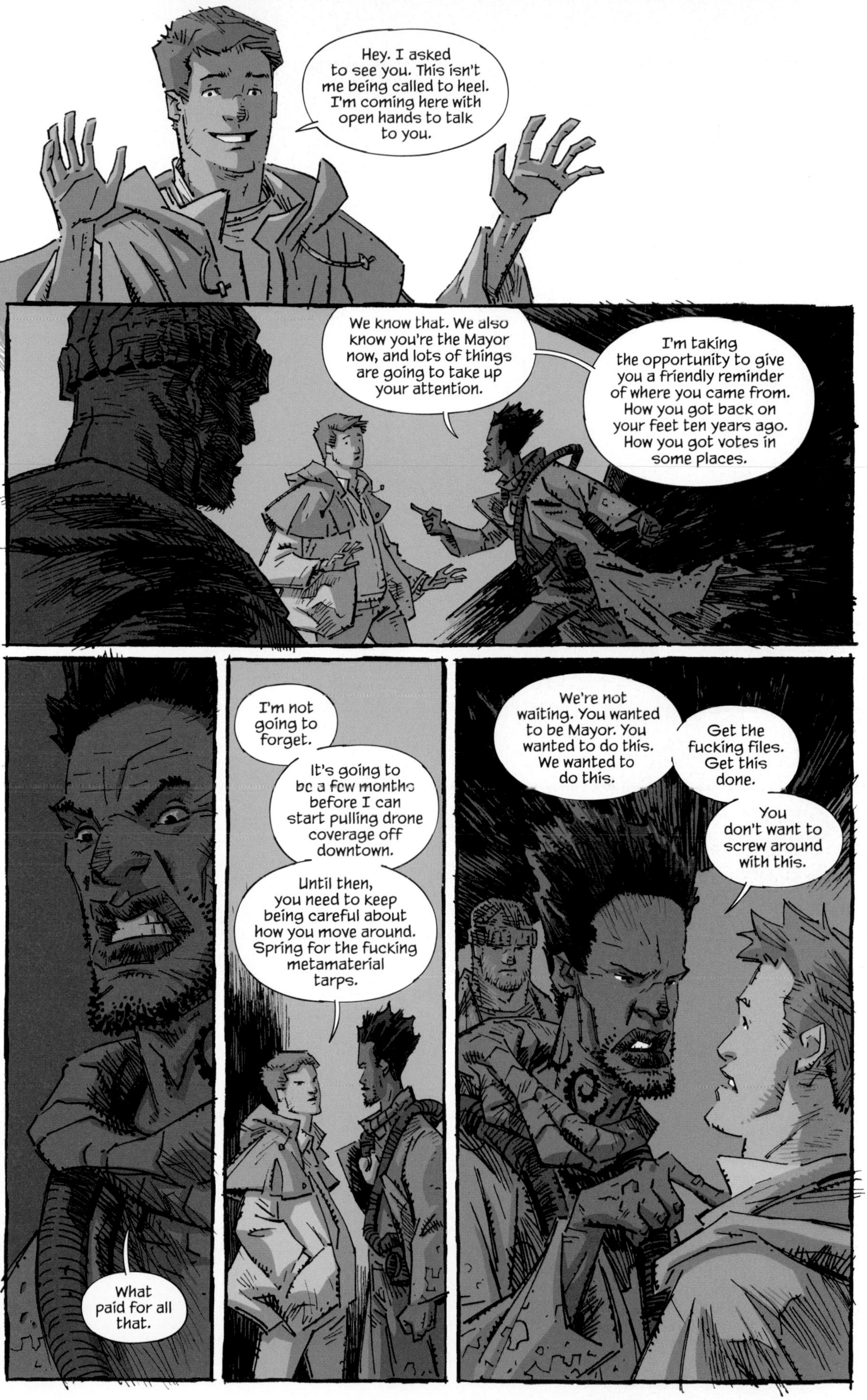
Hey. I asked to see you. This isn't me being called to heel. I'm coming here with open hands to talk to you.
We know that. We also know you're the Mayor now, and lots of things are going to take up your attention.
I'm taking the opportunity to give you a friendly reminder of where you came from. How you got back on your feet ten years ago. How you got votes in some places.
What paid for all that.
I'm not going to forget.
It's going to be a few months before I can start pulling drone coverage off downtown.
Until then, you need to keep being careful about how you move around. Spring for the fucking metamaterial tarps.
We're not waiting. You wanted to be Mayor. You wanted to do this. We wanted to do this.
Get the fucking files. Get this done.
You don't want to screw around with this.

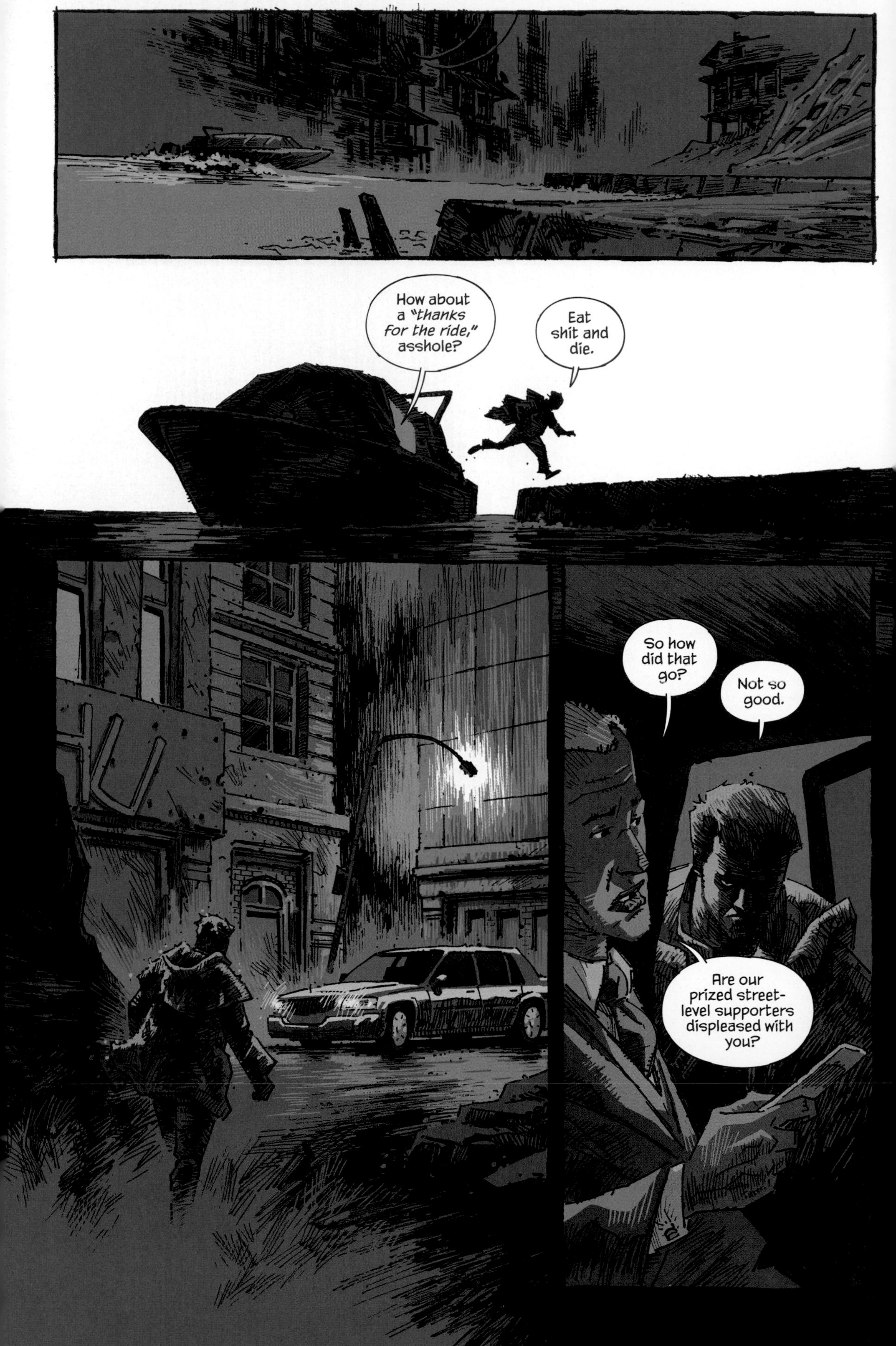
How about a "*thanks for the ride,*" asshole?
Eat shit and die.
So how did that go?
Not so good.
Are our prized street-level supporters displeased with you?

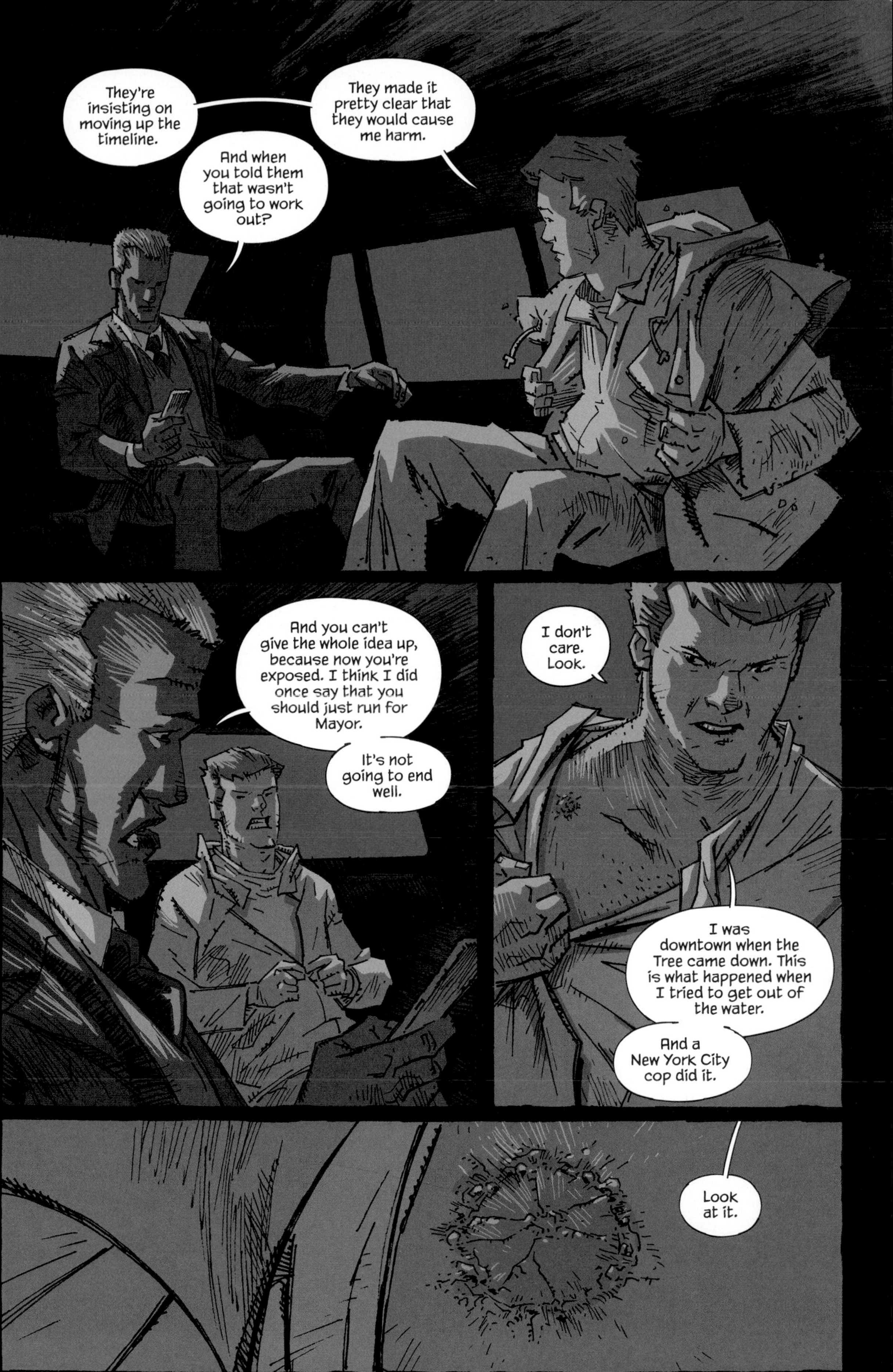
They're insisting on moving up the timeline.
They made it pretty clear that they would cause me harm.
And when you told them that wasn't going to work out?
And you can't give the whole idea up, because now you're exposed. I think I did once say that you should just run for Mayor.
It's not going to end well.
I don't care. Look.
I was downtown when the Tree came down. This is what happened when I tried to get out of the water.
And a New York City cop did it.
Look at it.

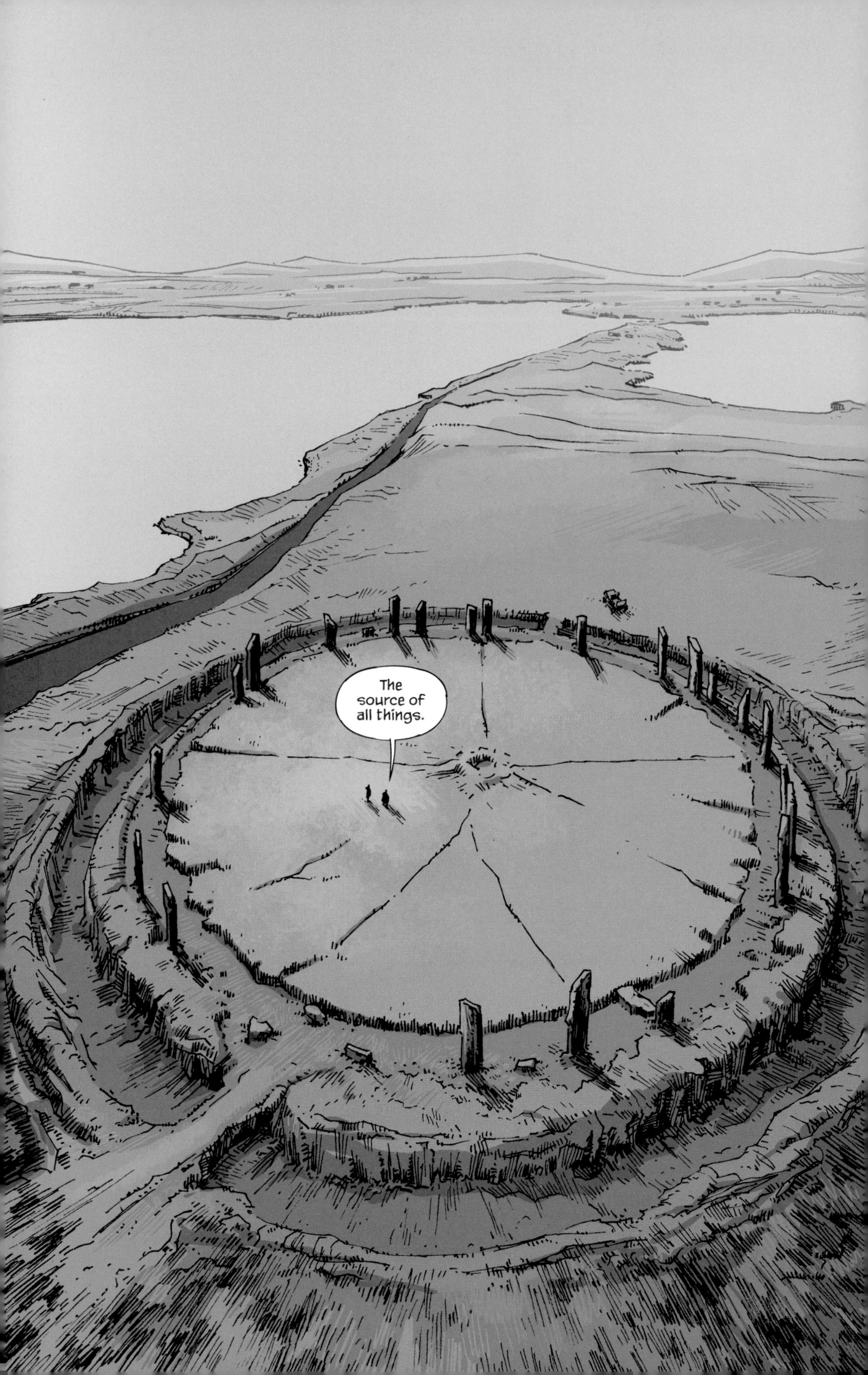
The source of all things.

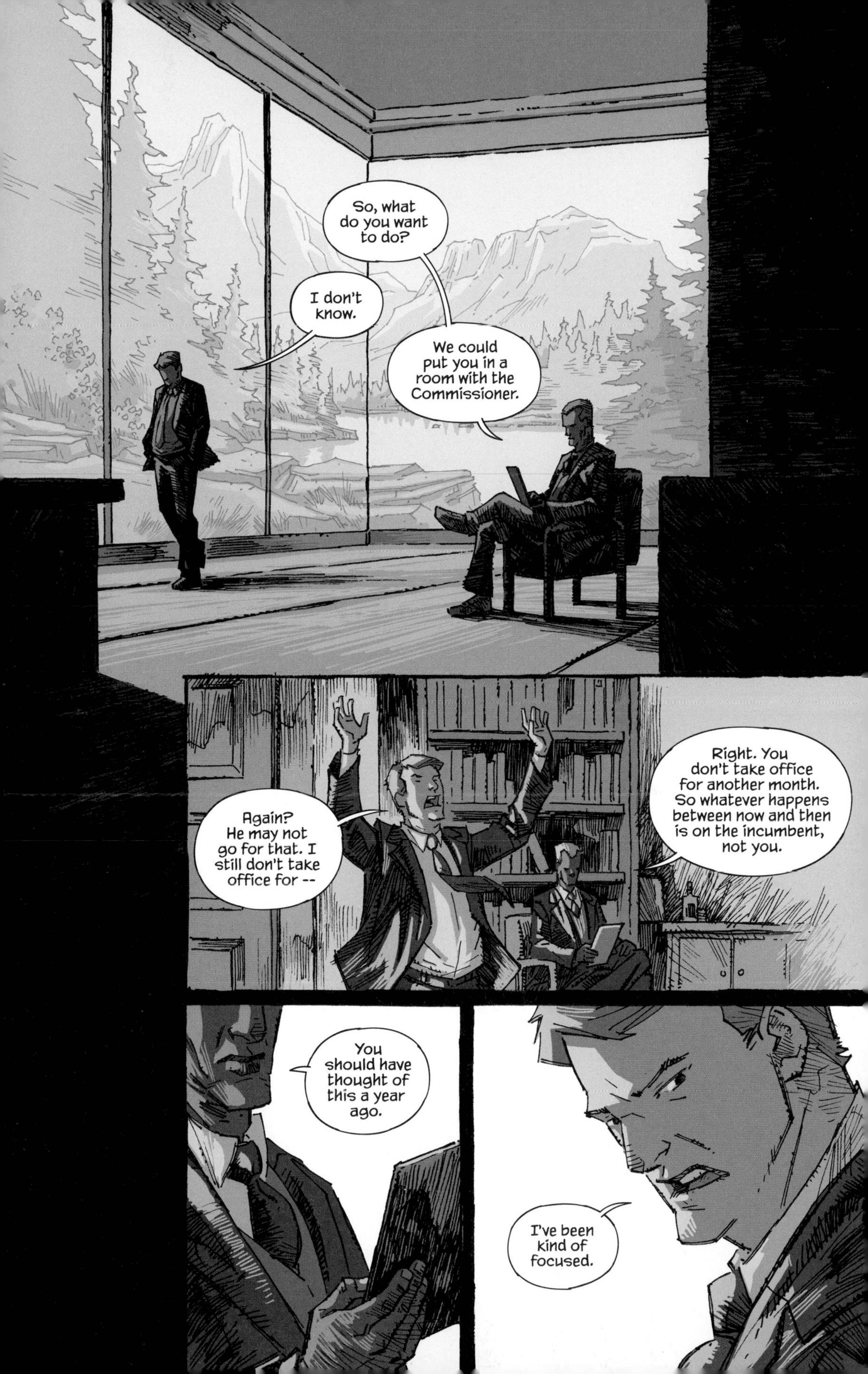
So, what do you want to do?
I don't know.
We could put you in a room with the Commissioner.
Again? He may not go for that. I still don't take office for --
Right. You don't take office for another month. So whatever happens between now and then is on the incumbent, not you.
You should have thought of this a year ago.
I've been kind of focused.

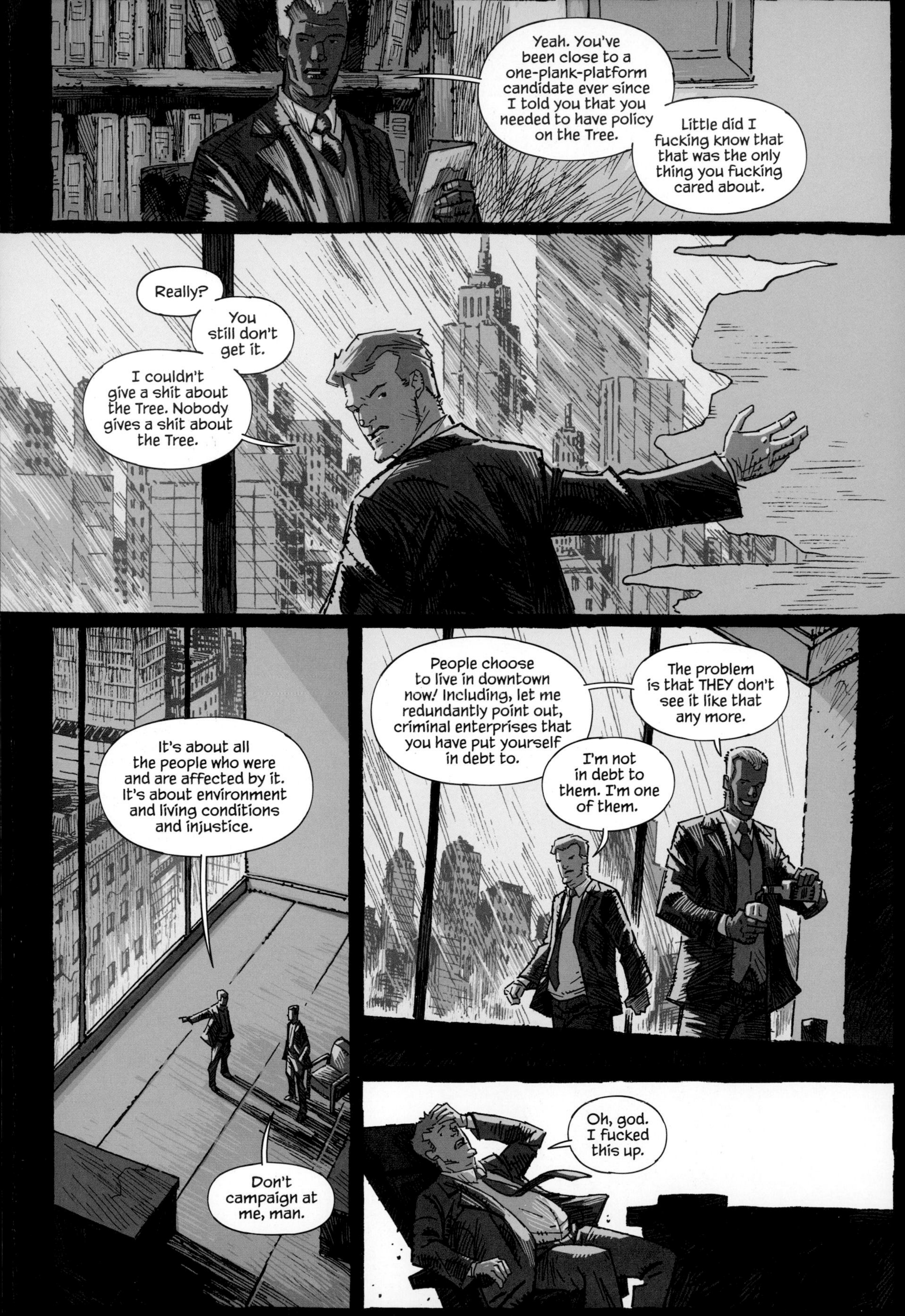
Yeah. You've been close to a one-plank-platform candidate ever since I told you that you needed to have policy on the Tree.
Little did I fucking know that that was the only thing you fucking cared about.
Really?
You still don't get it.
I couldn't give a shit about the Tree. Nobody gives a shit about the Tree.
It's about all the people who were and are affected by it. It's about environment and living conditions and injustice.
Don't campaign at me, man.
People choose to live in downtown now! Including, let me redundantly point out, criminal enterprises that you have put yourself in debt to.
The problem is that THEY don't see it like that any more.
I'm not in debt to them. I'm one of them.
Oh, god. I fucked this up.

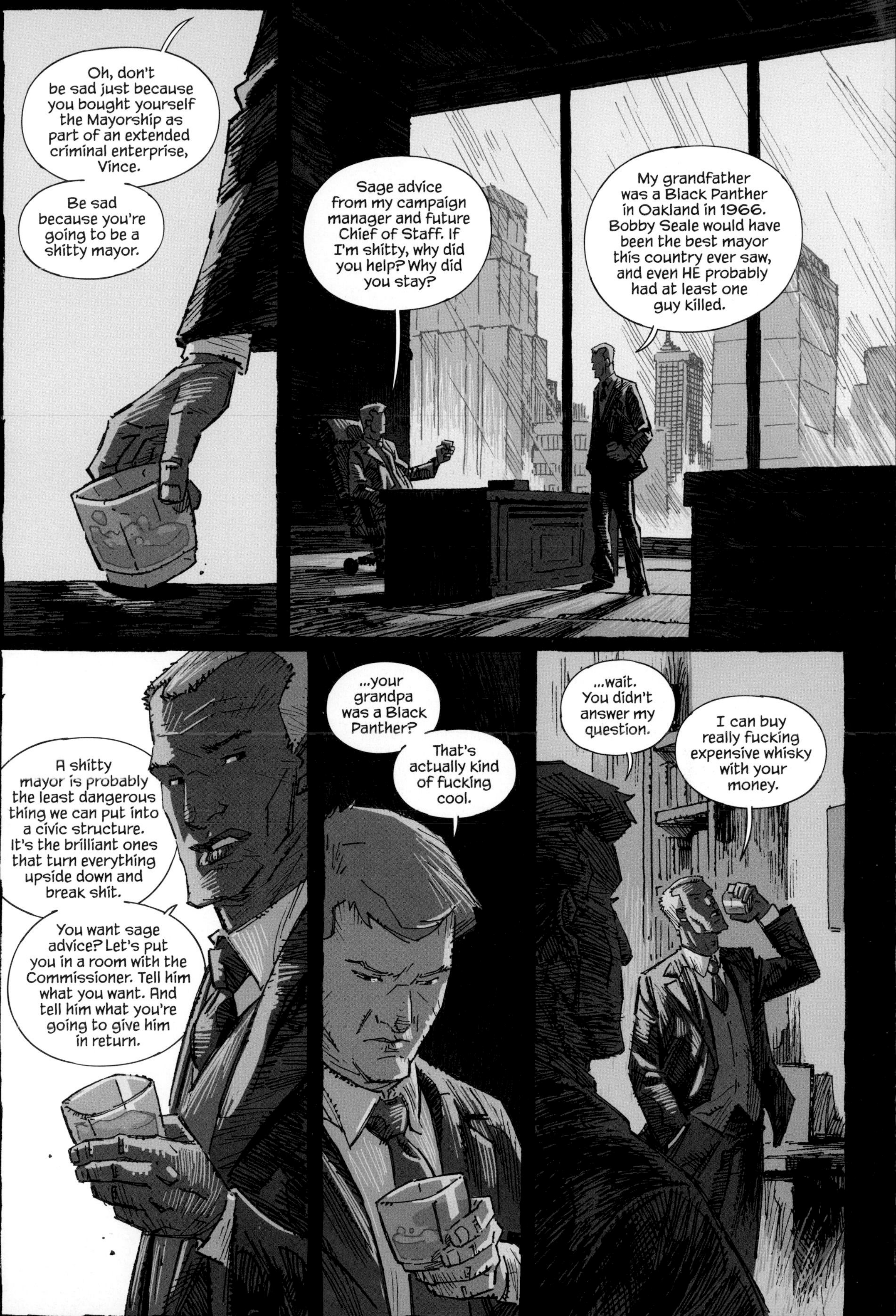
Oh, don't be sad just because you bought yourself the Mayorship as part of an extended criminal enterprise, Vince.
Be sad because you're going to be a shitty mayor.
Sage advice from my campaign manager and future Chief of Staff. If I'm shitty, why did you help? Why did you stay?
My grandfather was a Black Panther in Oakland in 1966. Bobby Seale would have been the best mayor this country ever saw, and even HE probably had at least one guy killed.
A shitty mayor is probably the least dangerous thing we can put into a civic structure. It's the brilliant ones that turn everything upside down and break shit.
You want sage advice? Let's put you in a room with the Commissioner. Tell him what you want. And tell him what you're going to give him in return.
...your grandpa was a Black Panther?
That's actually kind of fucking cool.
...wait. You didn't answer my question.
I can buy really fucking expensive whisky with your money.

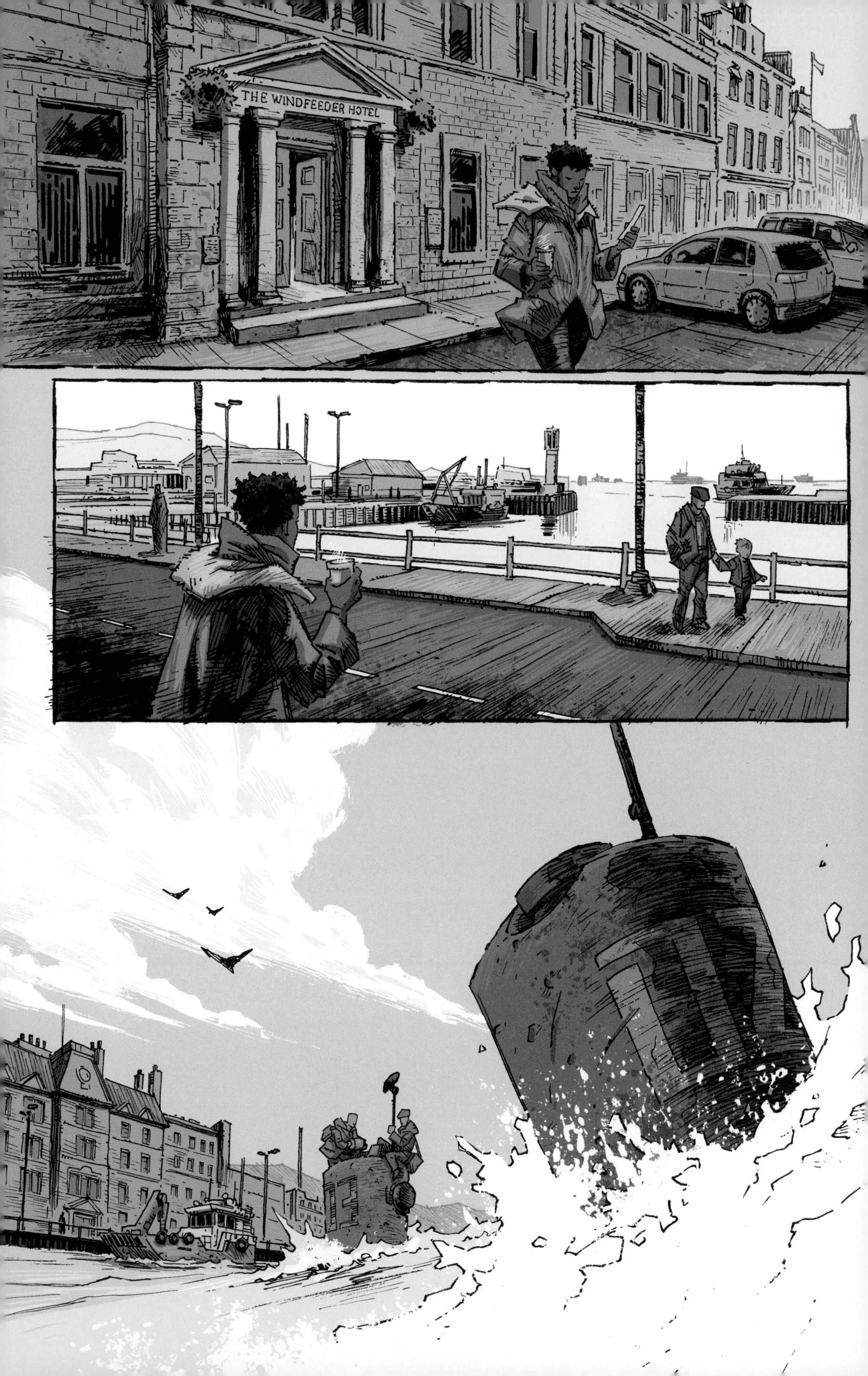
THE WINDFEEDER HOTEL

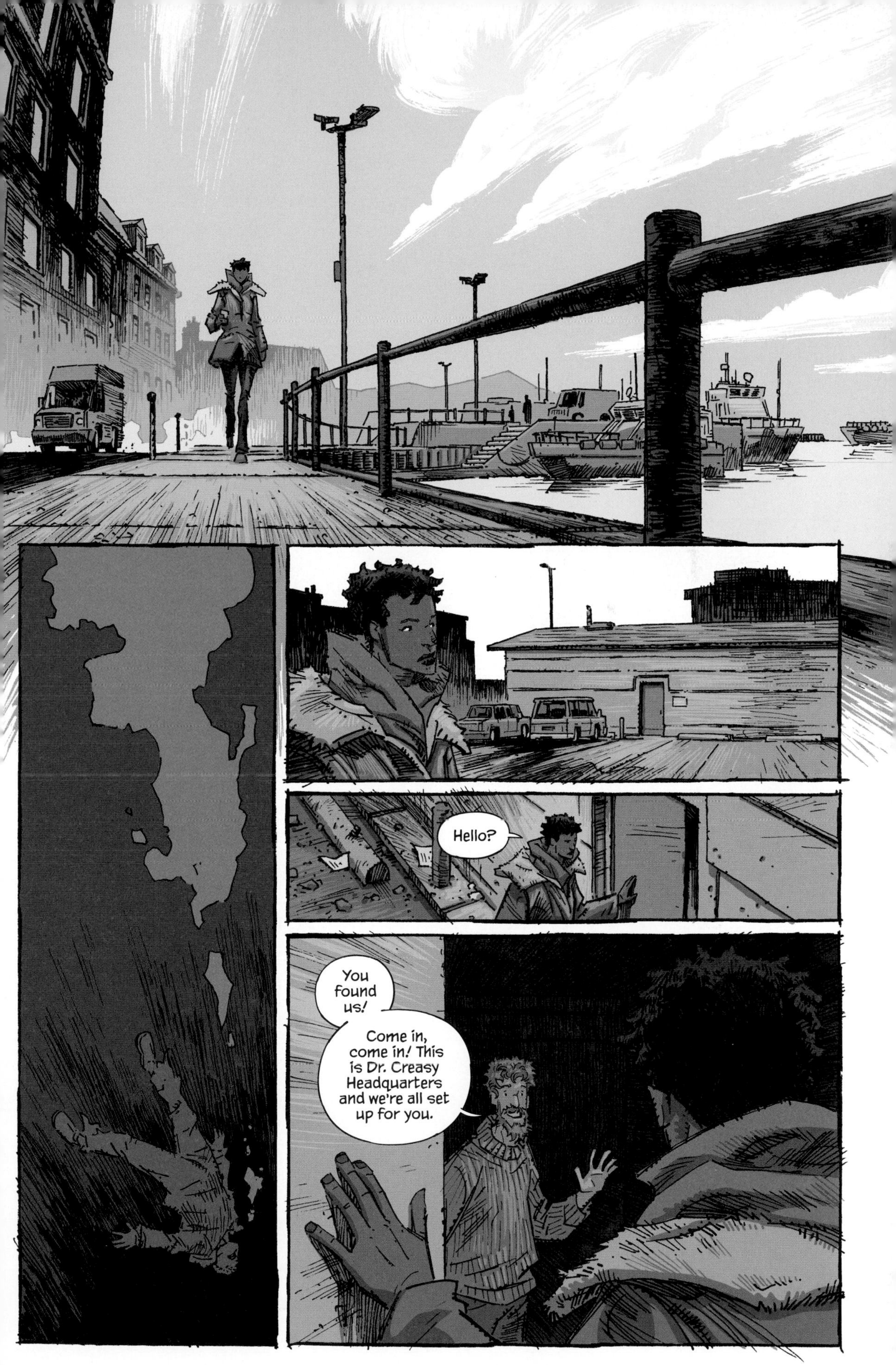
Hello?
You found us!
Come in, come in! This is Dr. Creasy Headquarters and we're all set up for you.

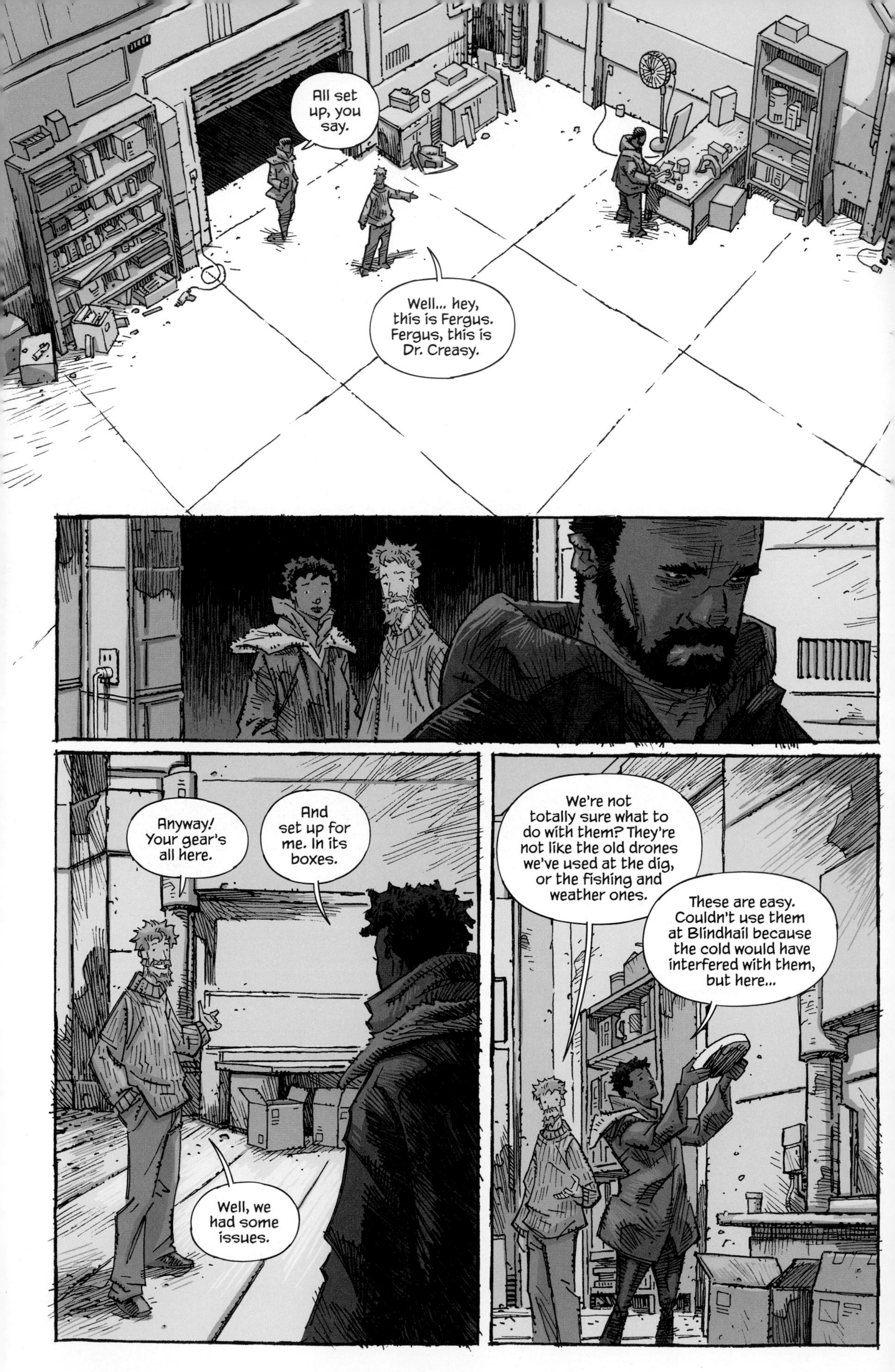
All set up, you say.
Well... hey, this is Fergus. Fergus, this is Dr. Creasy.
Anyway! Your gear's all here.
And set up for me. In its boxes.
Well, we had some issues.
We're not totally sure what to do with them? They're not like the old drones we've used at the dig, or the fishing and weather ones.
These are easy. Couldn't use them at Blindhail because the cold would have interfered with them, but here...

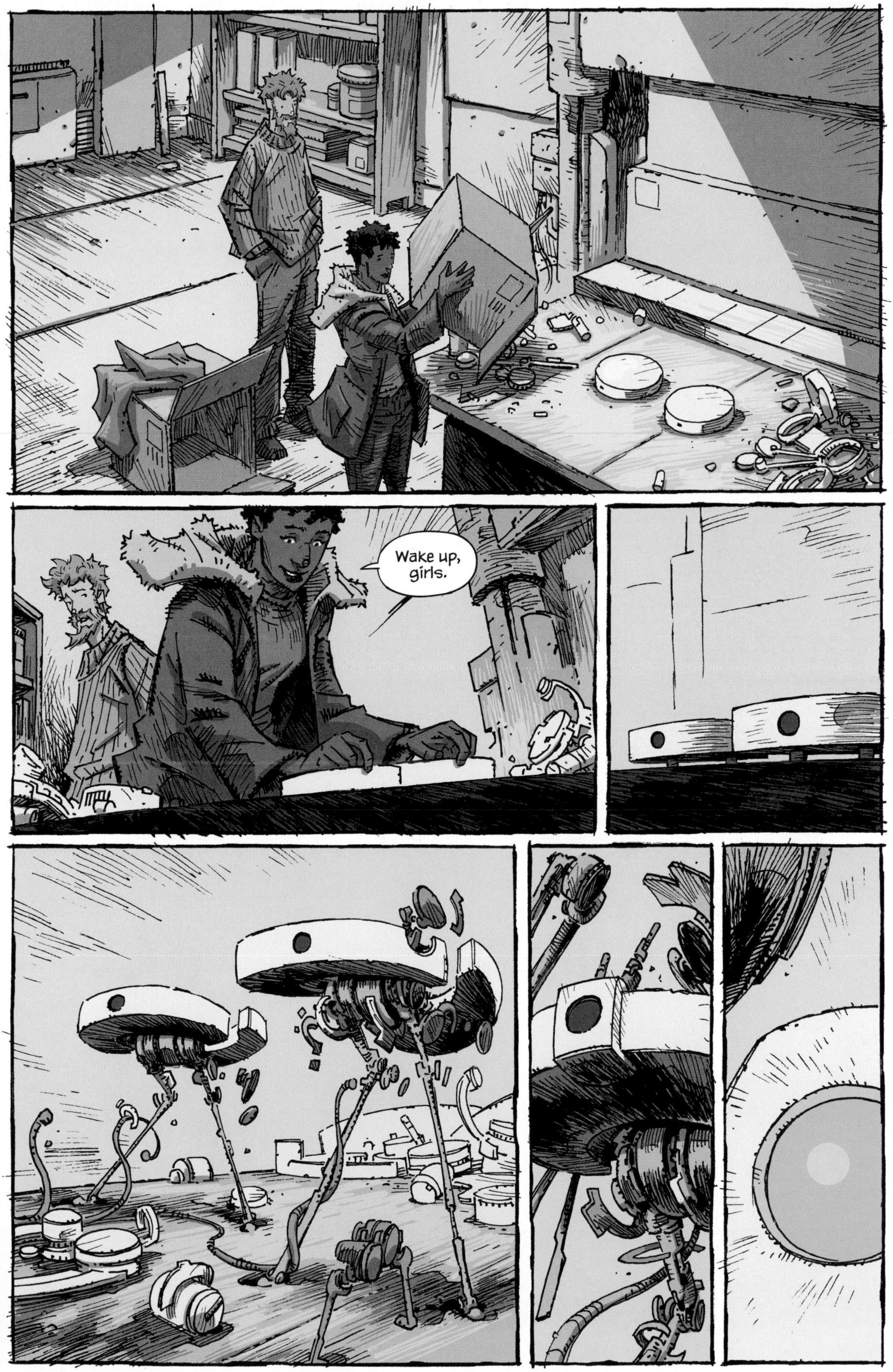
Wake up, girls.

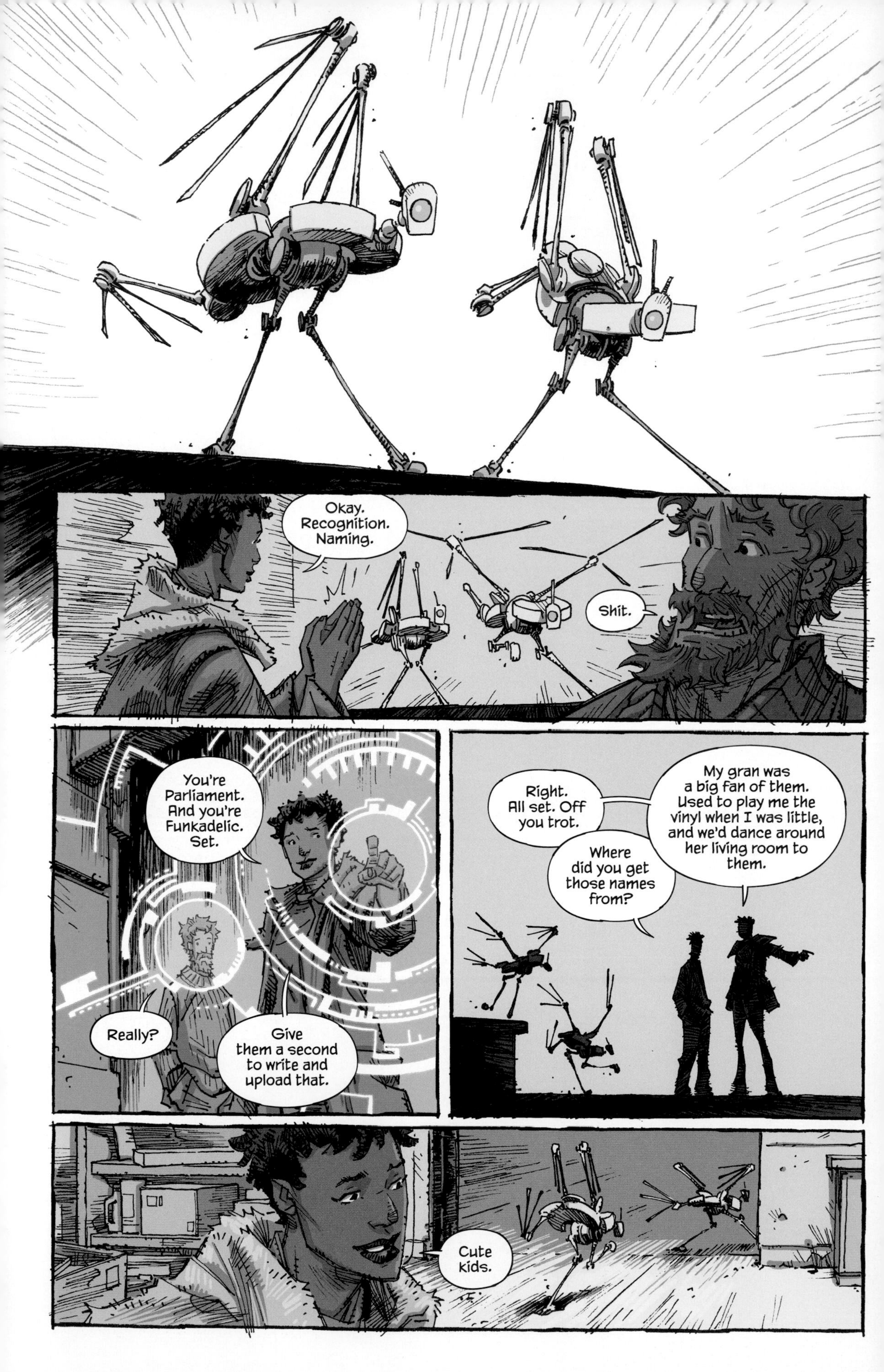
Okay. Recognition. Naming.
Shit.
You're Parliament. And you're Funkadelic. Set.
Really?
Give them a second to write and upload that.
Right. All set. Off you trot.
Where did you get those names from?
My gran was a big fan of them. Used to play me the vinyl when I was little, and we'd dance around her living room to them.
Cute kids.

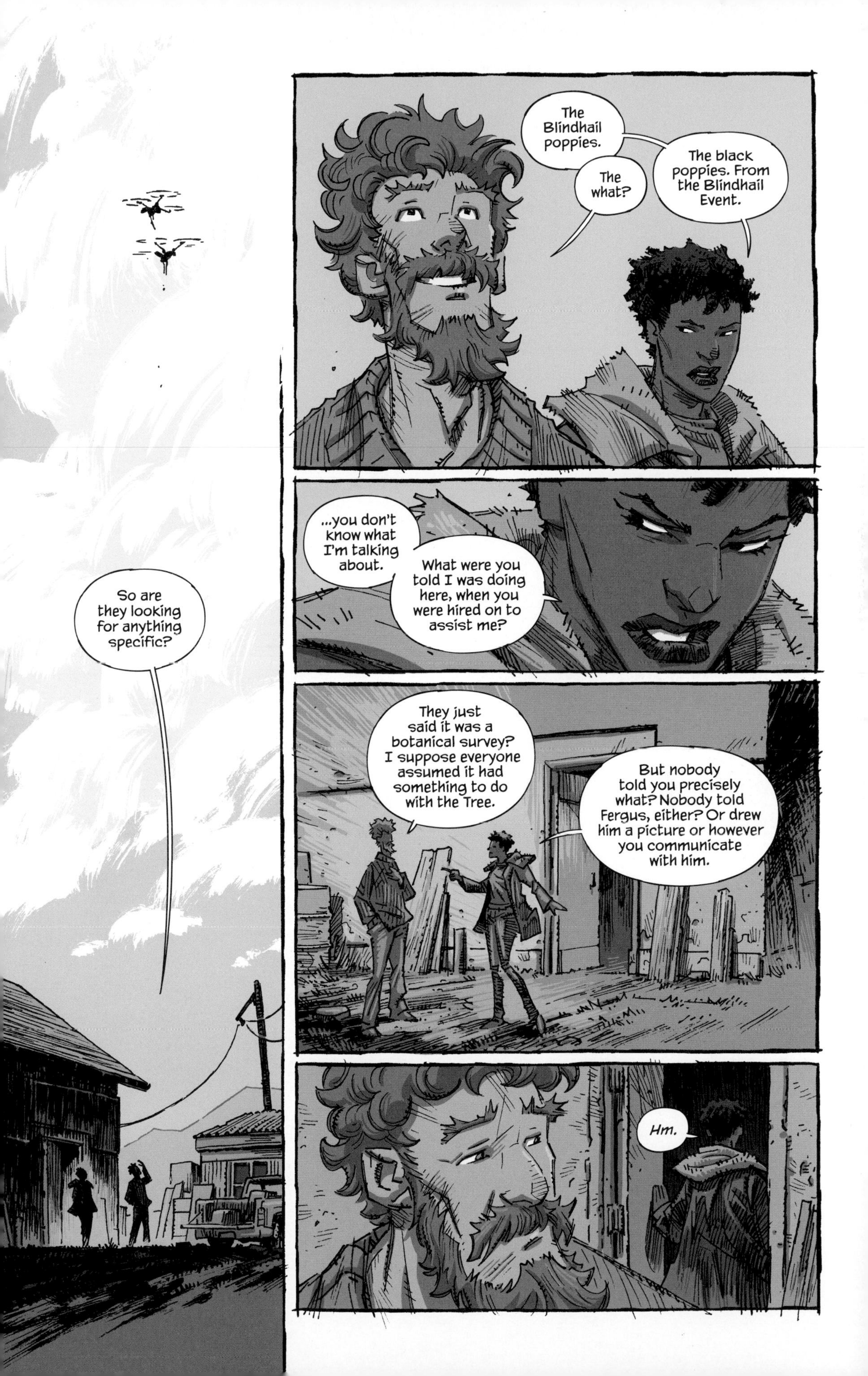
So are they looking for anything specific?
The Blindhail poppies.
The what?
The black poppies. From the Blindhail Event.
...you don't know what I'm talking about.
What were you told I was doing here, when you were hired on to assist me?
They just said it was a botanical survey? I suppose everyone assumed it had something to do with the Tree.
But nobody told you precisely what? Nobody told Fergus, either? Or drew him a picture or however you communicate with him.
Hm.

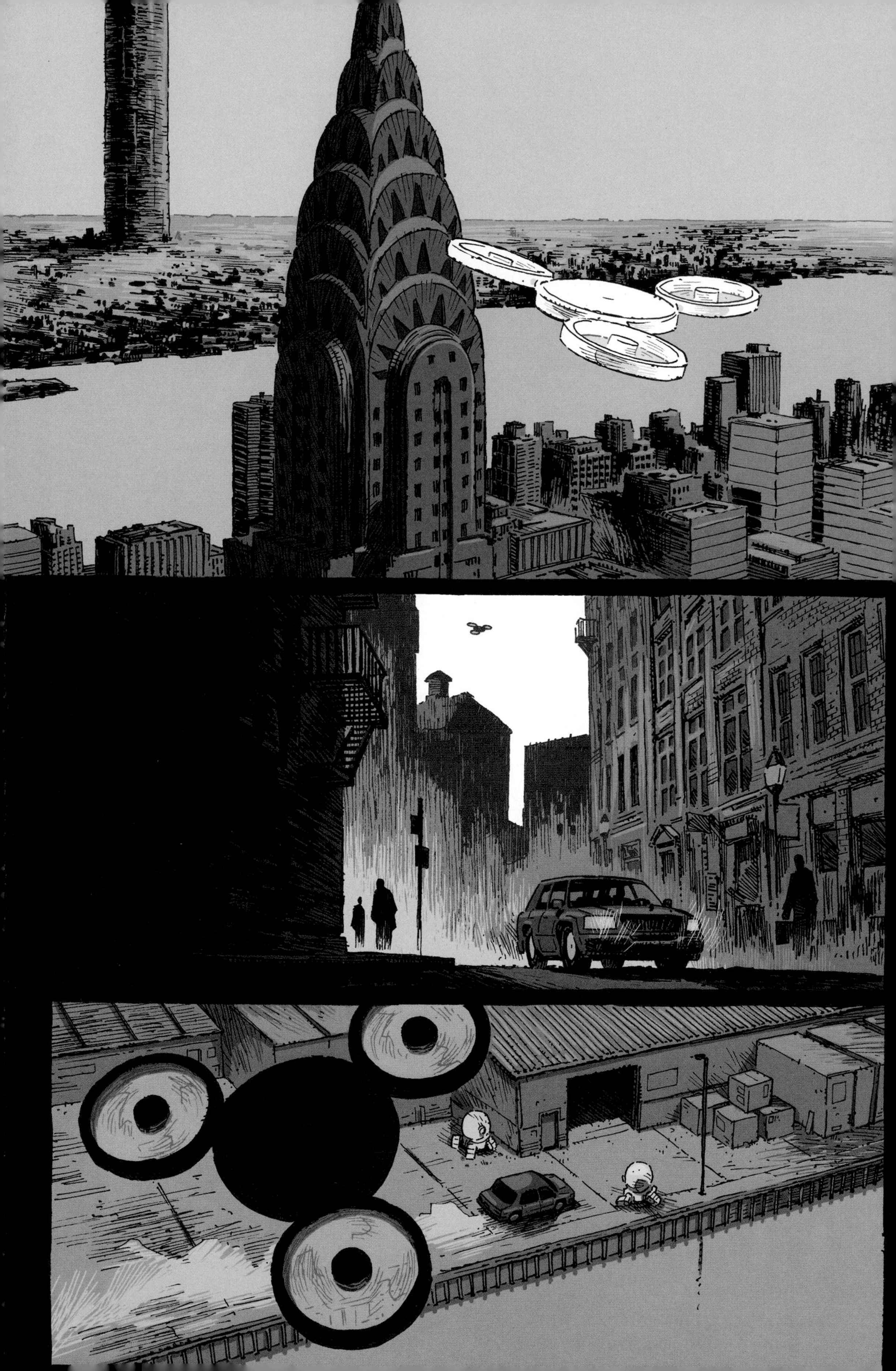

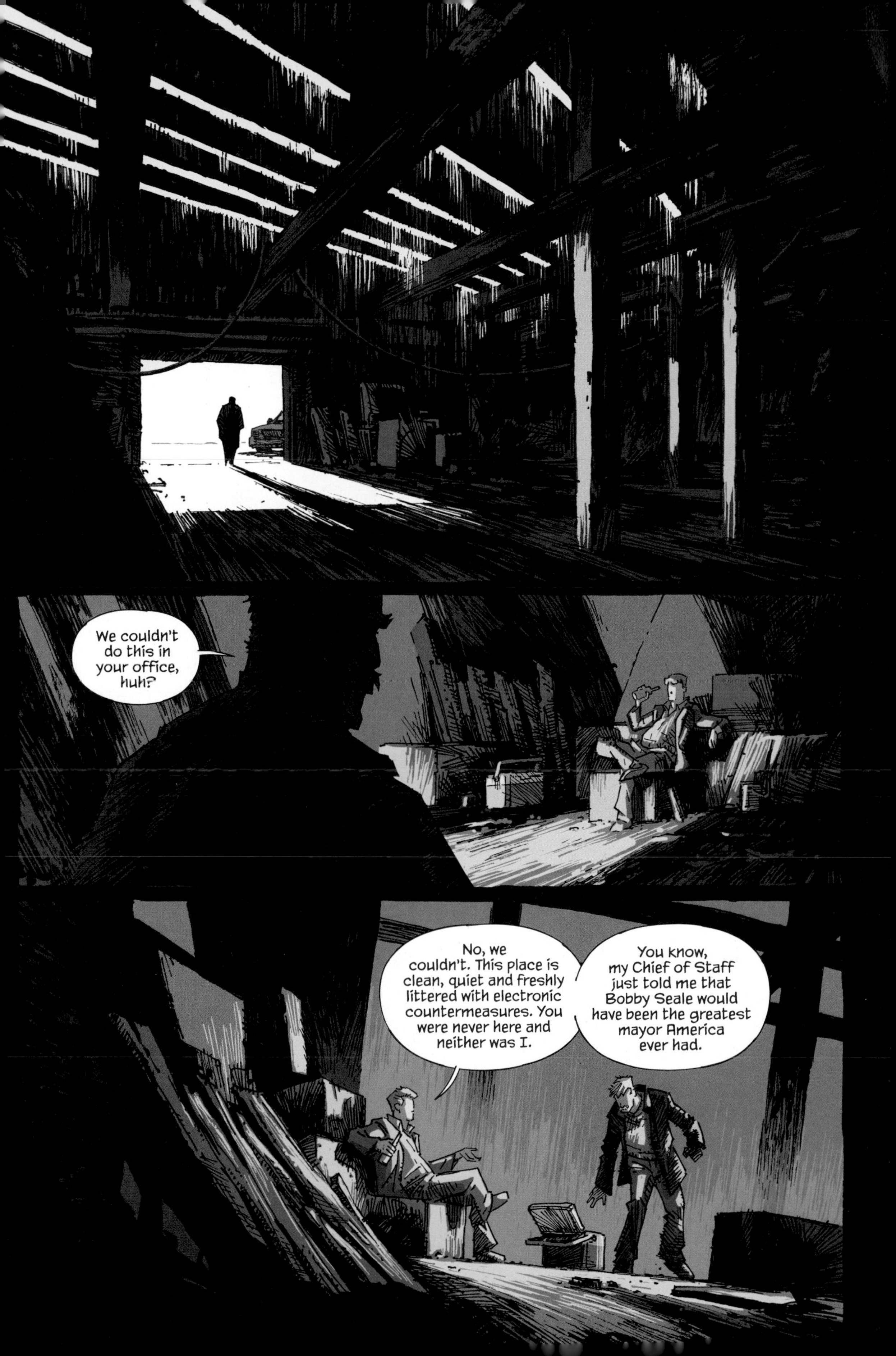
We couldn't do this in your office, huh?
No, we couldn't. This place is clean, quiet and freshly littered with electronic countermeasures. You were never here and neither was I.
You know, my Chief of Staff just told me that Bobby Seale would have been the greatest mayor America ever had.

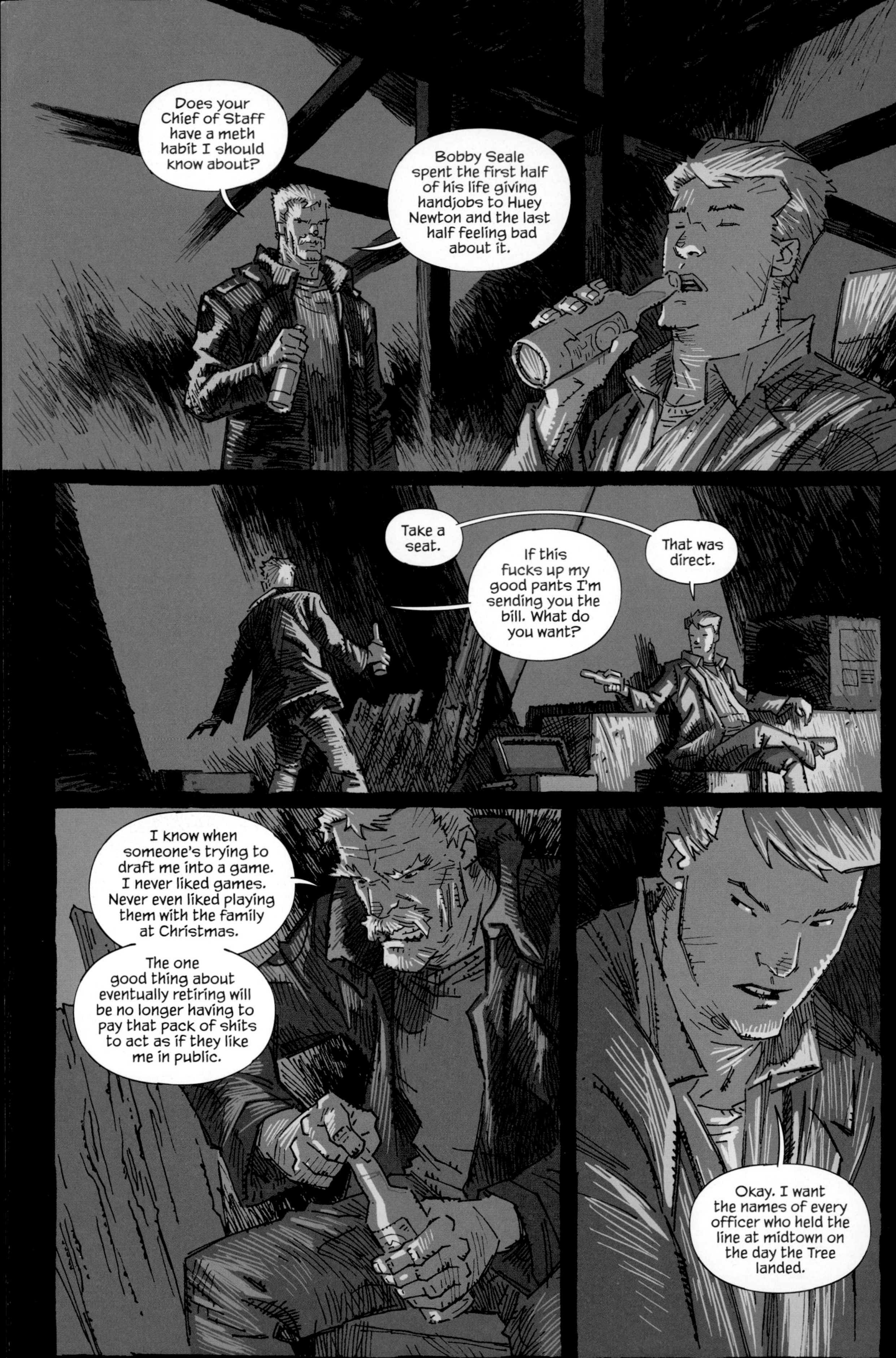
Does your Chief of Staff have a meth habit I should know about?
Bobby Seale spent the first half of his life giving handjobs to Huey Newton and the last half feeling bad about it.
Take a seat.
That was direct.
If this fucks up my good pants I'm sending you the bill. What do you want?
I know when someone's trying to draft me into a game. I never liked games. Never even liked playing them with the family at Christmas.
The one good thing about eventually retiring will be no longer having to pay that pack of shits to act as if they like me in public.
Okay. I want the names of every officer who held the line at midtown on the day the Tree landed.

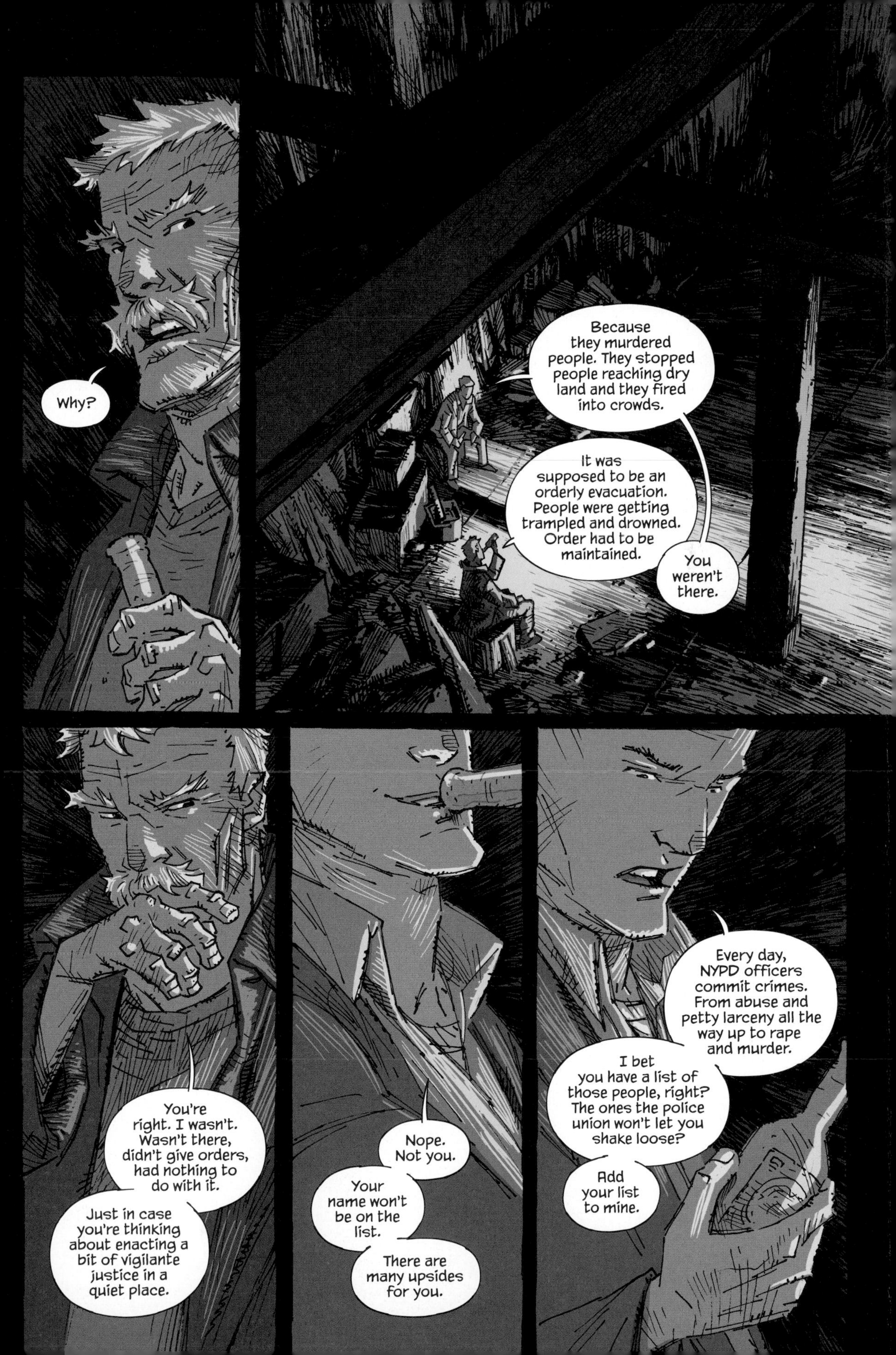
Why?
Because they murdered people. They stopped people reaching dry land and they fired into crowds.
It was supposed to be an orderly evacuation. People were getting trampled and drowned. Order had to be maintained.
You weren't there.
You're right. I wasn't. Wasn't there, didn't give orders, had nothing to do with it.
Just in case you're thinking about enacting a bit of vigilante justice in a quiet place.
Nope. Not you.
Your name won't be on the list.
There are many upsides for you.
Every day, NYPD officers commit crimes. From abuse and petty larceny all the way up to rape and murder.
I bet you have a list of those people, right? The ones the police union won't let you shake loose?
Add your list to mine.

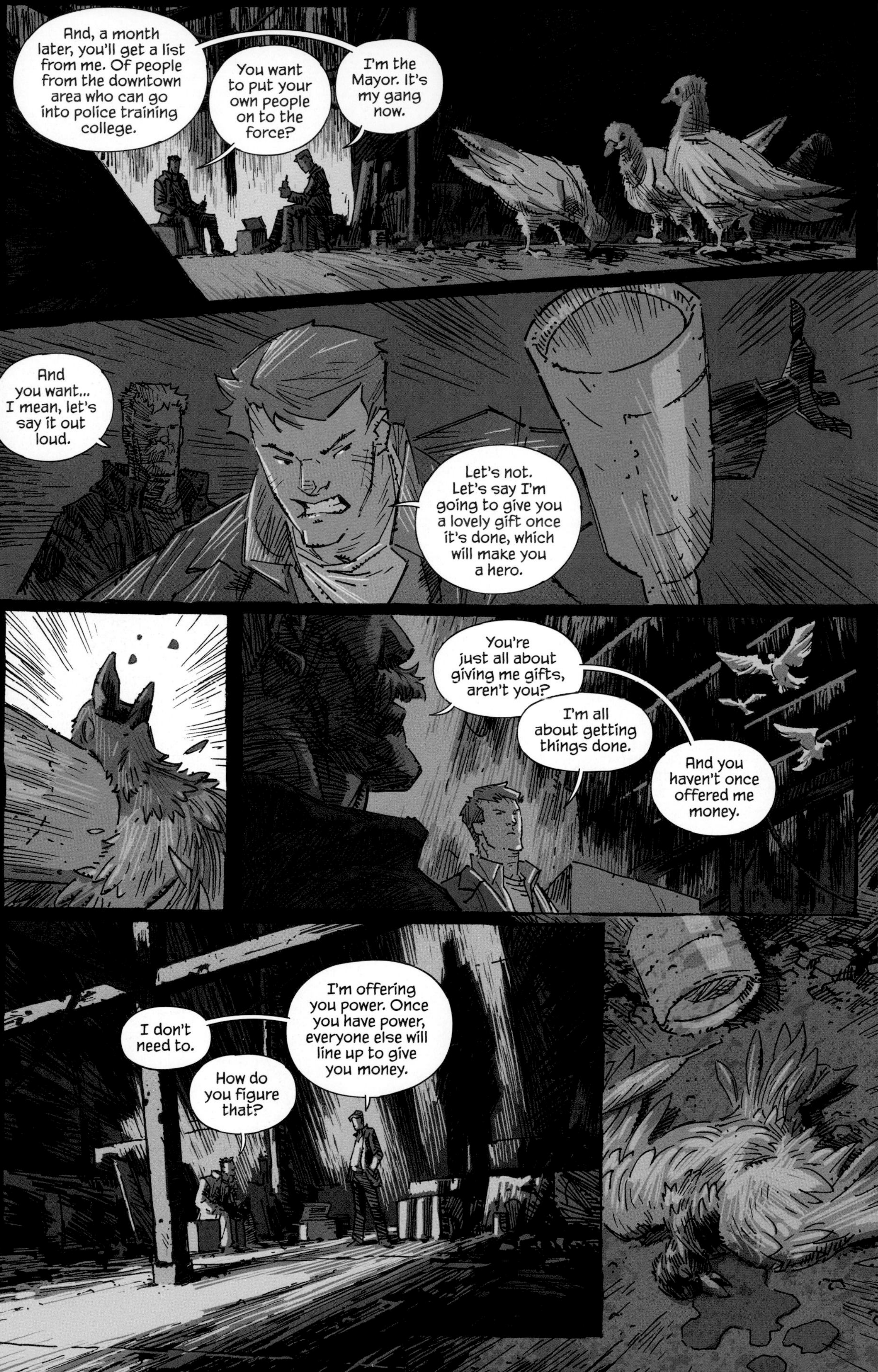
And, a month later, you'll get a list from me. Of people from the downtown area who can go into police training college.
You want to put your own people on to the force?
I'm the Mayor. It's my gang now.
And you want... I mean, let's say it out loud.
Let's not. Let's say I'm going to give you a lovely gift once it's done, which will make you a hero.
You're just all about giving me gifts, aren't you?
I'm all about getting things done.
And you haven't once offered me money.
I don't need to.
I'm offering you power. Once you have power, everyone else will line up to give you money.
How do you figure that?

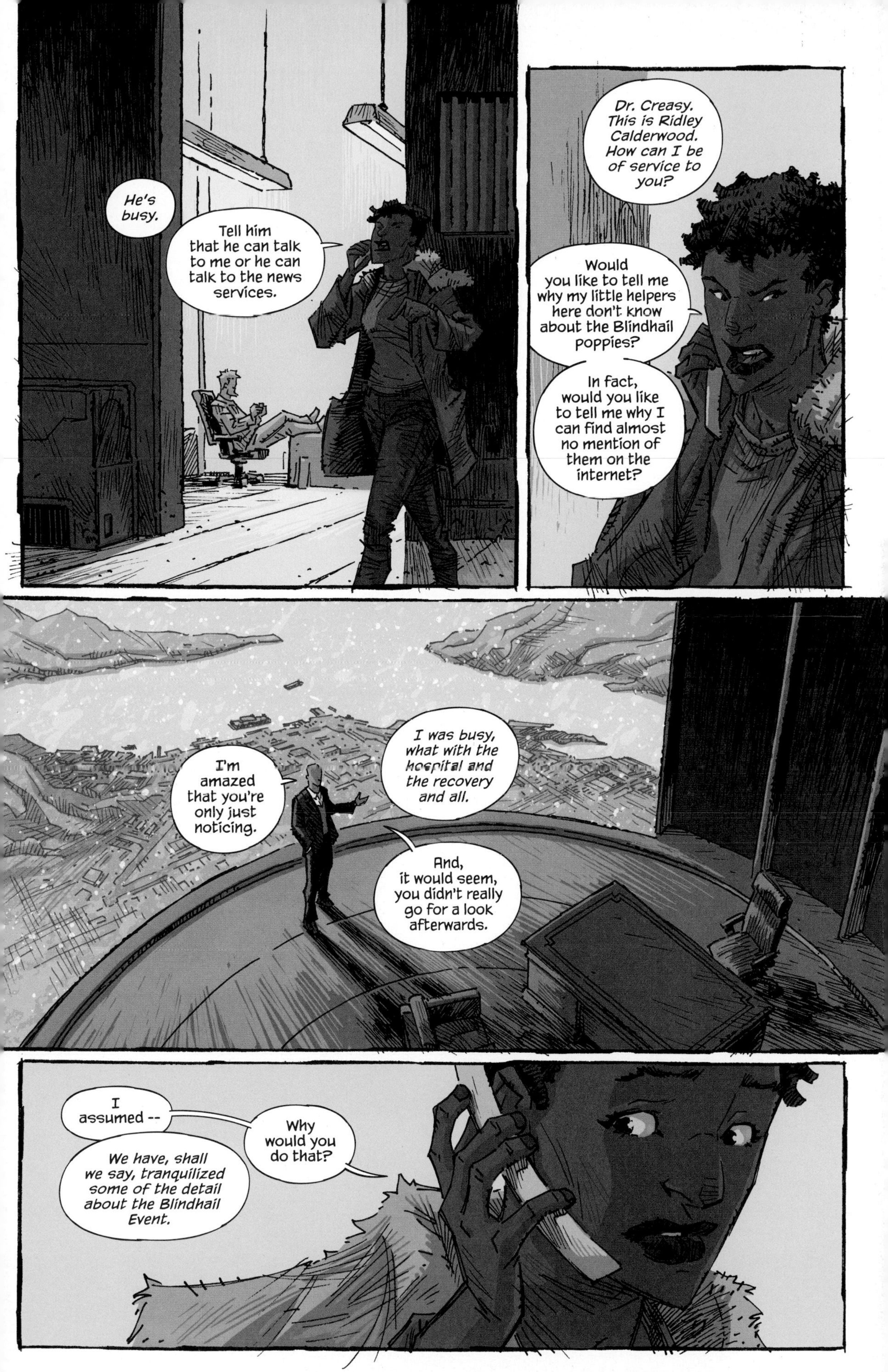
He's busy.
Tell him that he can talk to me or he can talk to the news services.
Dr. Creasy. This is Ridley Calderwood. How can I be of service to you?
Would you like to tell me why my little helpers here don't know about the Blindhail poppies?
In fact, would you like to tell me why I can find almost no mention of them on the internet?
I'm amazed that you're only just noticing.
I was busy, what with the hospital and the recovery and all.
And, it would seem, you didn't really go for a look afterwards.
I assumed --
Why would you do that?
We have, shall we say, tranquilized some of the detail about the Blindhail Event.

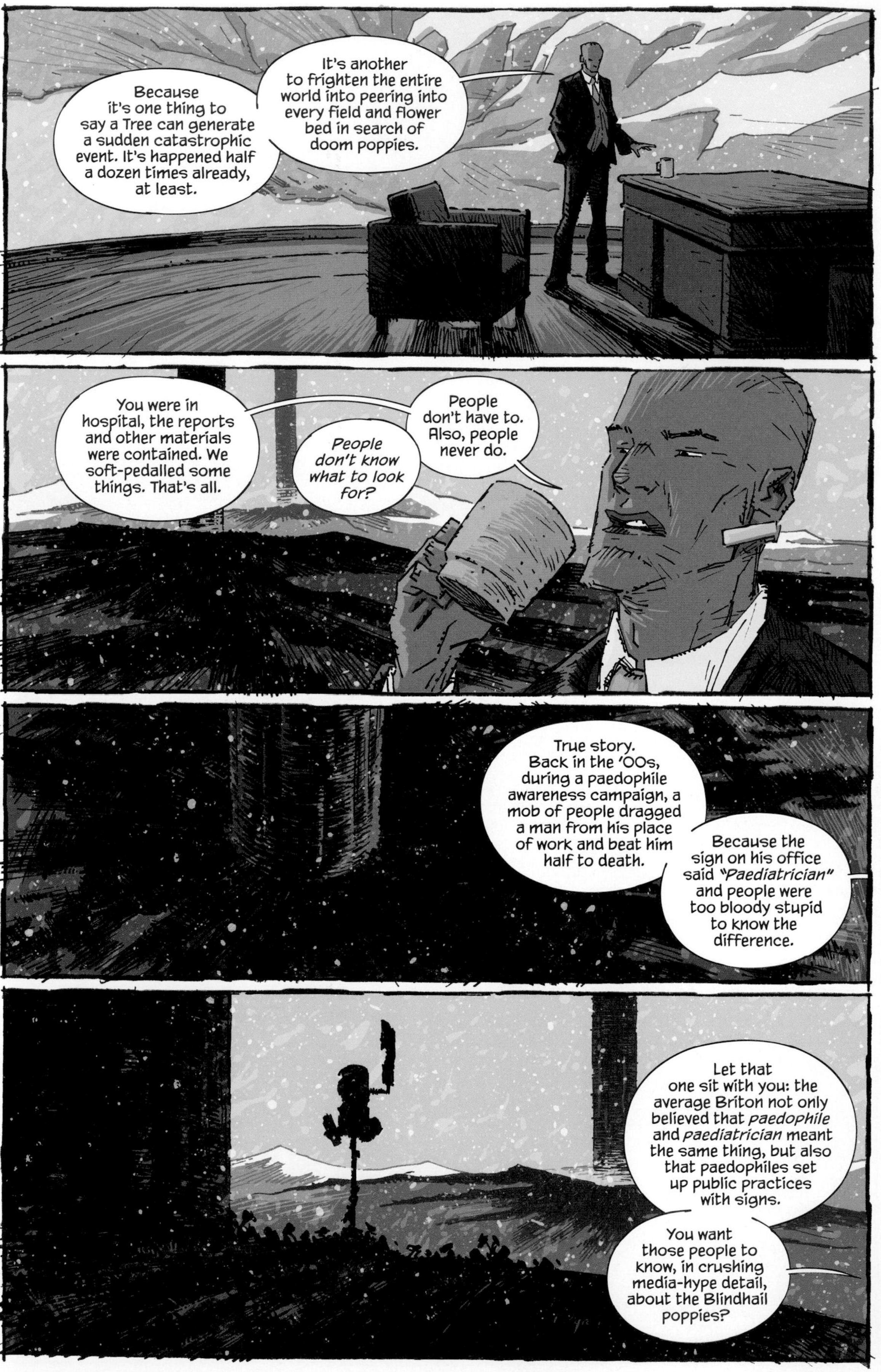
Because it's one thing to say a Tree can generate a sudden catastrophic event. It's happened half a dozen times already, at least.
It's another to frighten the entire world into peering into every field and flower bed in search of doom poppies.
You were in hospital, the reports and other materials were contained. We soft-pedalled some things. That's all.
People don't know what to look for?
People don't have to. Also, people never do.
True story. Back in the '00s, during a paedophile awareness campaign, a mob of people dragged a man from his place of work and beat him half to death.
Because the sign on his office said *"Paediatrician"* and people were too bloody stupid to know the difference.
Let that one sit with you: the average Briton not only believed that *paedophile* and *paediatrician* meant the same thing, but also that paedophiles set up public practices with signs.
You want those people to know, in crushing media-hype detail, about the Blindhail poppies?

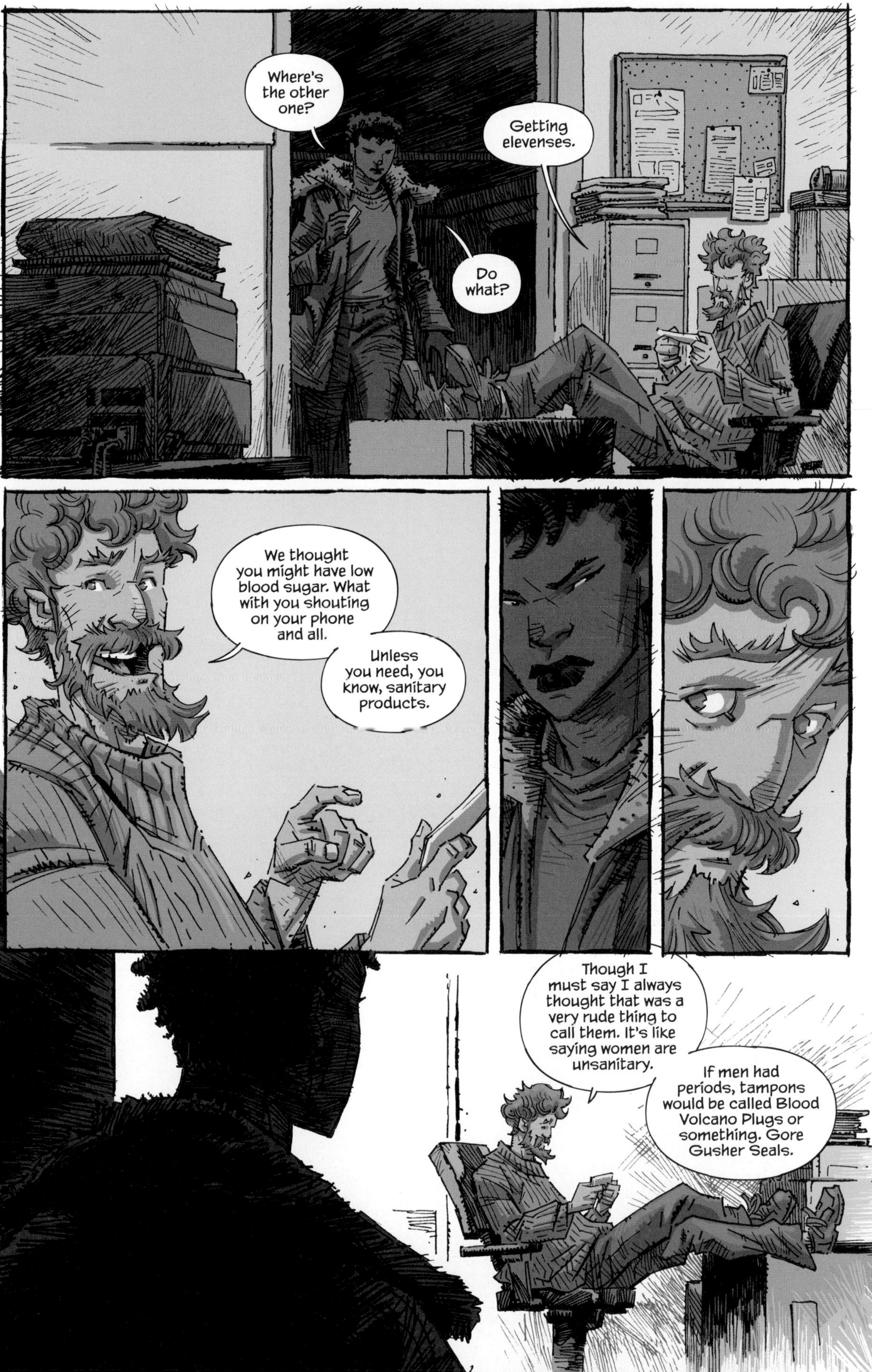
Where's the other one?
Getting elevenses.
Do what?
We thought you might have low blood sugar. What with you shouting on your phone and all.
Unless you need, you know, sanitary products.
Though I must say I always thought that was a very rude thing to call them. It's like saying women are unsanitary.
If men had periods, tampons would be called Blood Volcano Plugs or something. Gore Gusher Seals.

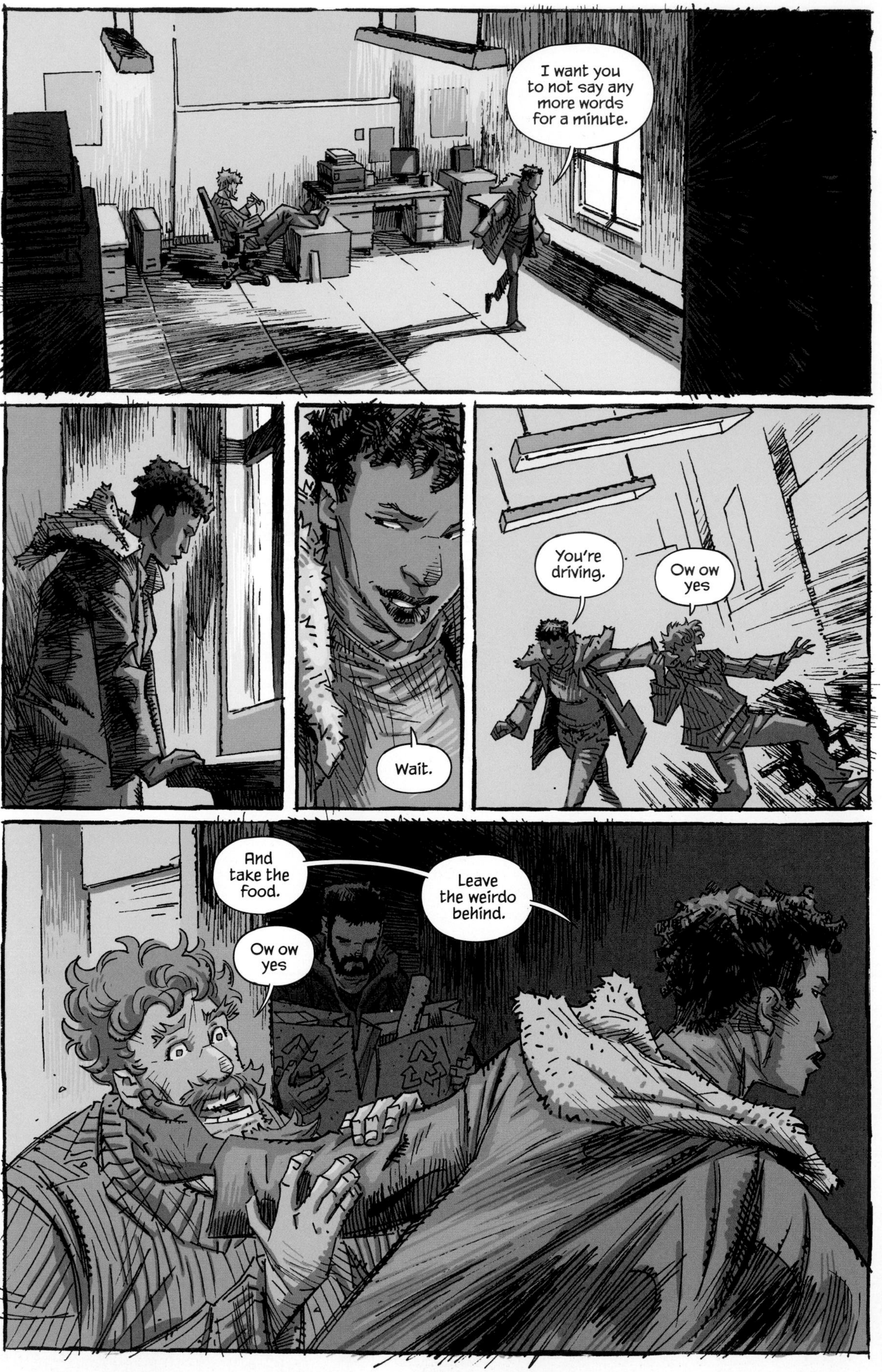
I want you to not say any more words for a minute.
Wait.
You're driving.
Ow ow yes
And take the food.
Leave the weirdo behind.
Ow ow yes

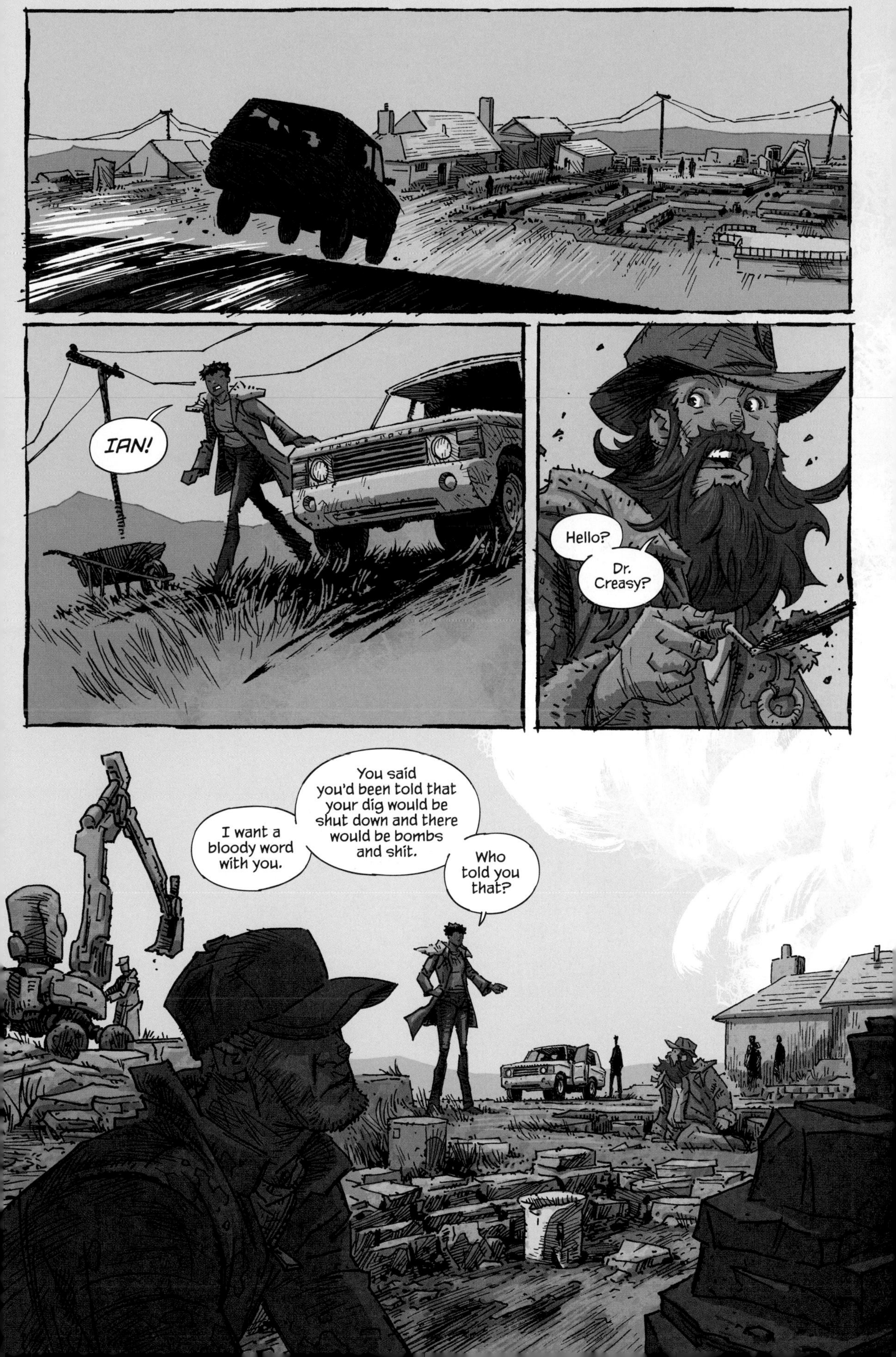
IAN!
Hello?
Dr. Creasy?
I want a bloody word with you.
You said you'd been told that your dig would be shut down and there would be bombs and shit.
Who told you that?

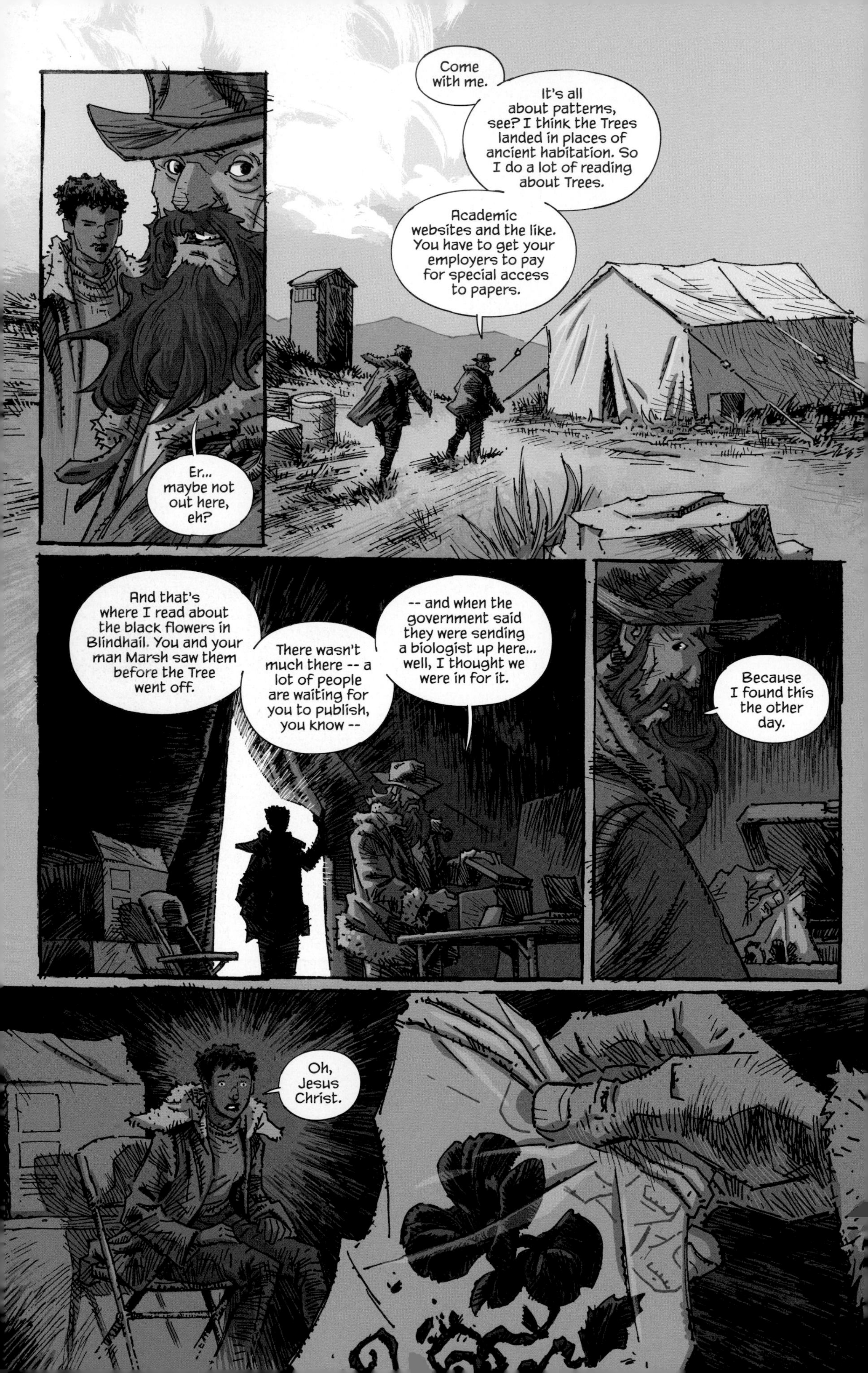
Come with me.
It's all about patterns, see? I think the Trees landed in places of ancient habitation. So I do a lot of reading about Trees.
Academic websites and the like. You have to get your employers to pay for special access to papers.
Er... maybe not out here, eh?
And that's where I read about the black flowers in Blindhail. You and your man Marsh saw them before the Tree went off.
There wasn't much there -- a lot of people are waiting for you to publish, you know --
-- and when the government said they were sending a biologist up here... well, I thought we were in for it.
Because I found this the other day.
Oh, Jesus Christ.

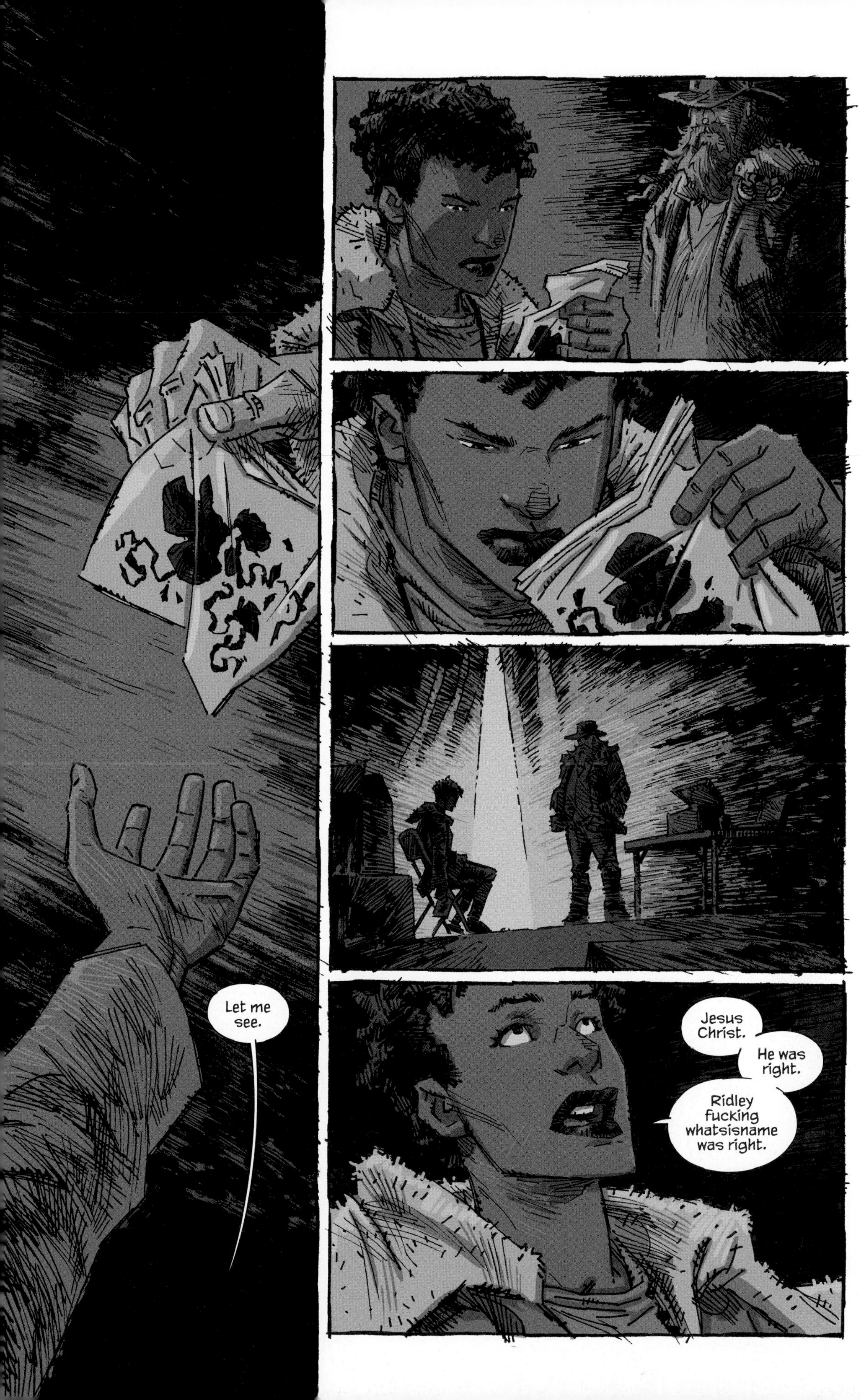
Let me see.
Jesus Christ.
He was right.
Ridley fucking whatsisname was right.

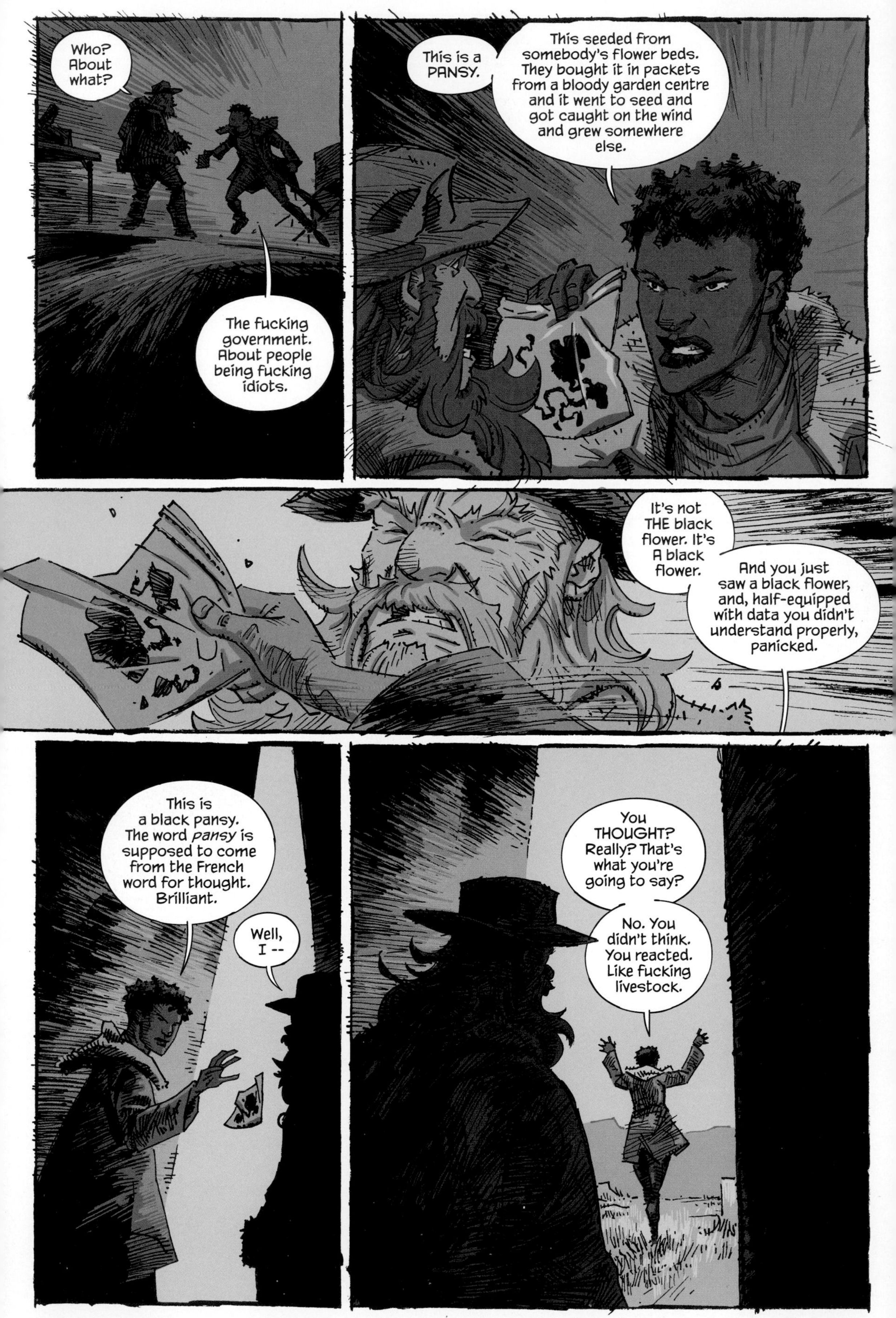
Who? About what?
The fucking government. About people being fucking idiots.
This is a PANSY.
This seeded from somebody's flower beds. They bought it in packets from a bloody garden centre and it went to seed and got caught on the wind and grew somewhere else.
It's not THE black flower. It's A black flower.
And you just saw a black flower, and, half-equipped with data you didn't understand properly, panicked.
This is a black pansy. The word *pansy* is supposed to come from the French word for thought. Brilliant.
Well, I --
You THOUGHT? Really? That's what you're going to say?
No. You didn't think. You reacted. Like fucking livestock.

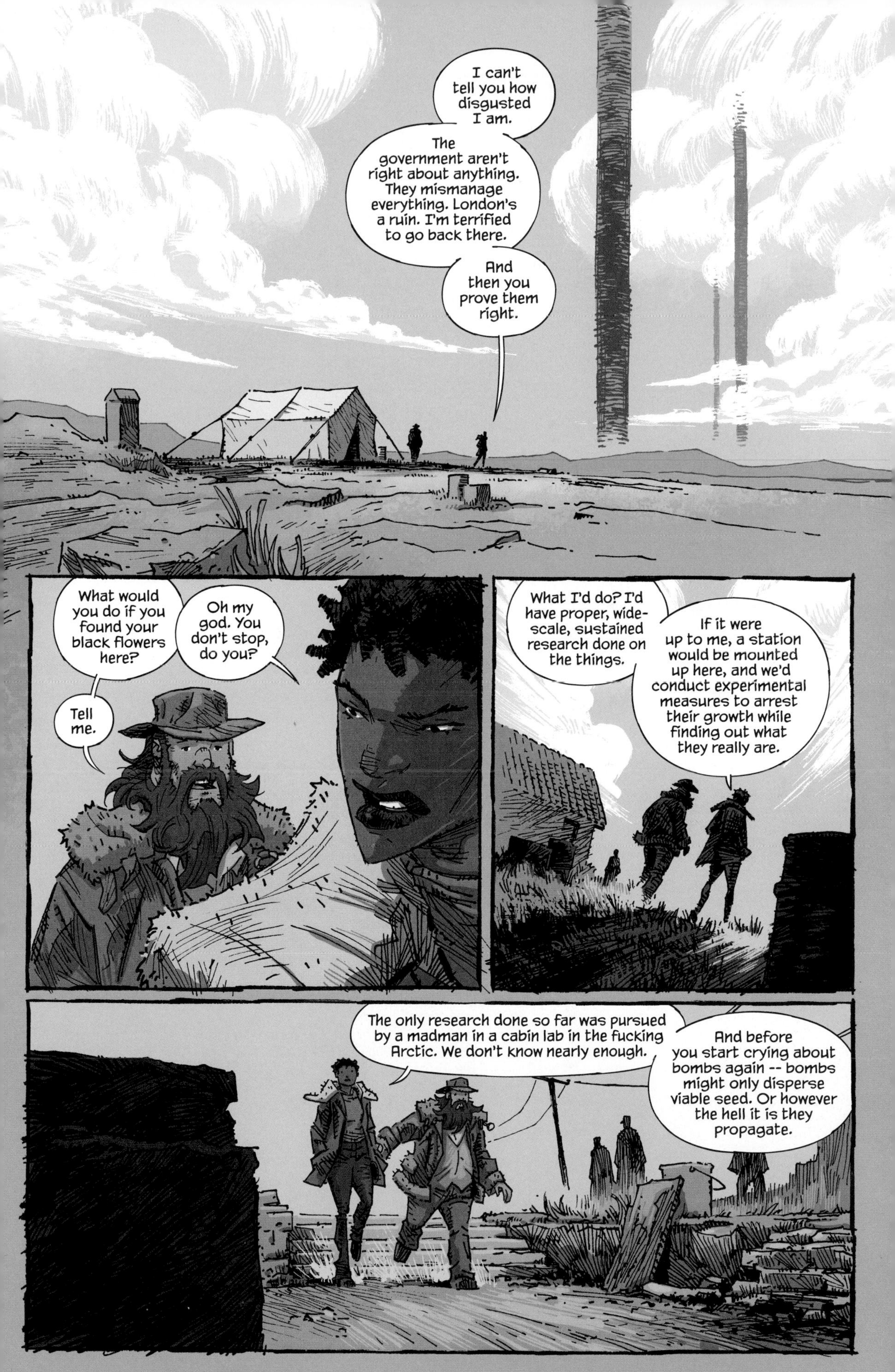
I can't tell you how disgusted I am.
The government aren't right about anything. They mismanage everything. London's a ruin. I'm terrified to go back there.
And then you prove them right.
What would you do if you found your black flowers here?
Tell me.
Oh my god. You don't stop, do you?
What I'd do? I'd have proper, wide-scale, sustained research done on the things.
If it were up to me, a station would be mounted up here, and we'd conduct experimental measures to arrest their growth while finding out what they really are.
The only research done so far was pursued by a madman in a cabin lab in the fucking Arctic. We don't know nearly enough.
And before you start crying about bombs again -- bombs might only disperse viable seed. Or however the hell it is they propagate.

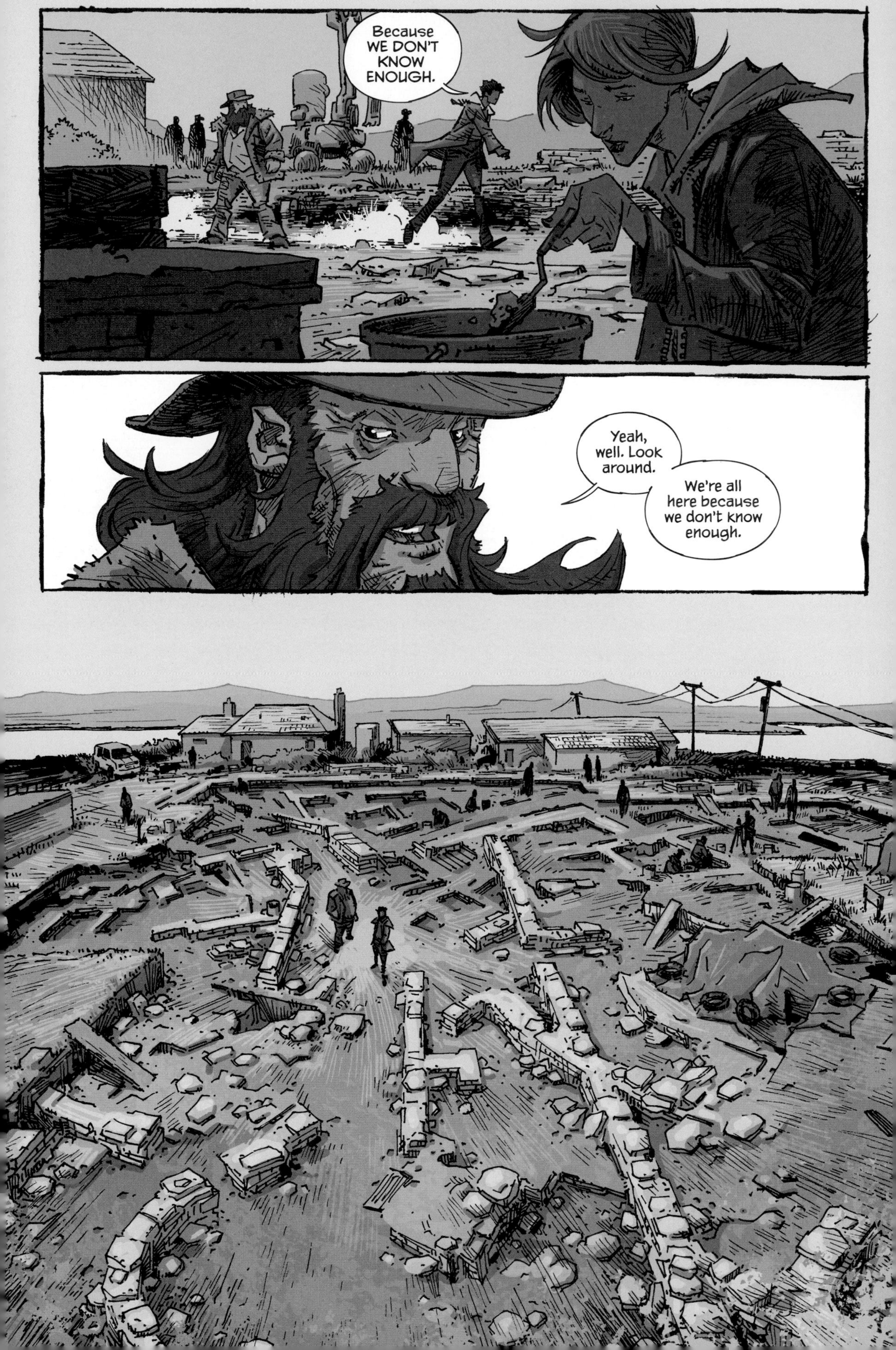
Because WE DON'T KNOW ENOUGH.
Yeah, well. Look around.
We're all here because we don't know enough.

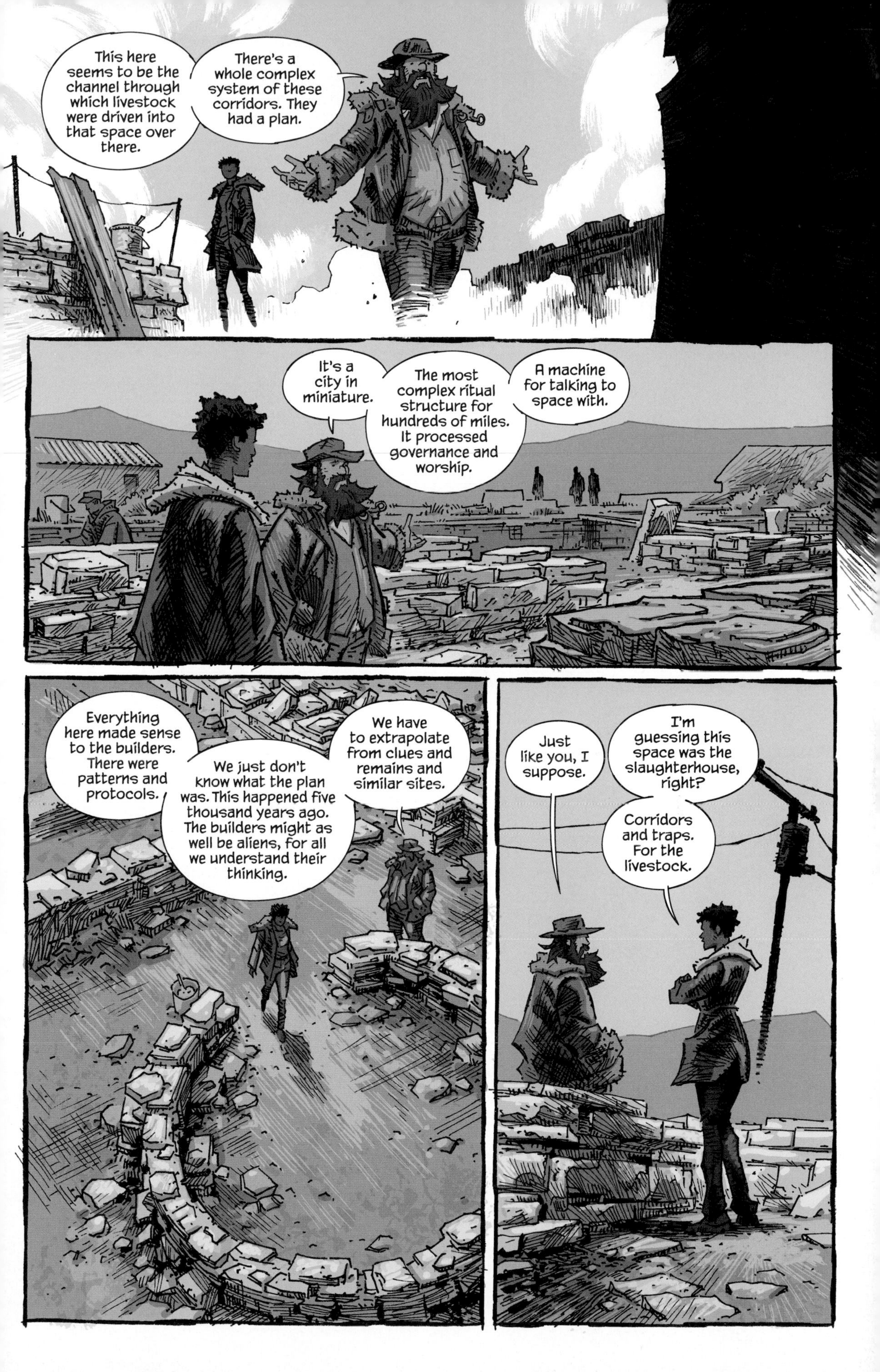
This here seems to be the channel through which livestock were driven into that space over there.
There's a whole complex system of these corridors. They had a plan.
It's a city in miniature.
The most complex ritual structure for hundreds of miles. It processed governance and worship.
A machine for talking to space with.
Everything here made sense to the builders. There were patterns and protocols.
We just don't know what the plan was. This happened five thousand years ago. The builders might as well be aliens, for all we understand their thinking.
We have to extrapolate from clues and remains and similar sites.
I'm guessing this space was the slaughterhouse, right?
Just like you, I suppose.
Corridors and traps. For the livestock.

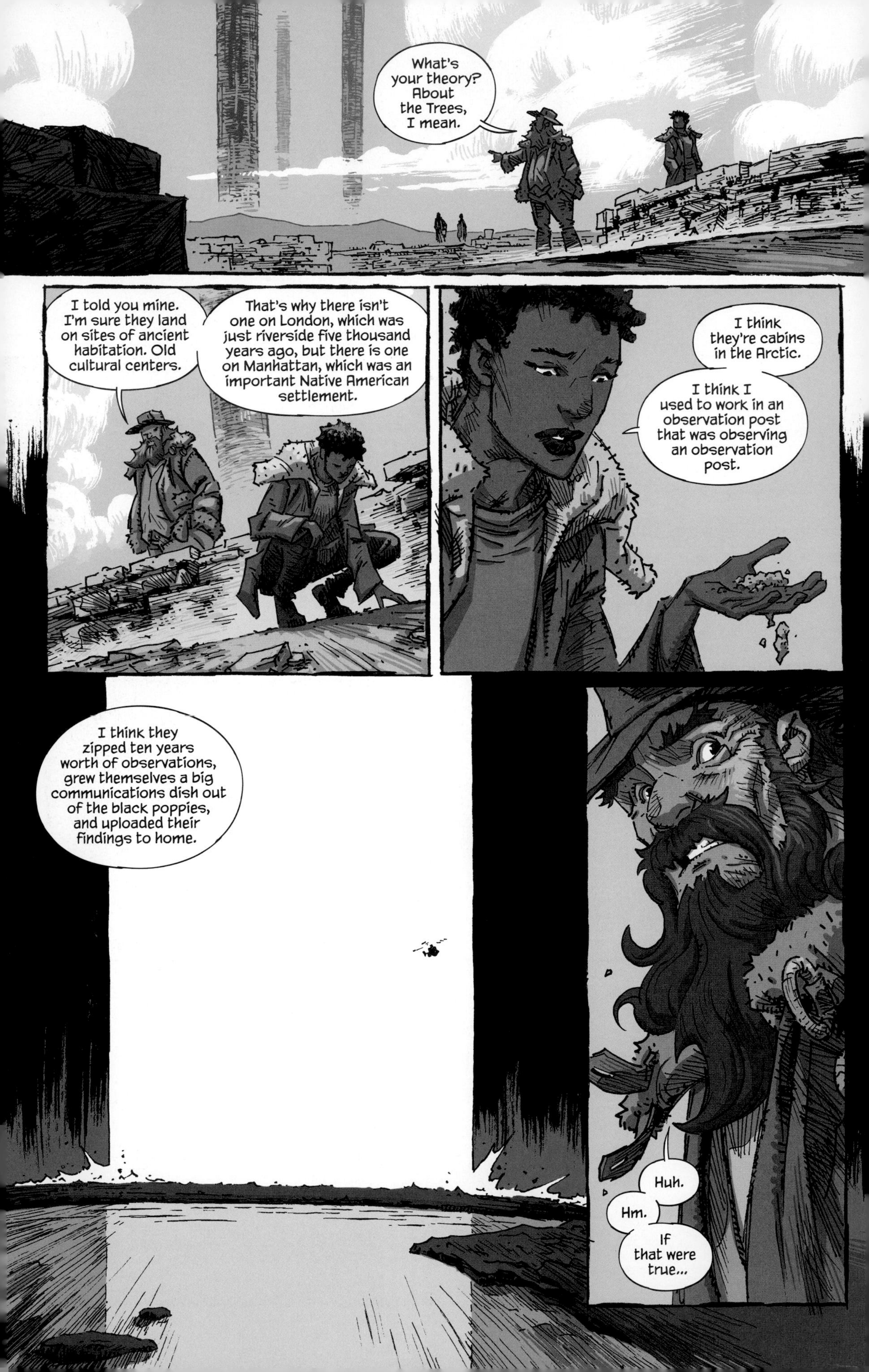
What's your theory? About the Trees, I mean.
I told you mine. I'm sure they land on sites of ancient habitation. Old cultural centers.
That's why there isn't one on London, which was just riverside five thousand years ago, but there is one on Manhattan, which was an important Native American settlement.
I think they're cabins in the Arctic.
I think I used to work in an observation post that was observing an observation post.
I think they zipped ten years worth of observations, grew themselves a big communications dish out of the black poppies, and uploaded their findings to home.
Huh.
Hm.
If that were true...

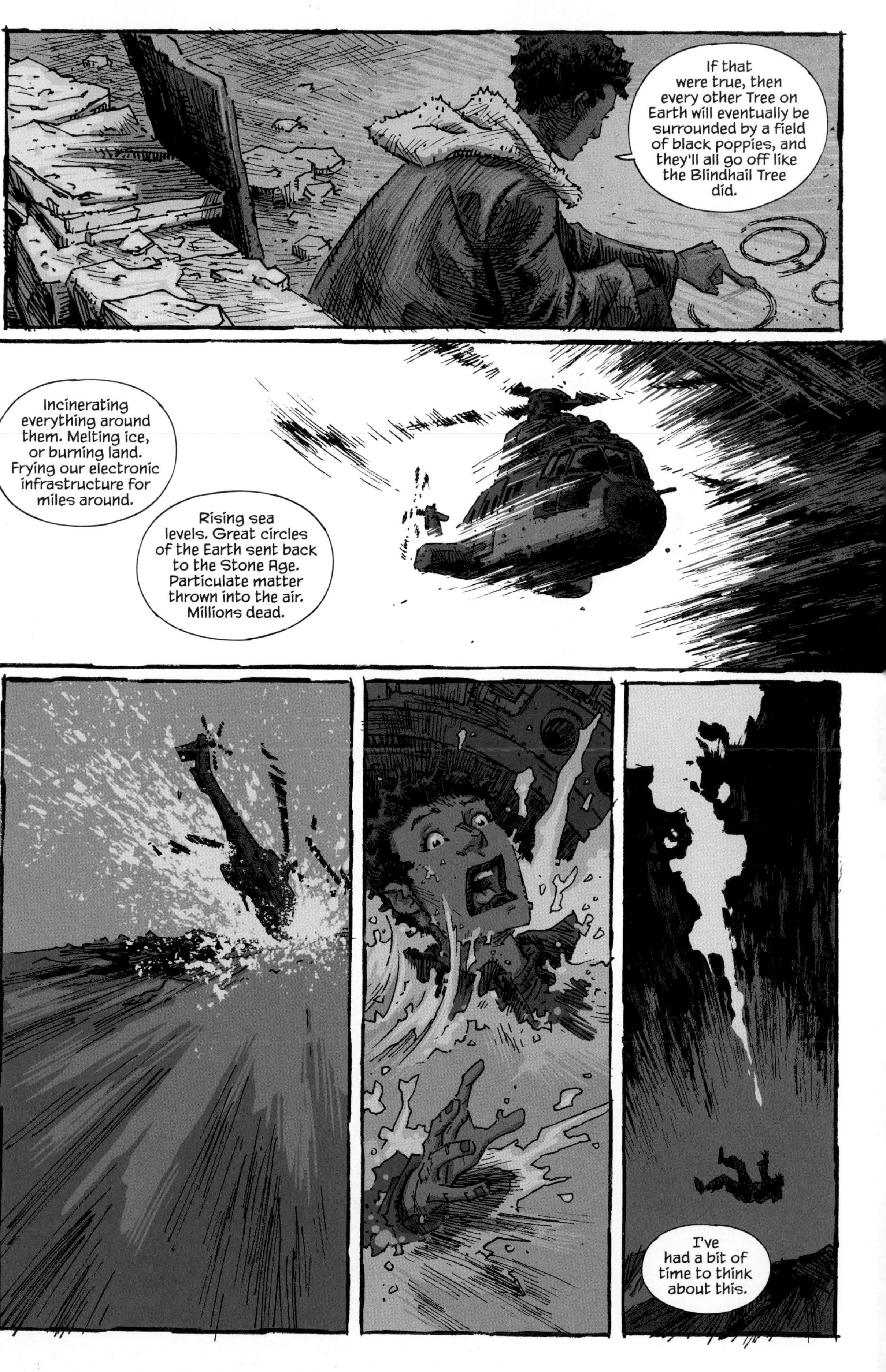
If that were true, then every other Tree on Earth will eventually be surrounded by a field of black poppies, and they'll all go off like the Blindhail Tree did.
Incinerating everything around them. Melting ice, or burning land. Frying our electronic infrastructure for miles around.
Rising sea levels. Great circles of the Earth sent back to the Stone Age. Particulate matter thrown into the air. Millions dead.
I've had a bit of time to think about this.

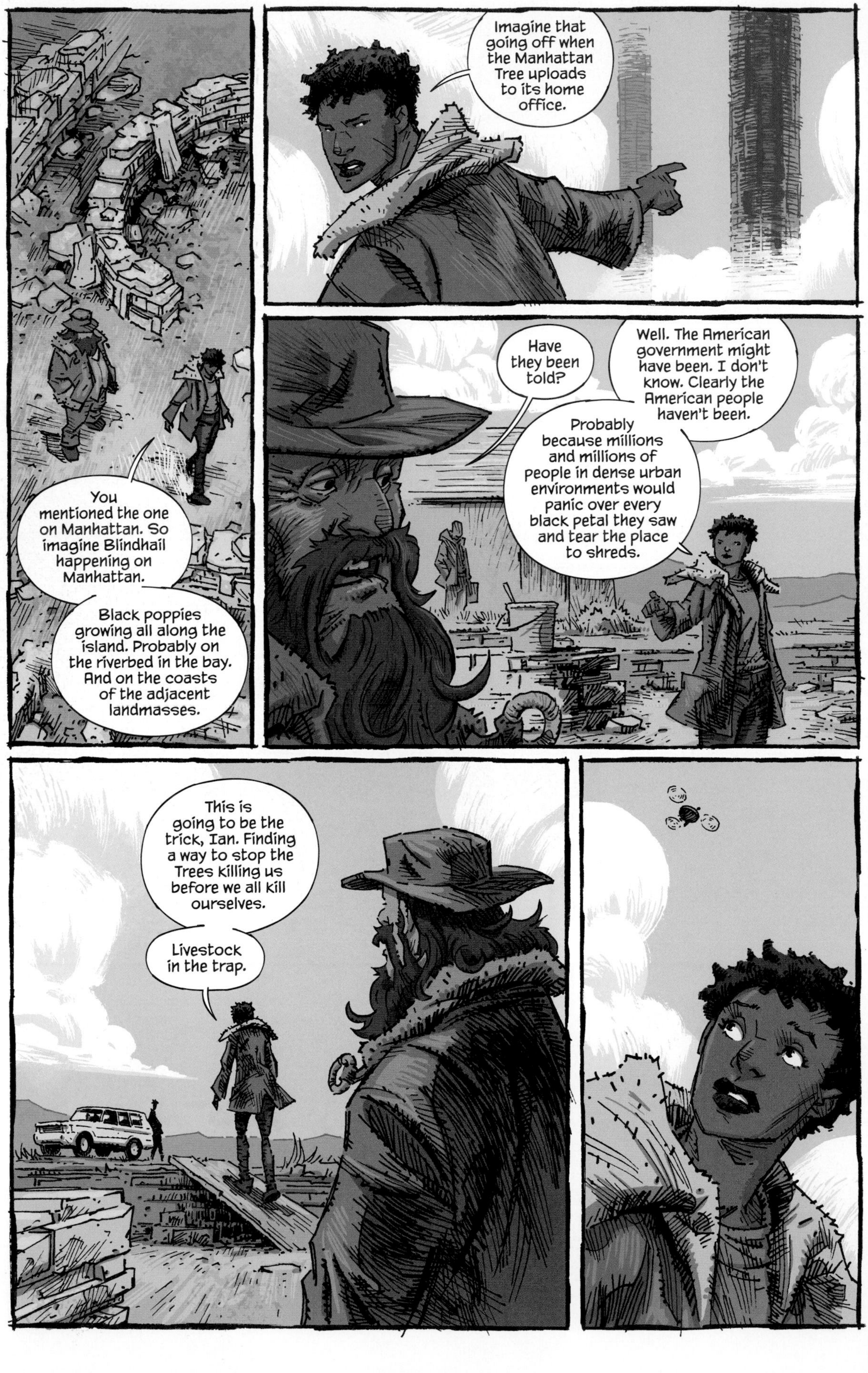
Imagine that going off when the Manhattan Tree uploads to its home office.
You mentioned the one on Manhattan. So imagine Blindhail happening on Manhattan.
Black poppies growing all along the island. Probably on the riverbed in the bay. And on the coasts of the adjacent landmasses.
Have they been told?
Well. The American government might have been. I don't know. Clearly the American people haven't been.
Probably because millions and millions of people in dense urban environments would panic over every black petal they saw and tear the place to shreds.
This is going to be the trick, Ian. Finding a way to stop the Trees killing us before we all kill ourselves.
Livestock in the trap.

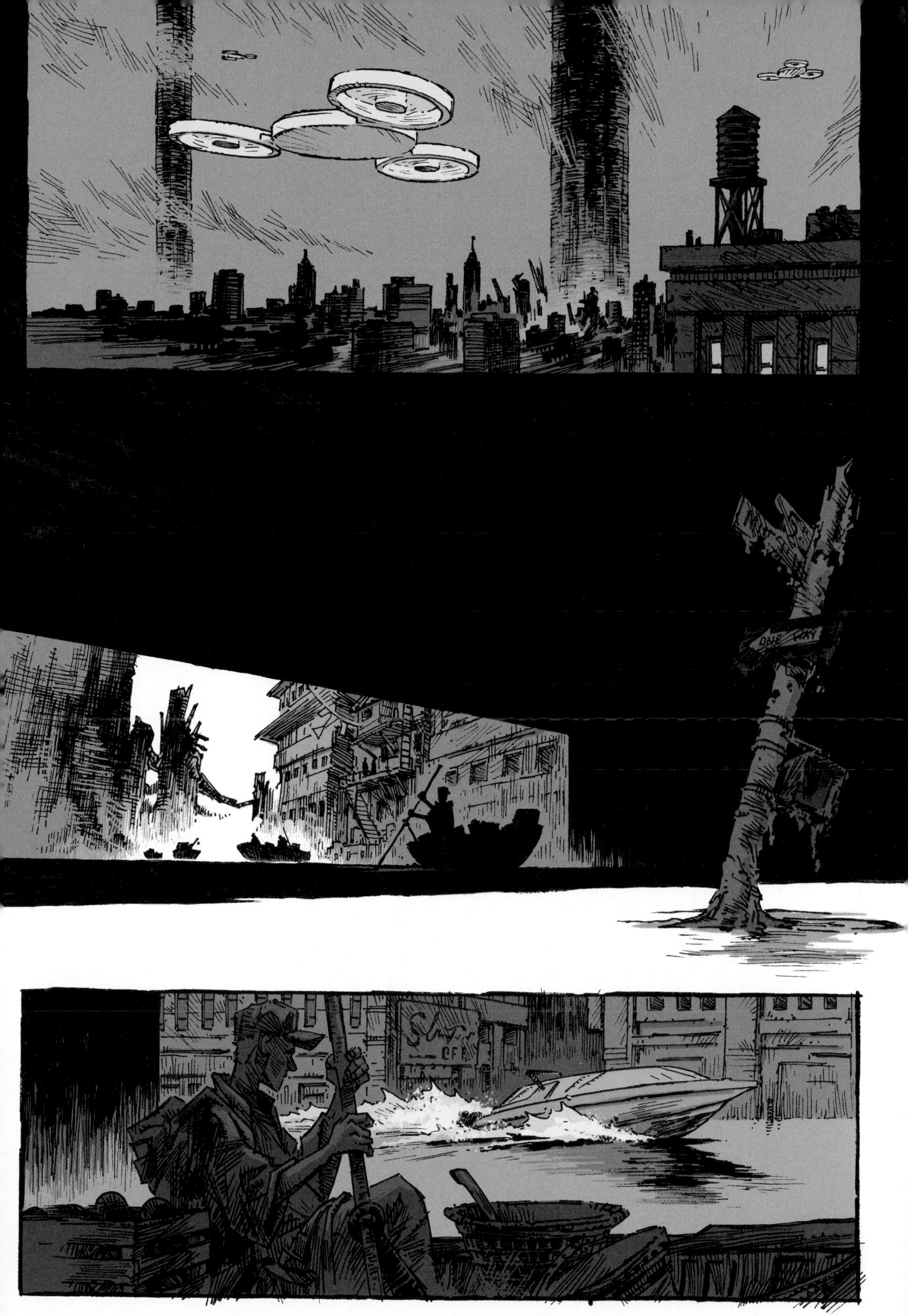
ONE WAY

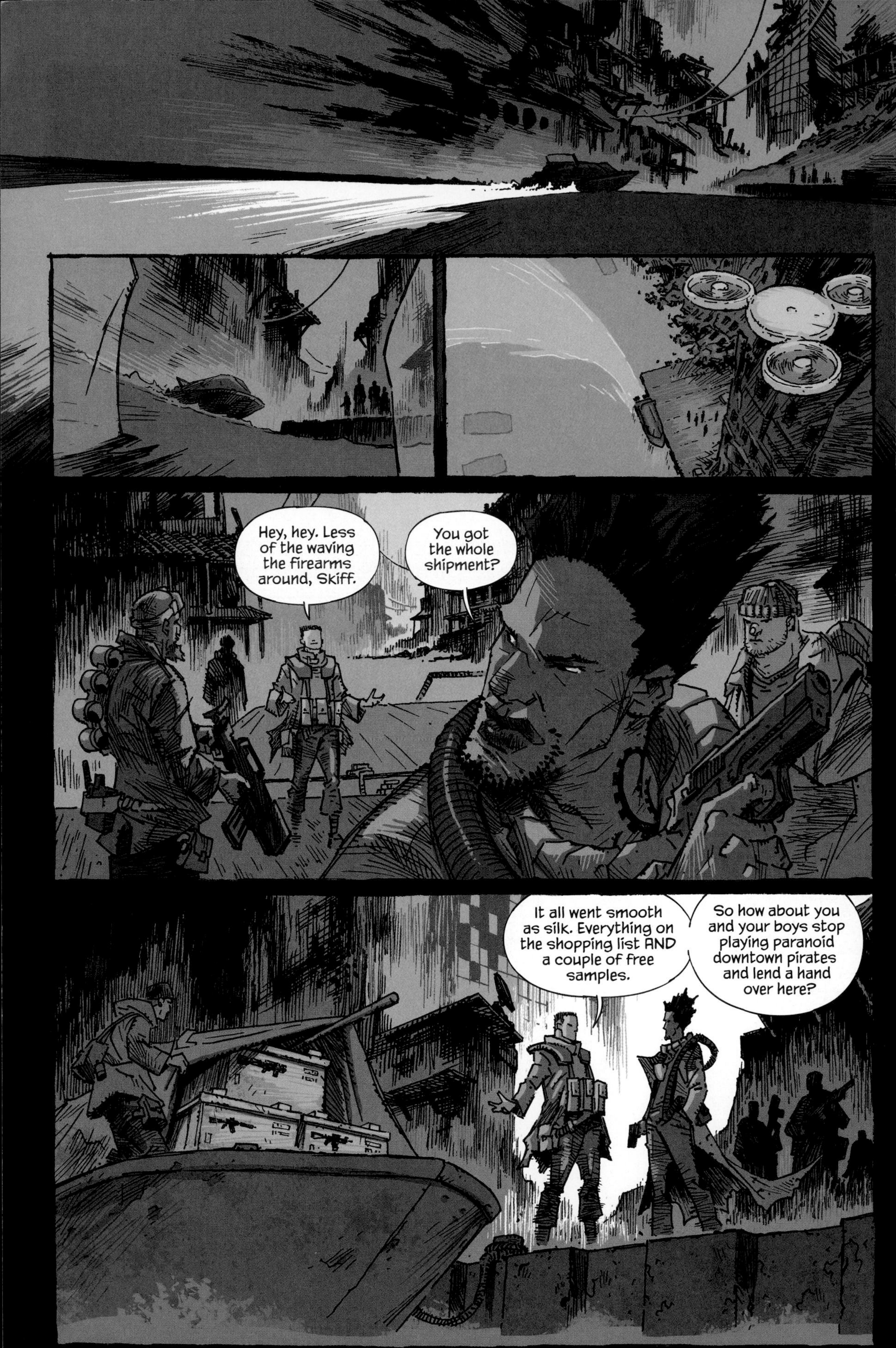
Hey, hey. Less of the waving the firearms around, Skiff.
You got the whole shipment?
It all went smooth as silk. Everything on the shopping list AND a couple of free samples.
So how about you and your boys stop playing paranoid downtown pirates and lend a hand over here?

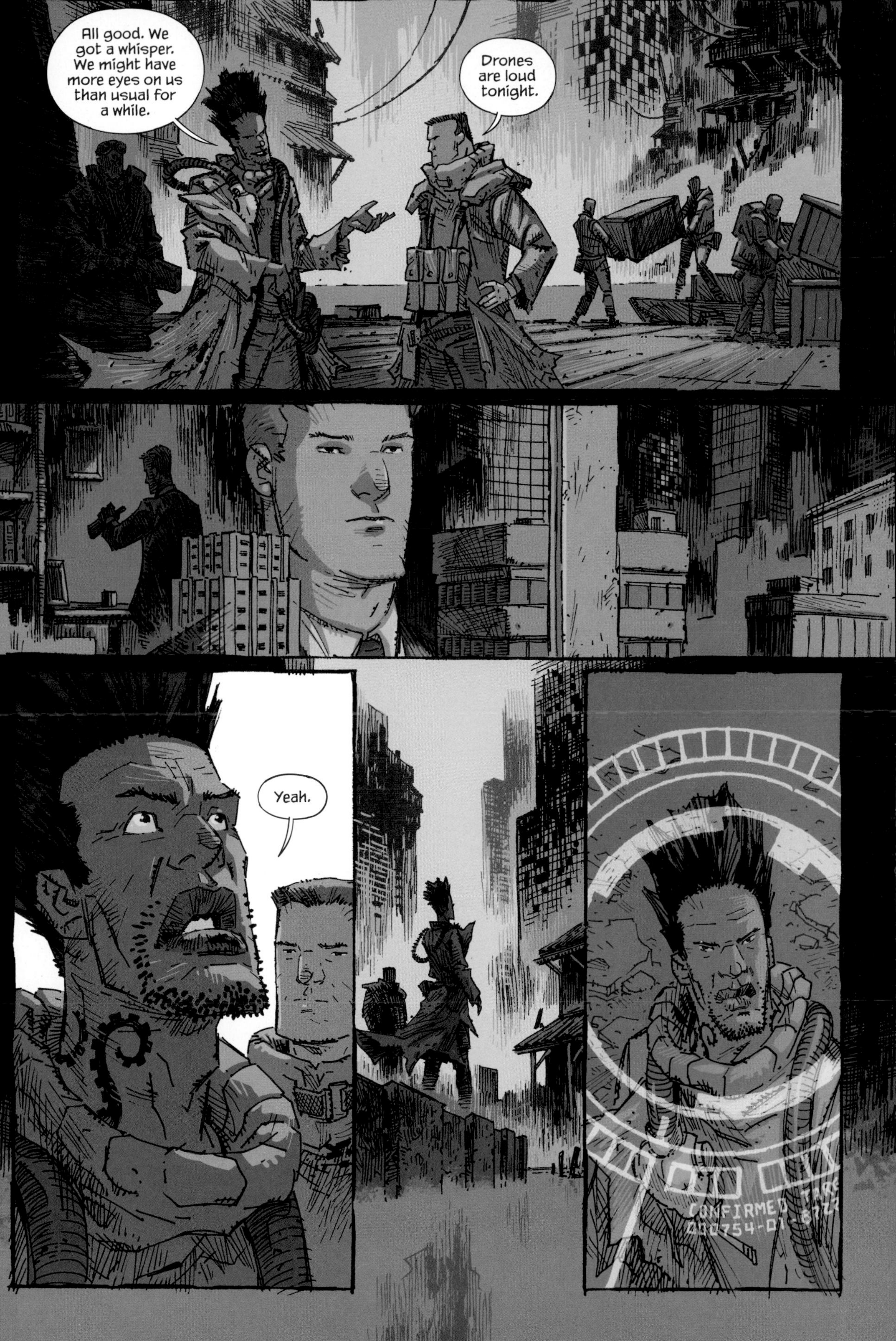
All good. We got a whisper. We might have more eyes on us than usual for a while.
Drones are loud tonight.
Yeah.
CONFIRMED

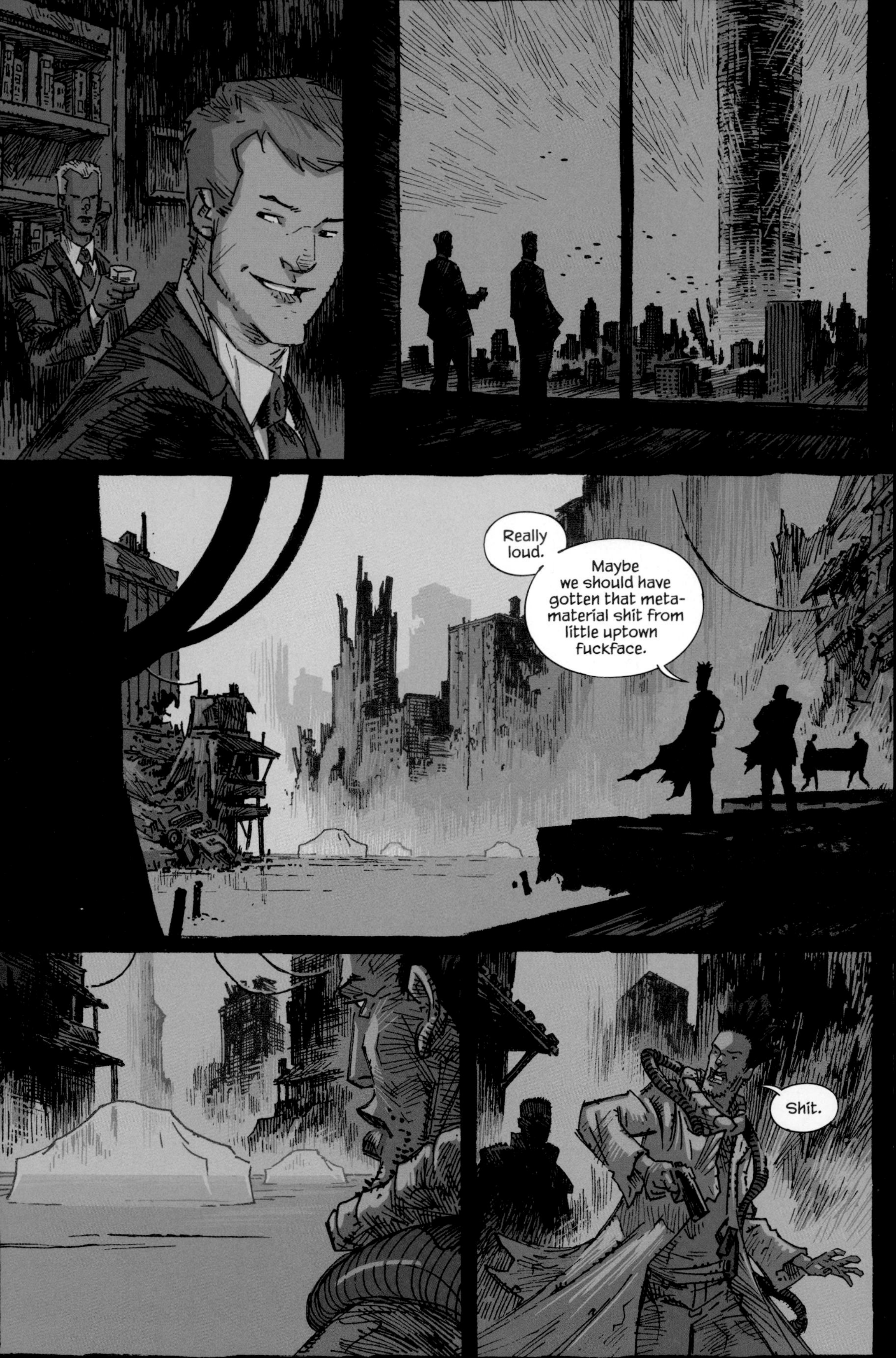
Really loud.
Maybe we should have gotten that meta-material shit from little uptown fuckface.
Shit.

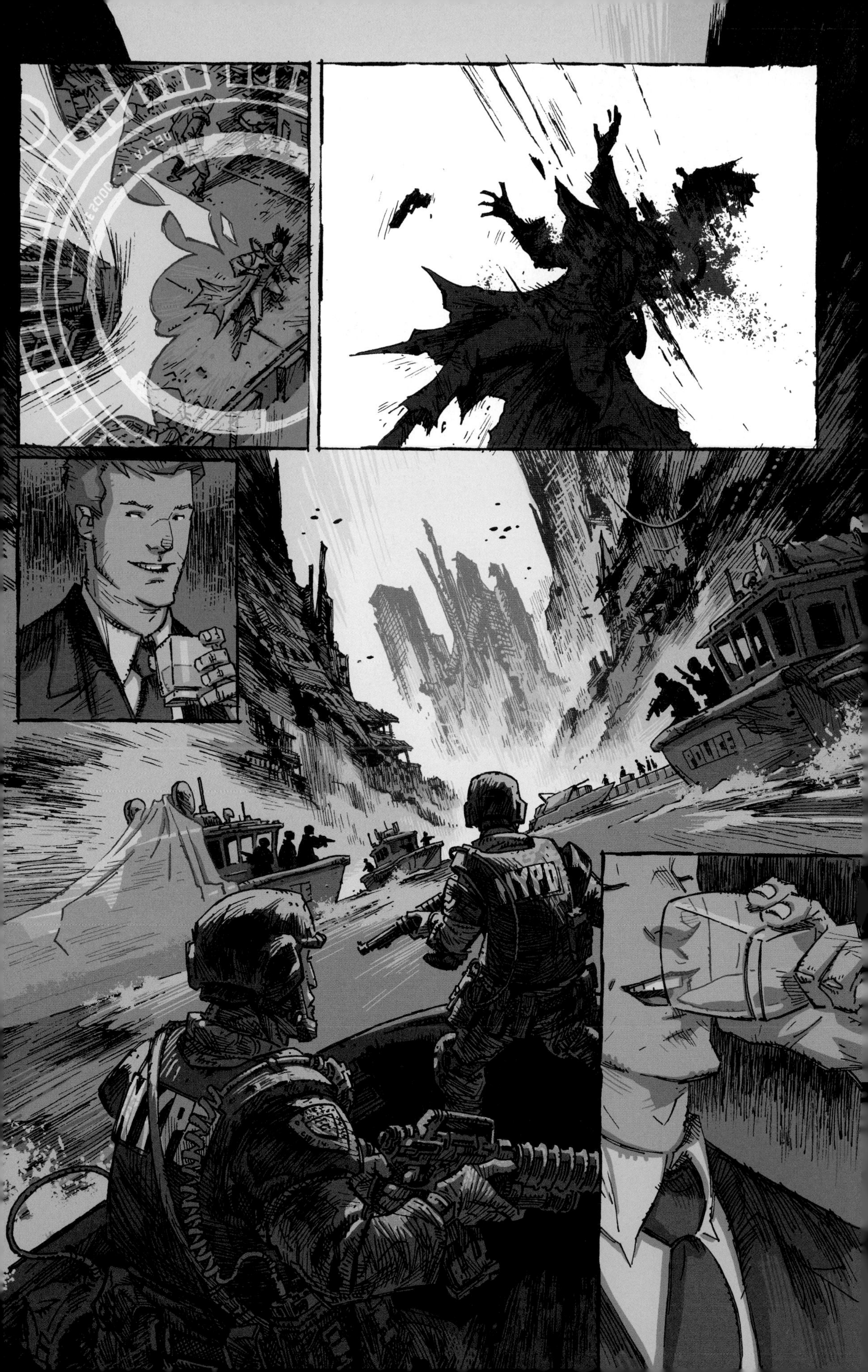
POLICE

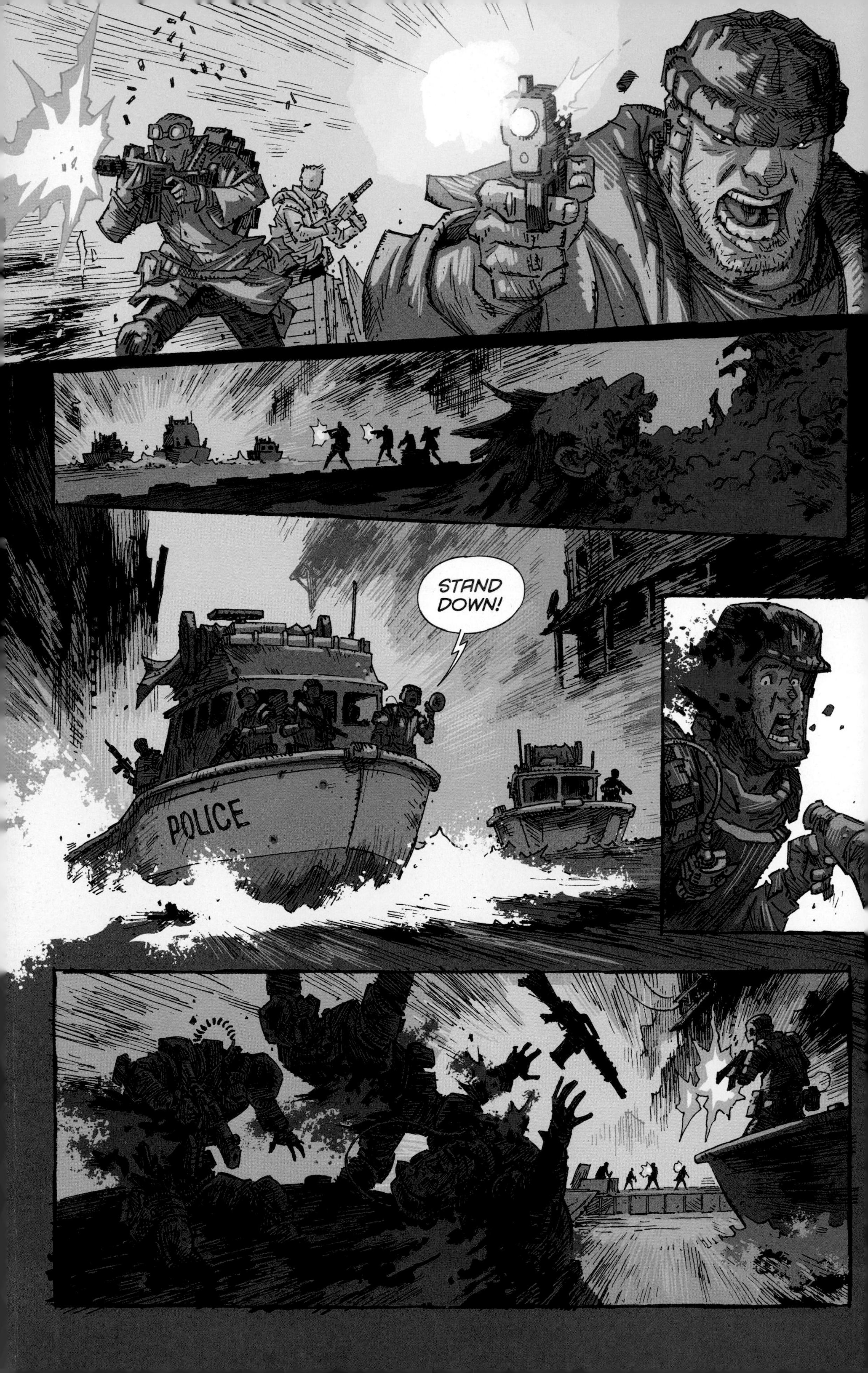
STAND DOWN!
POLICE

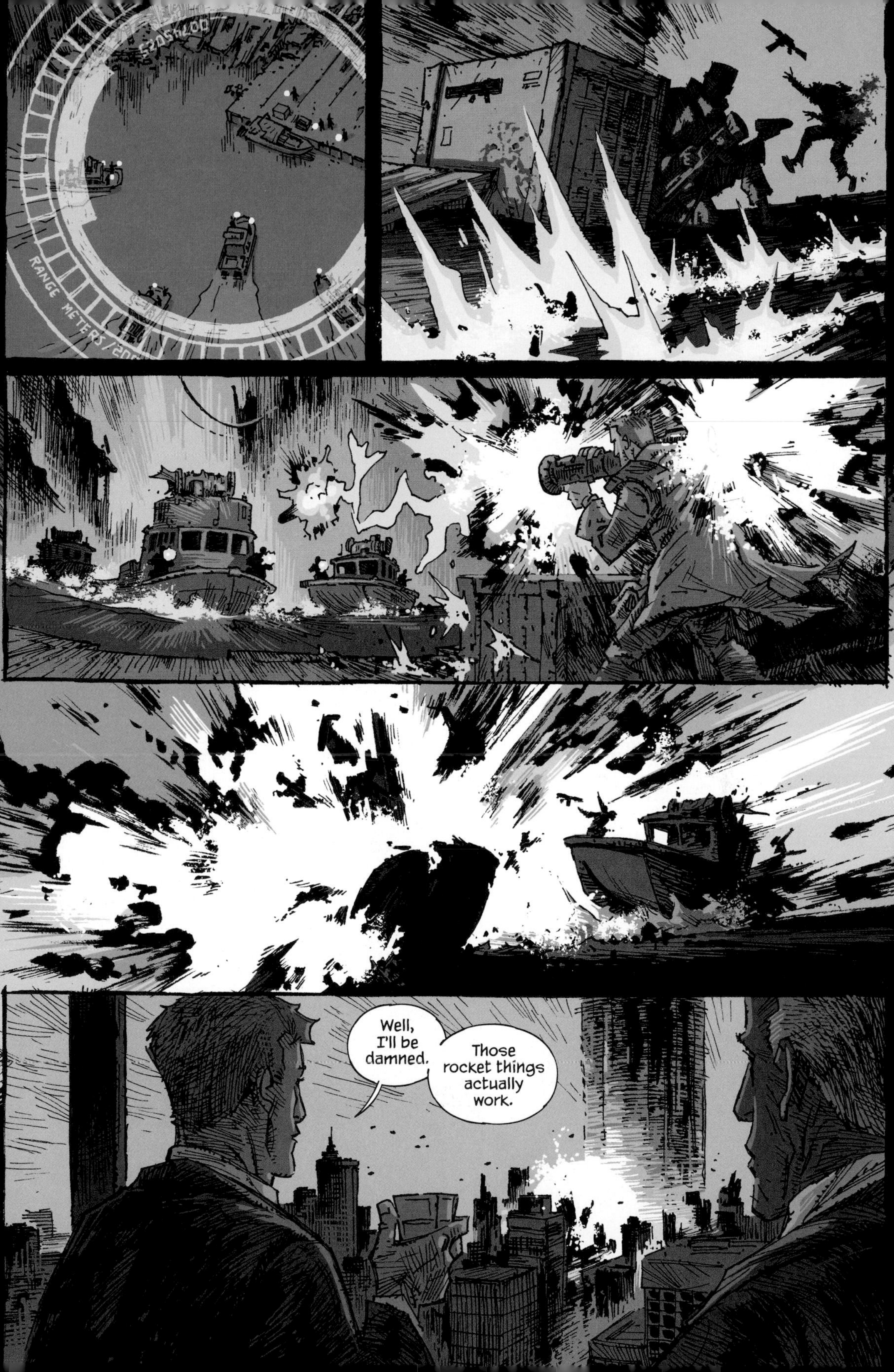
RANGE METERS
Well, I'll be damned.
Those rocket things actually work.

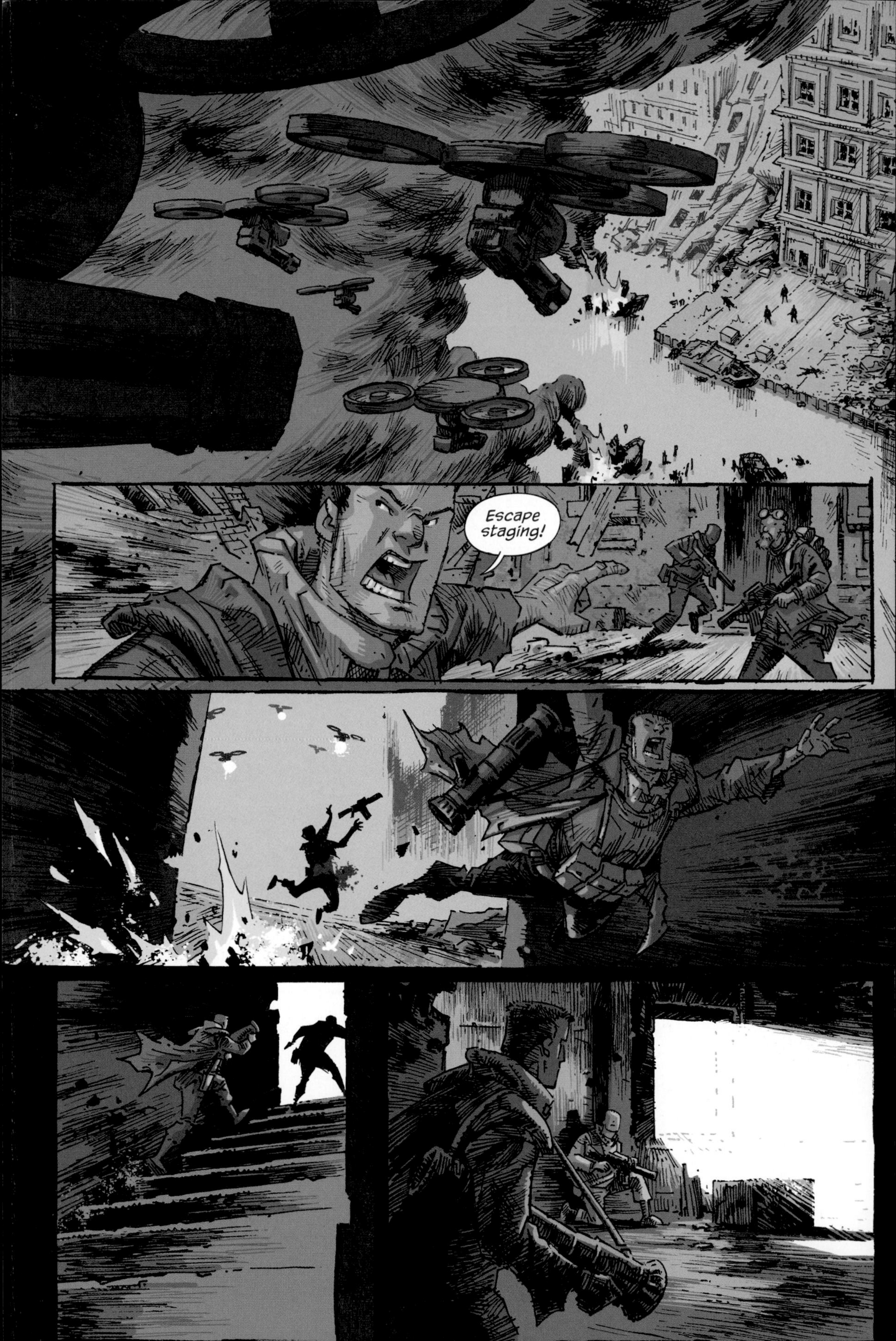
Escape staging!

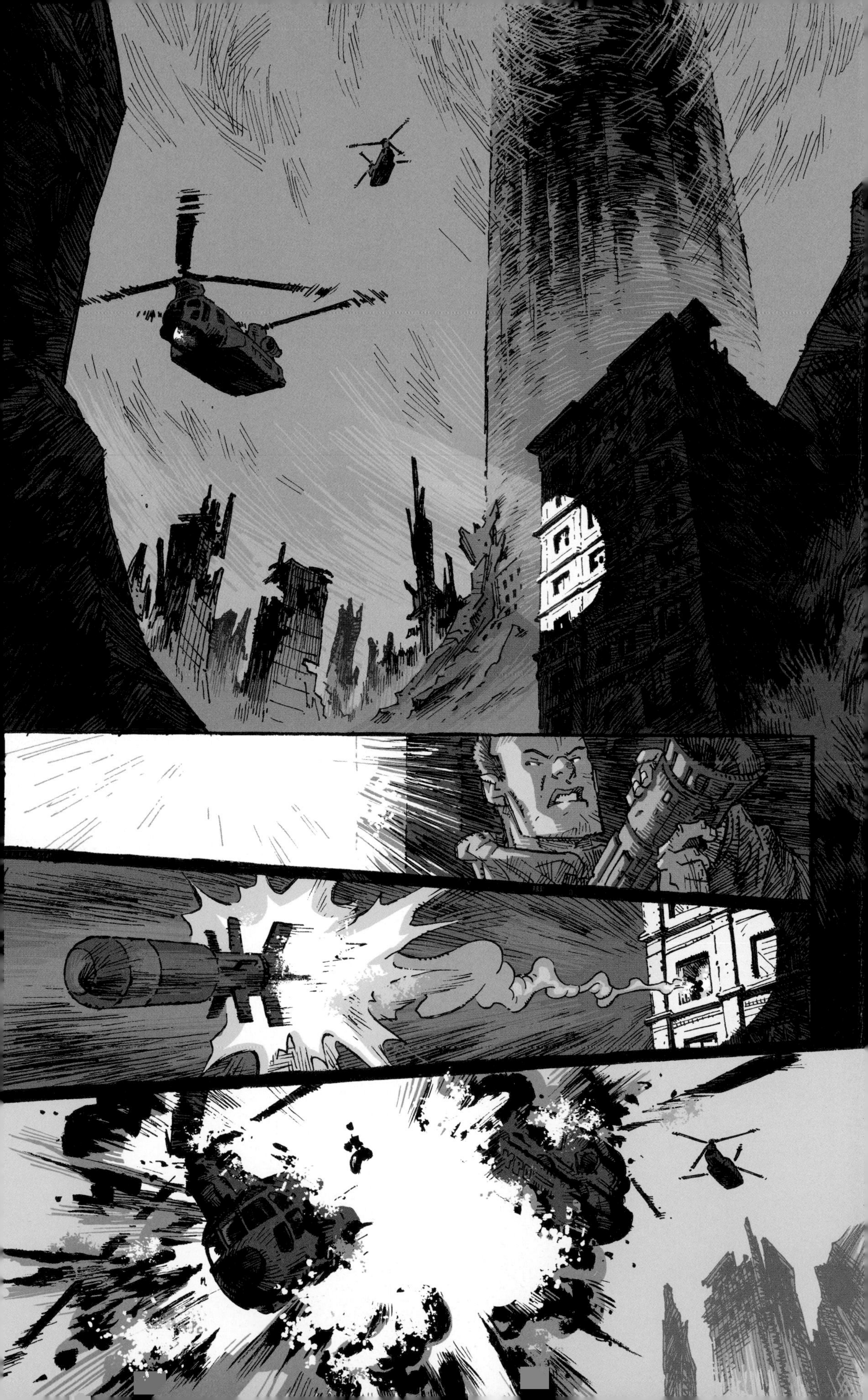

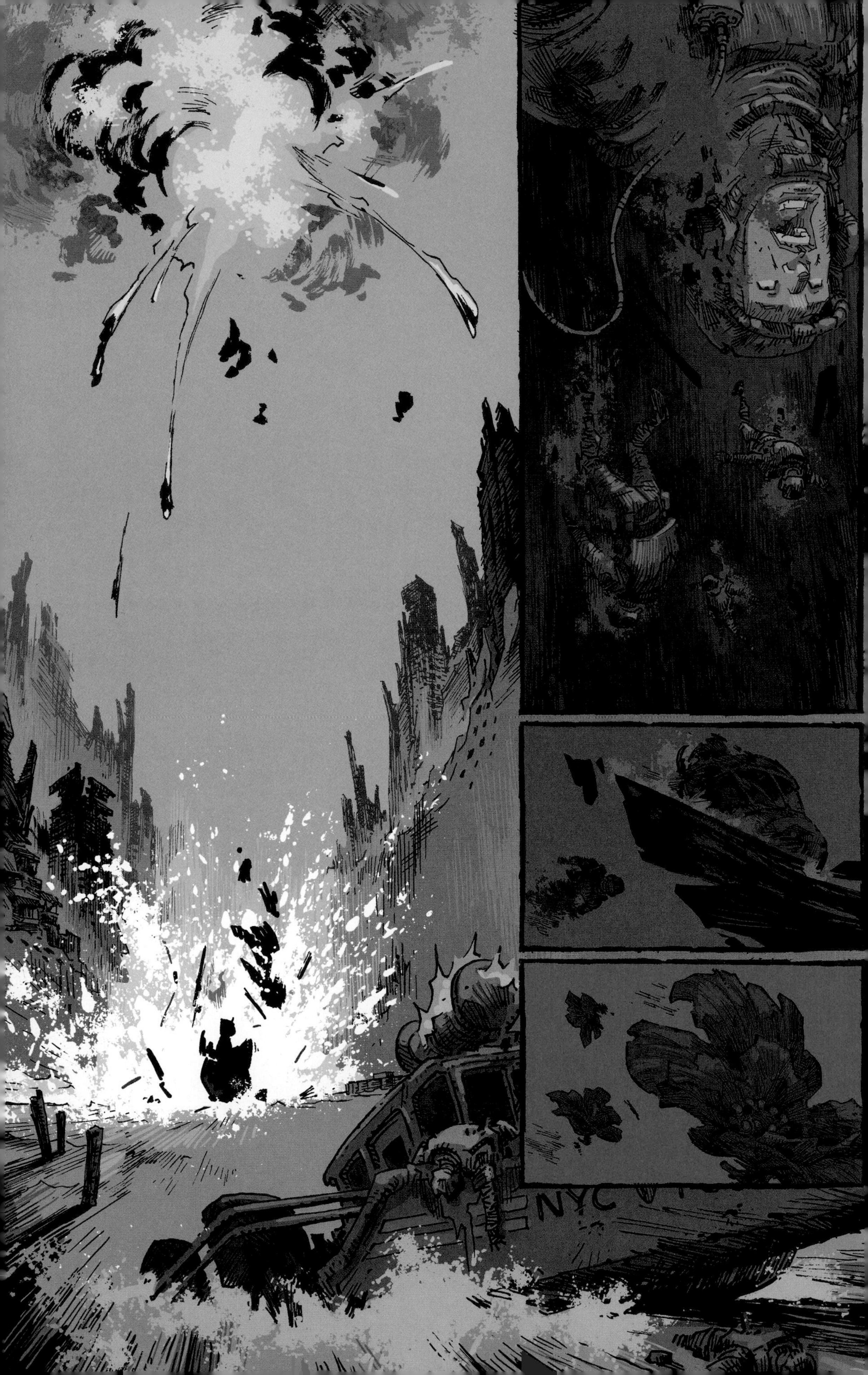
NYC

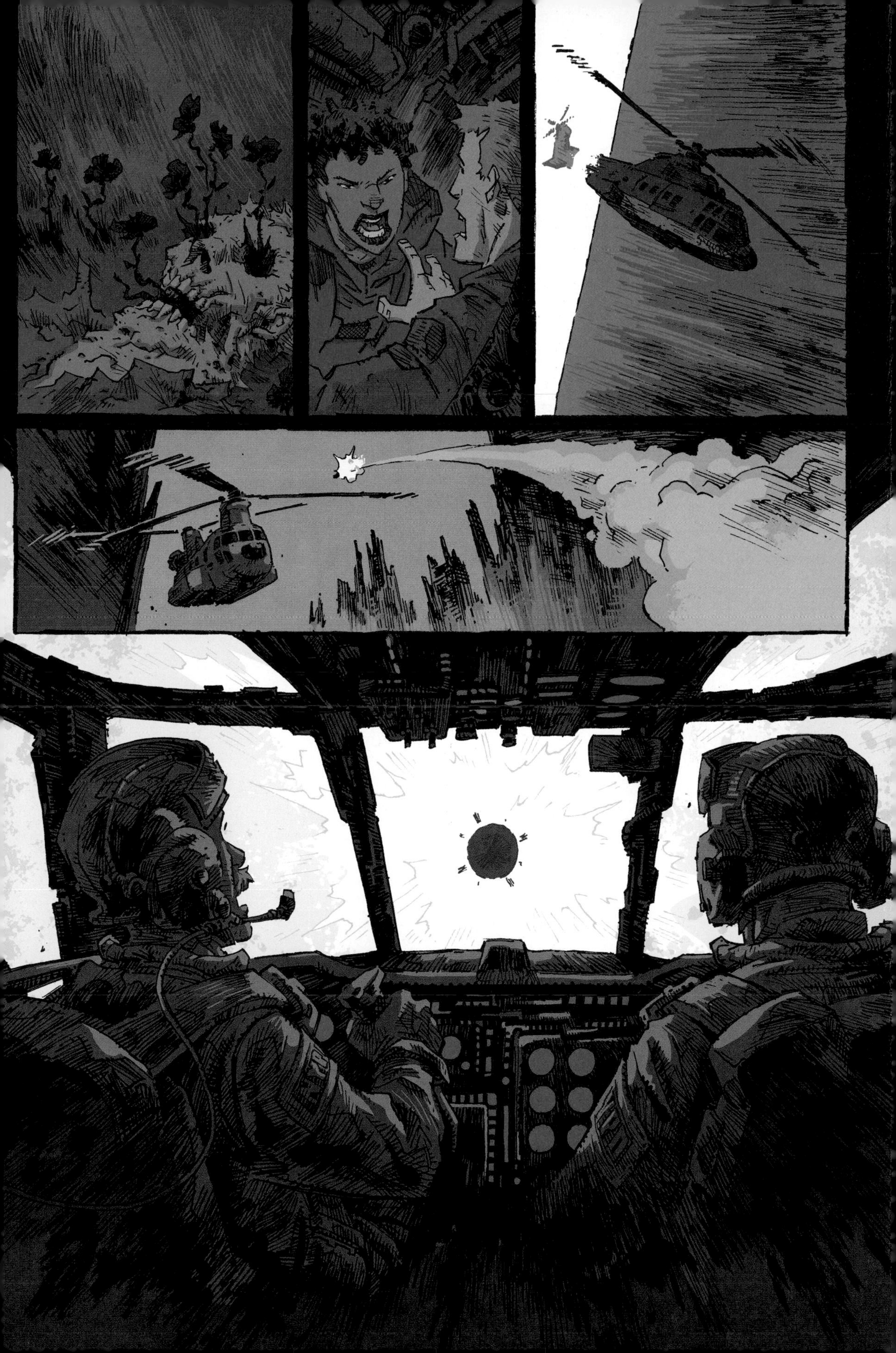

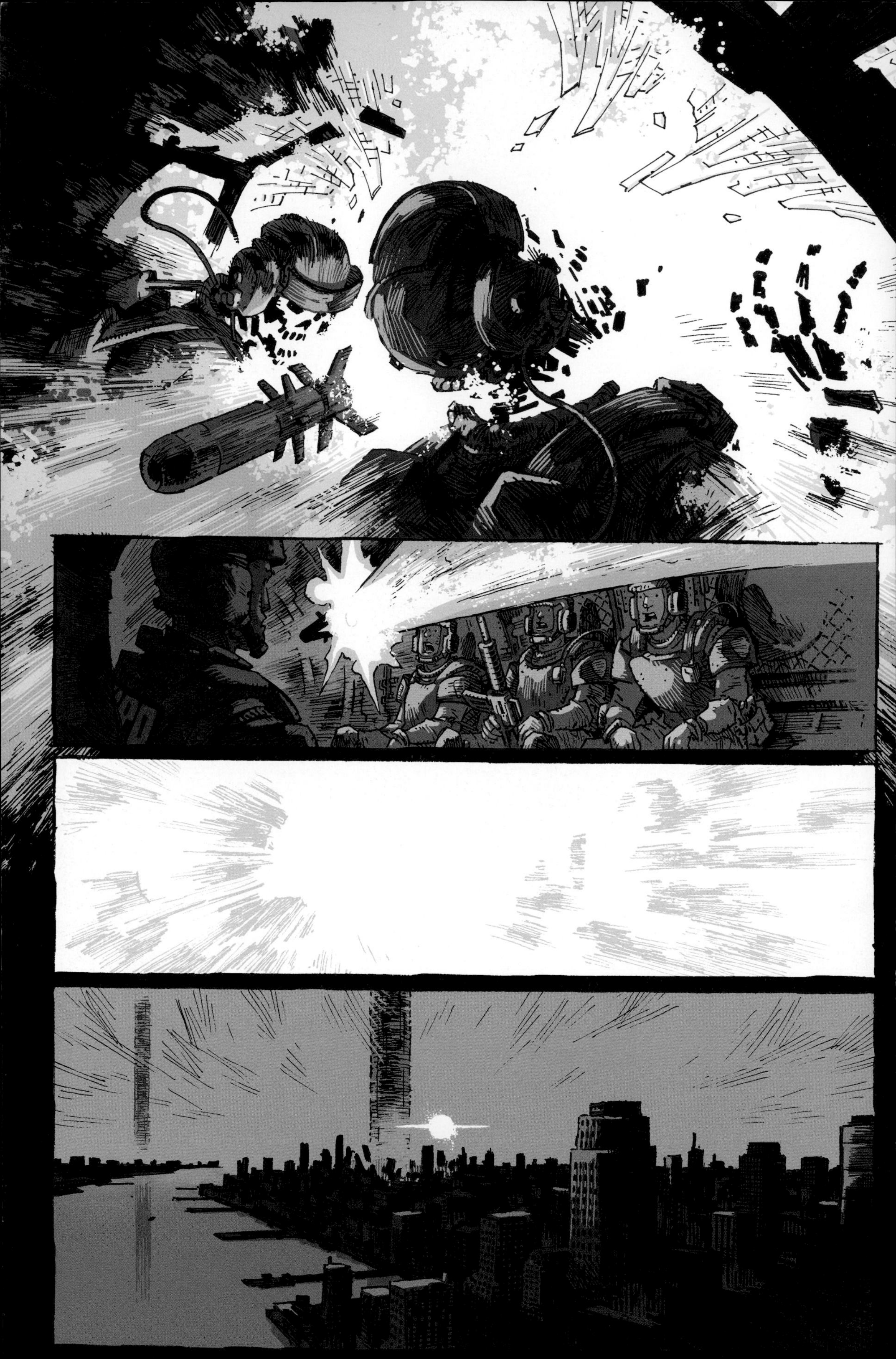

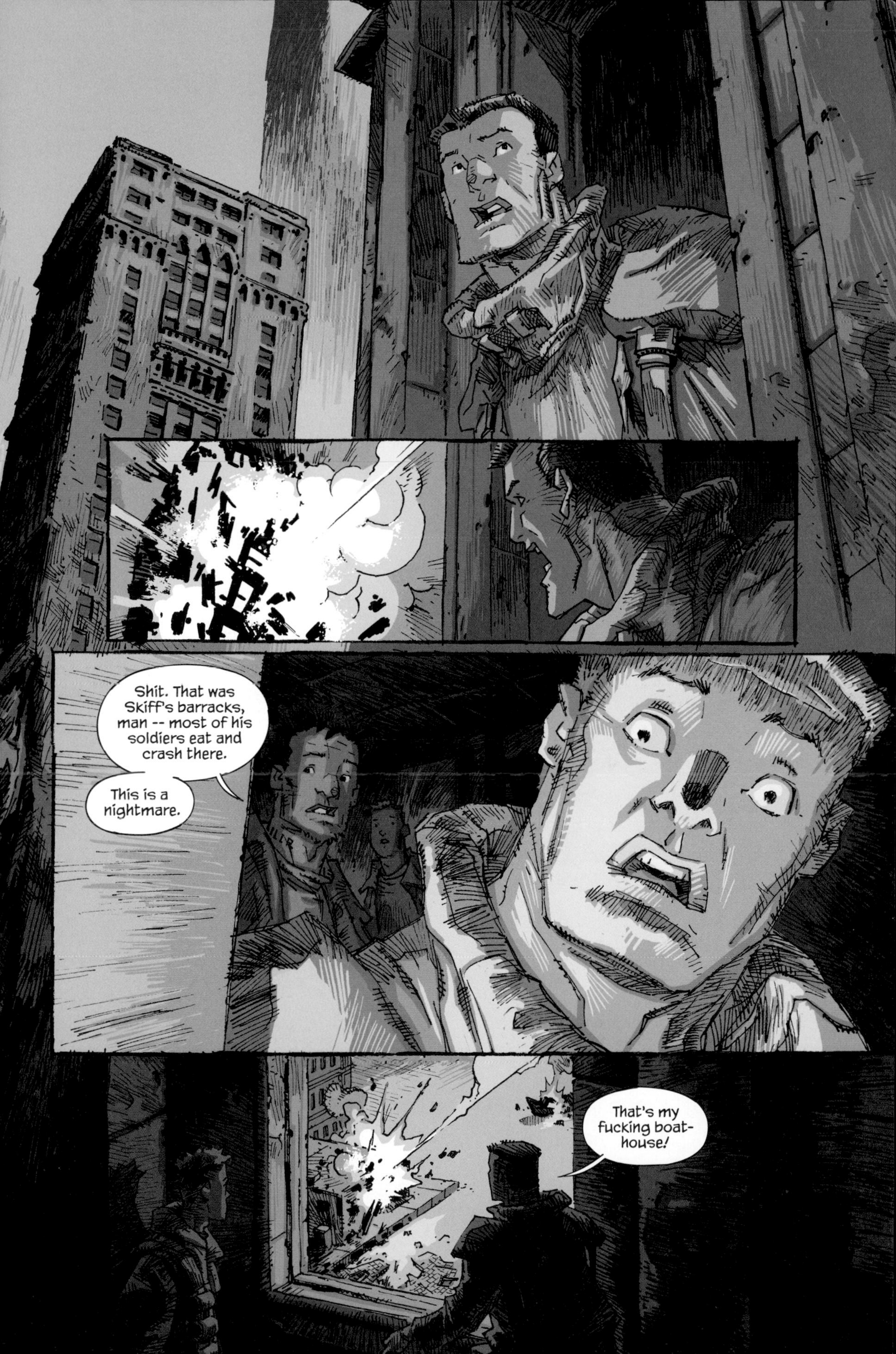
Shit. That was Skiff's barracks, man -- most of his soldiers eat and crash there.
This is a nightmare.
That's my fucking boat-house!

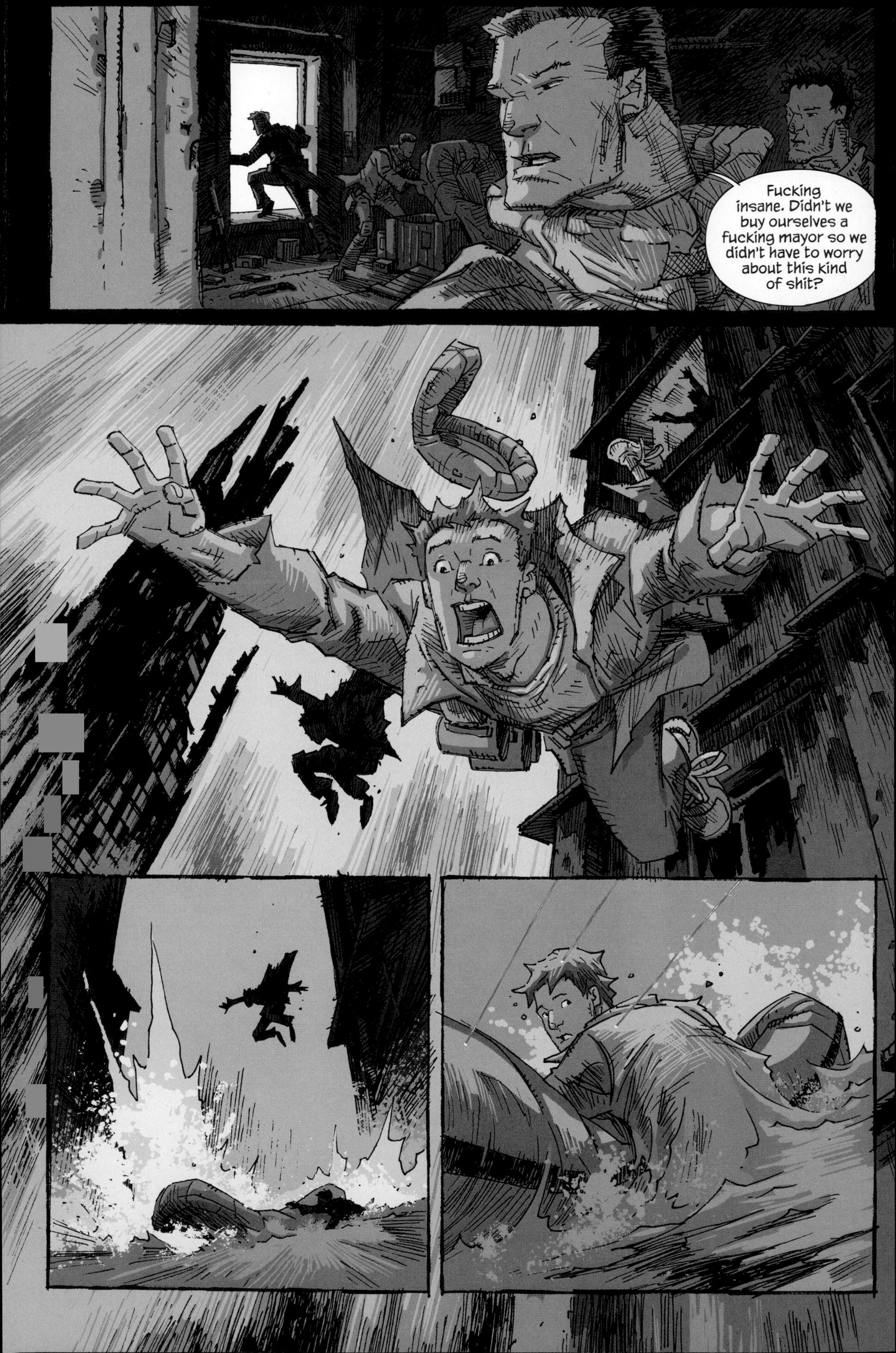
Fucking insane. Didn't we buy ourselves a fucking mayor so we didn't have to worry about this kind of shit?

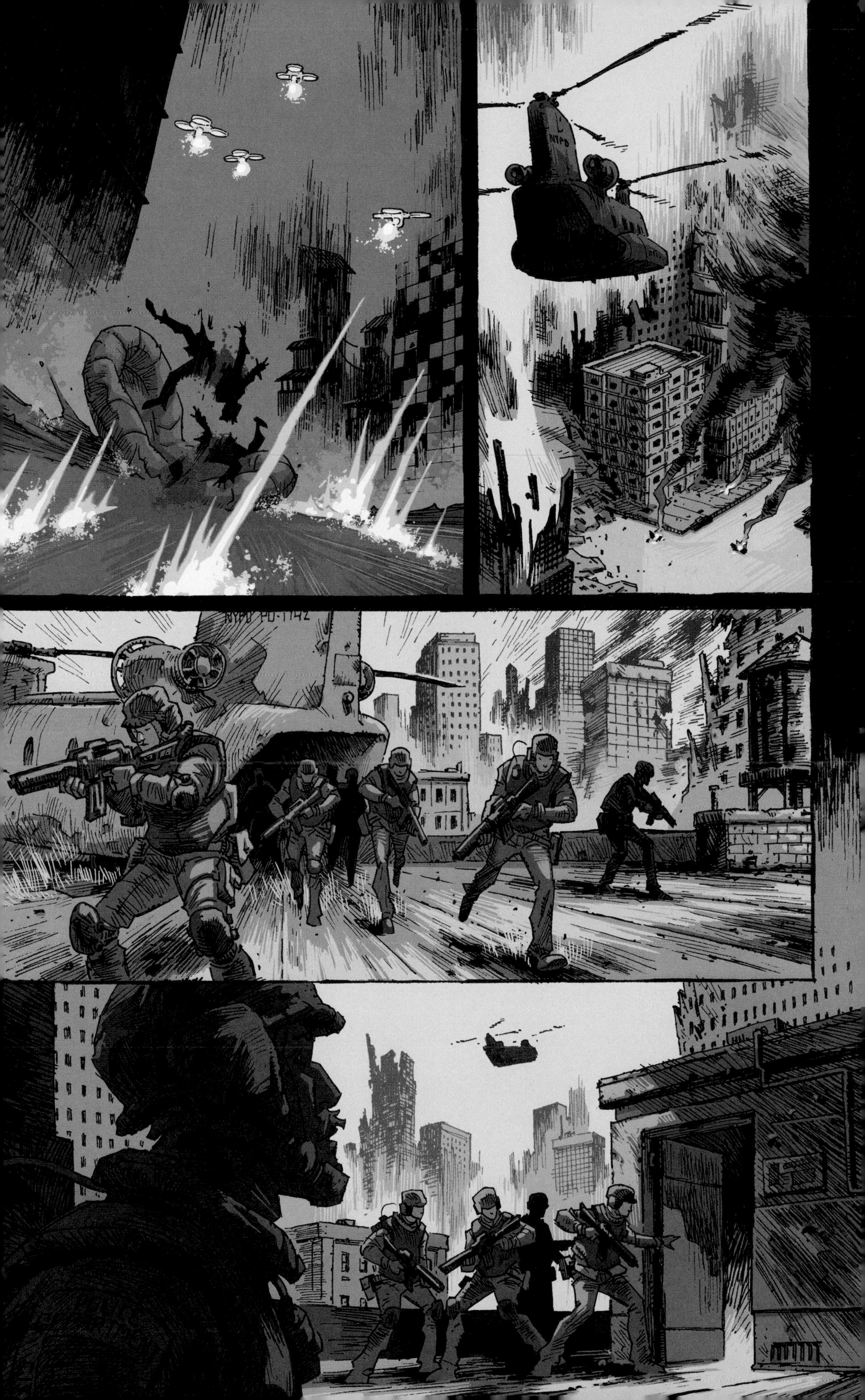

NYPD
NYPD PD-1142

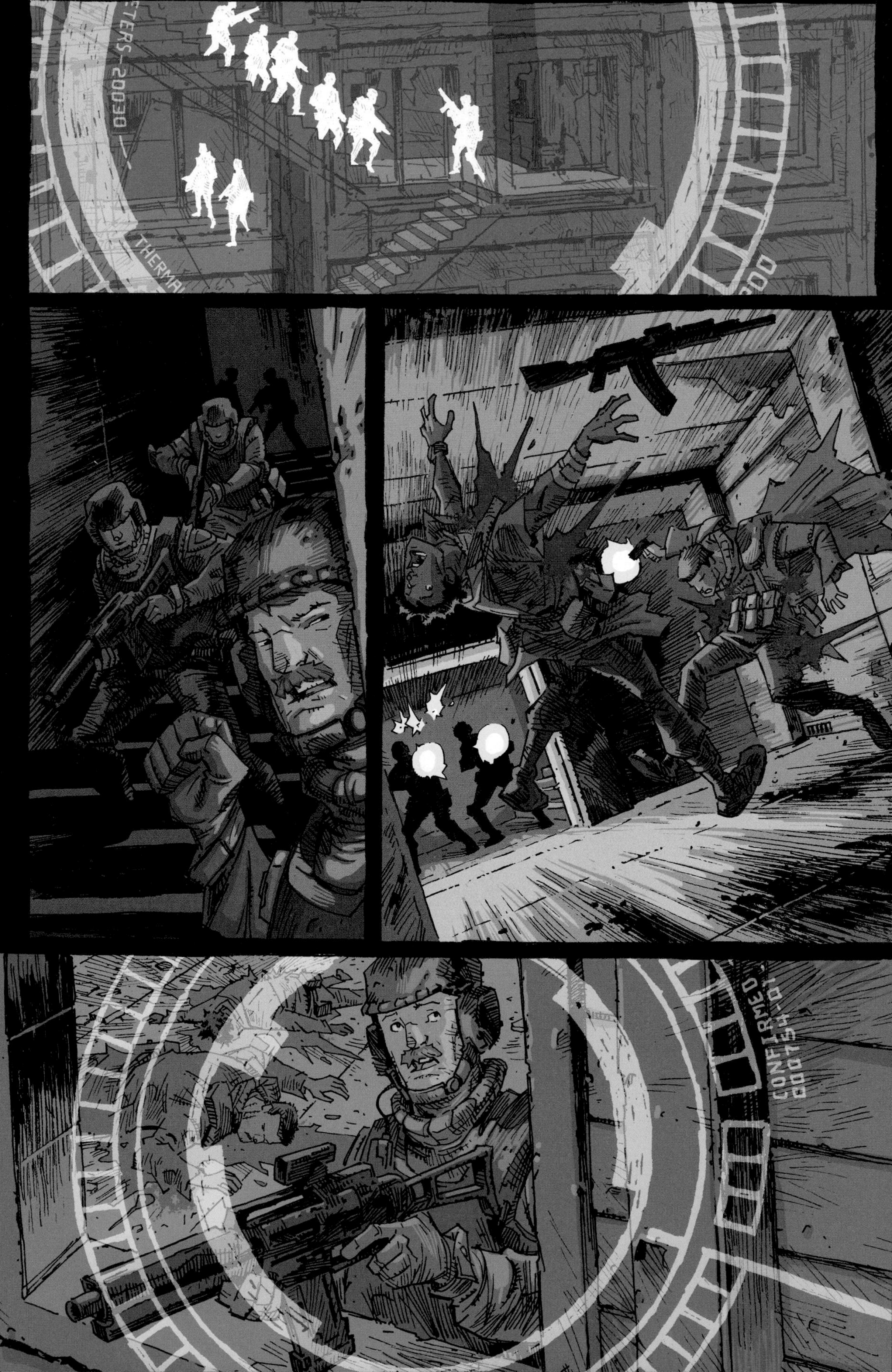
CONFIRMED

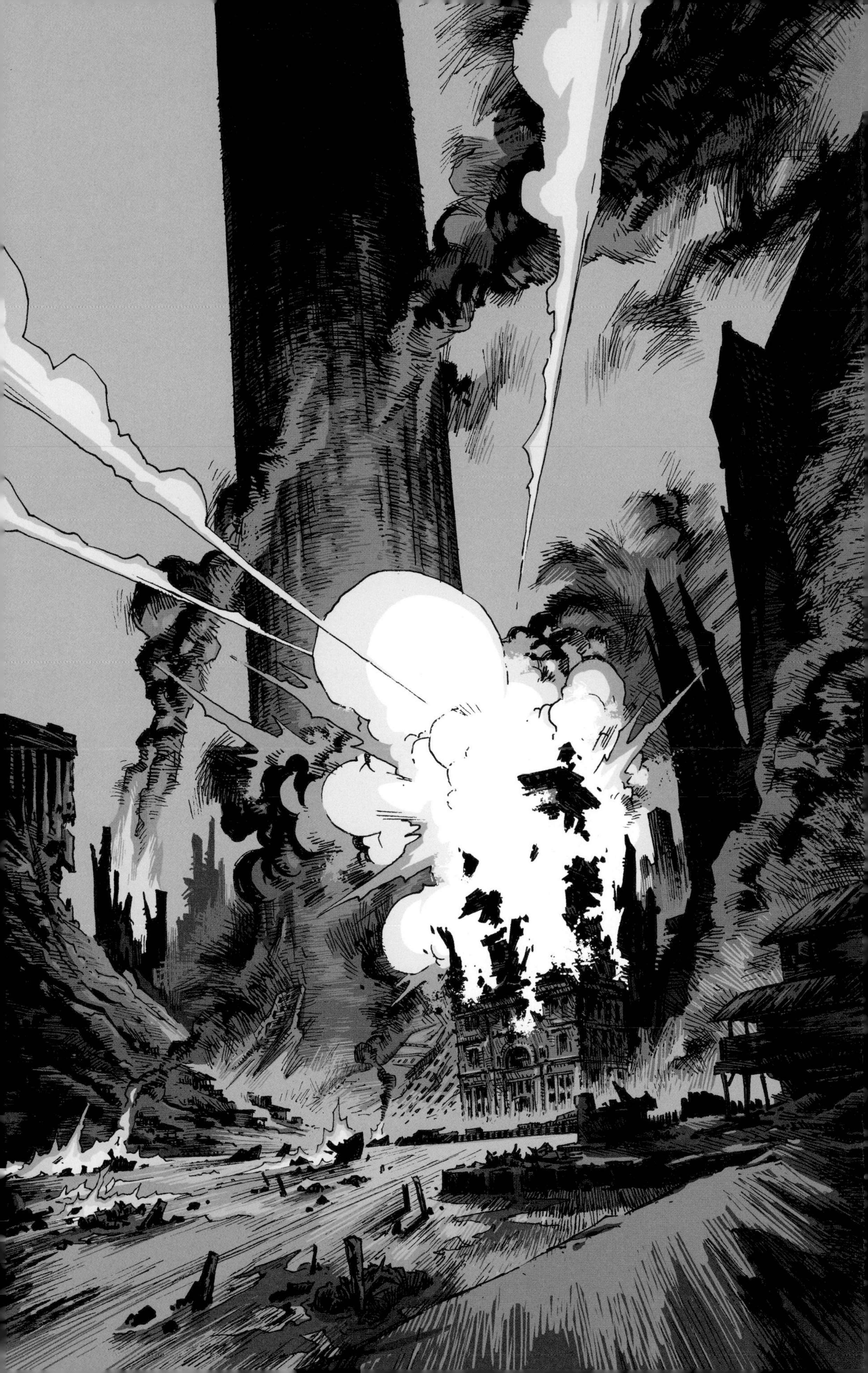

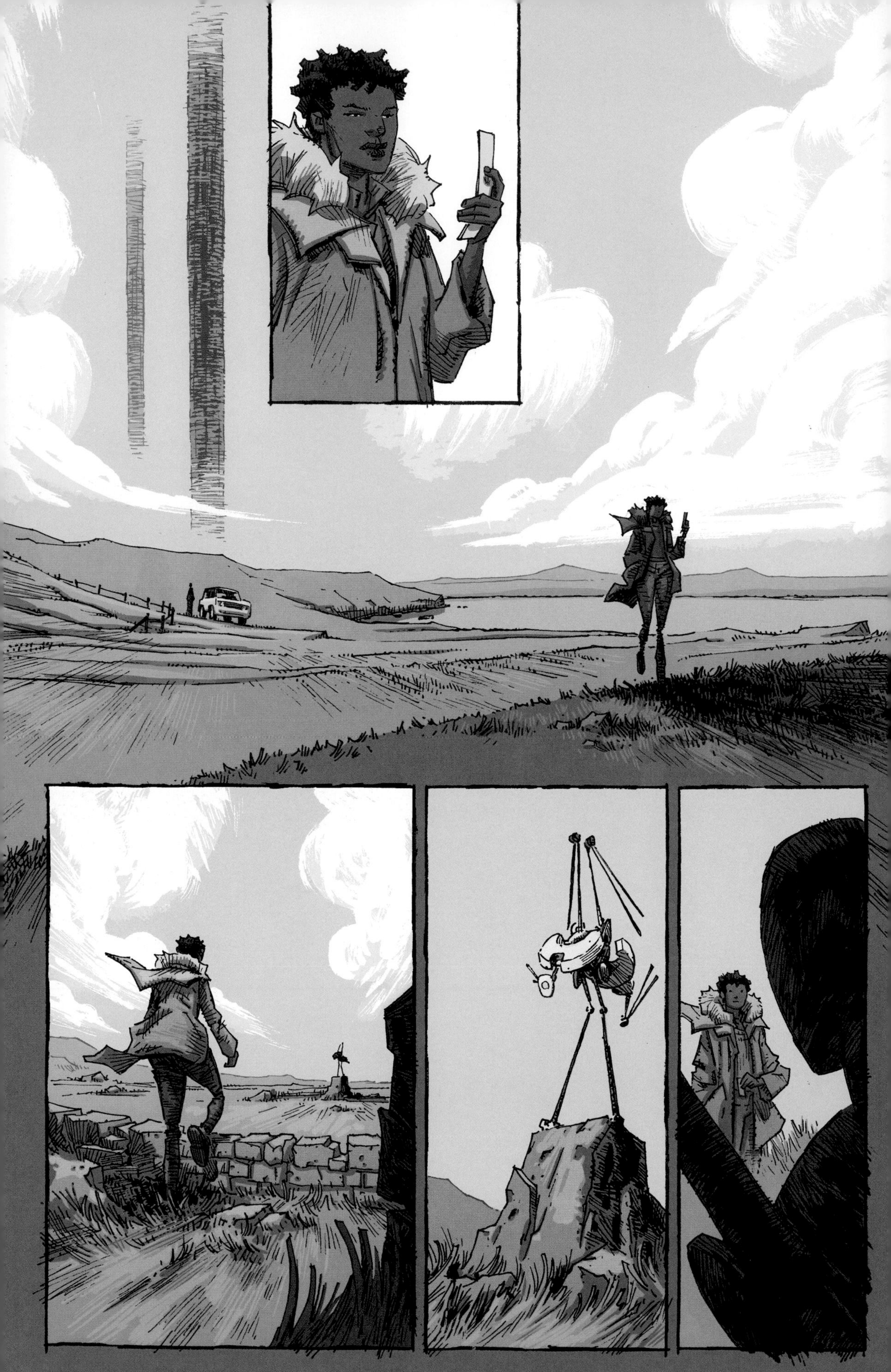

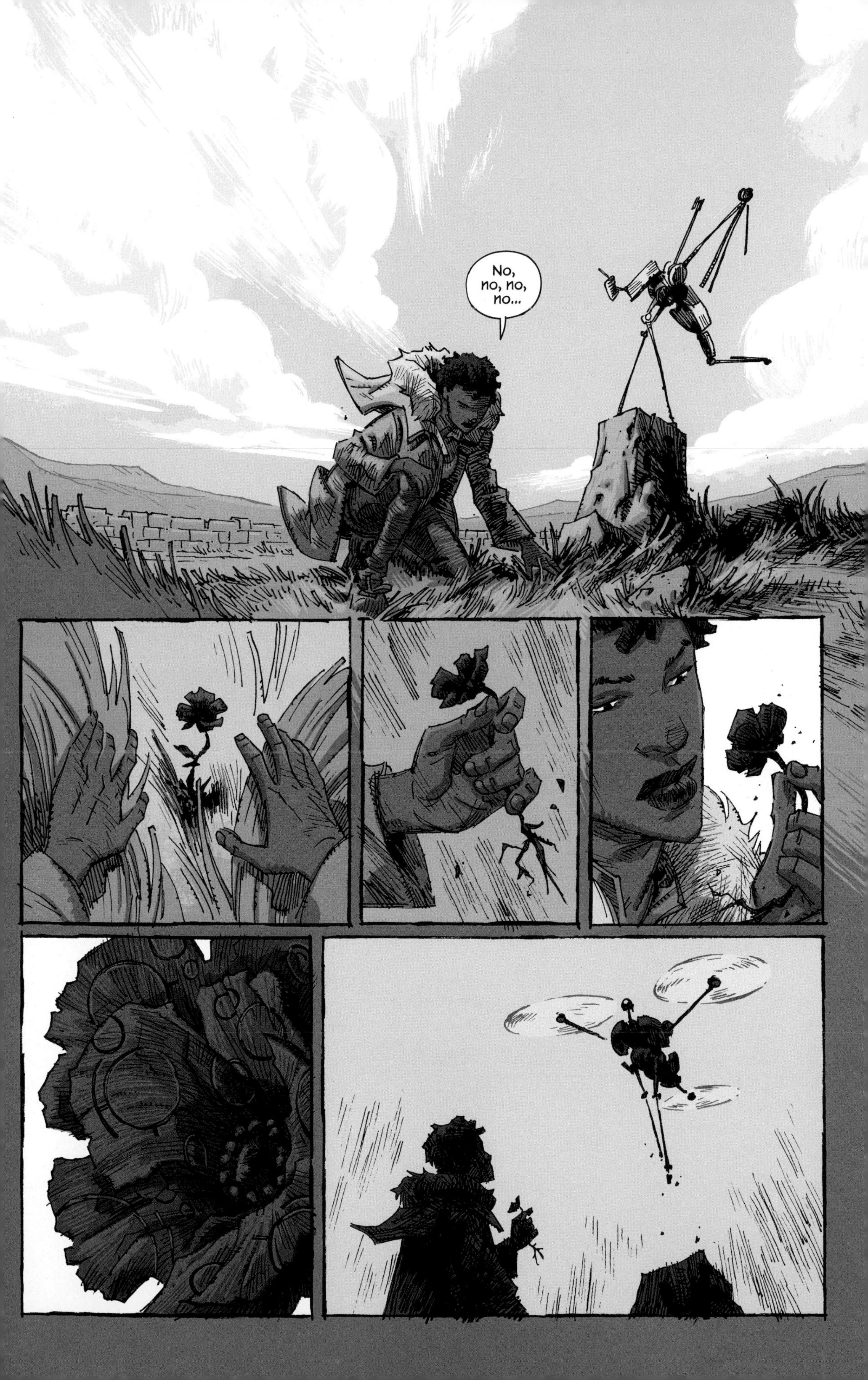
No, no, no, no...

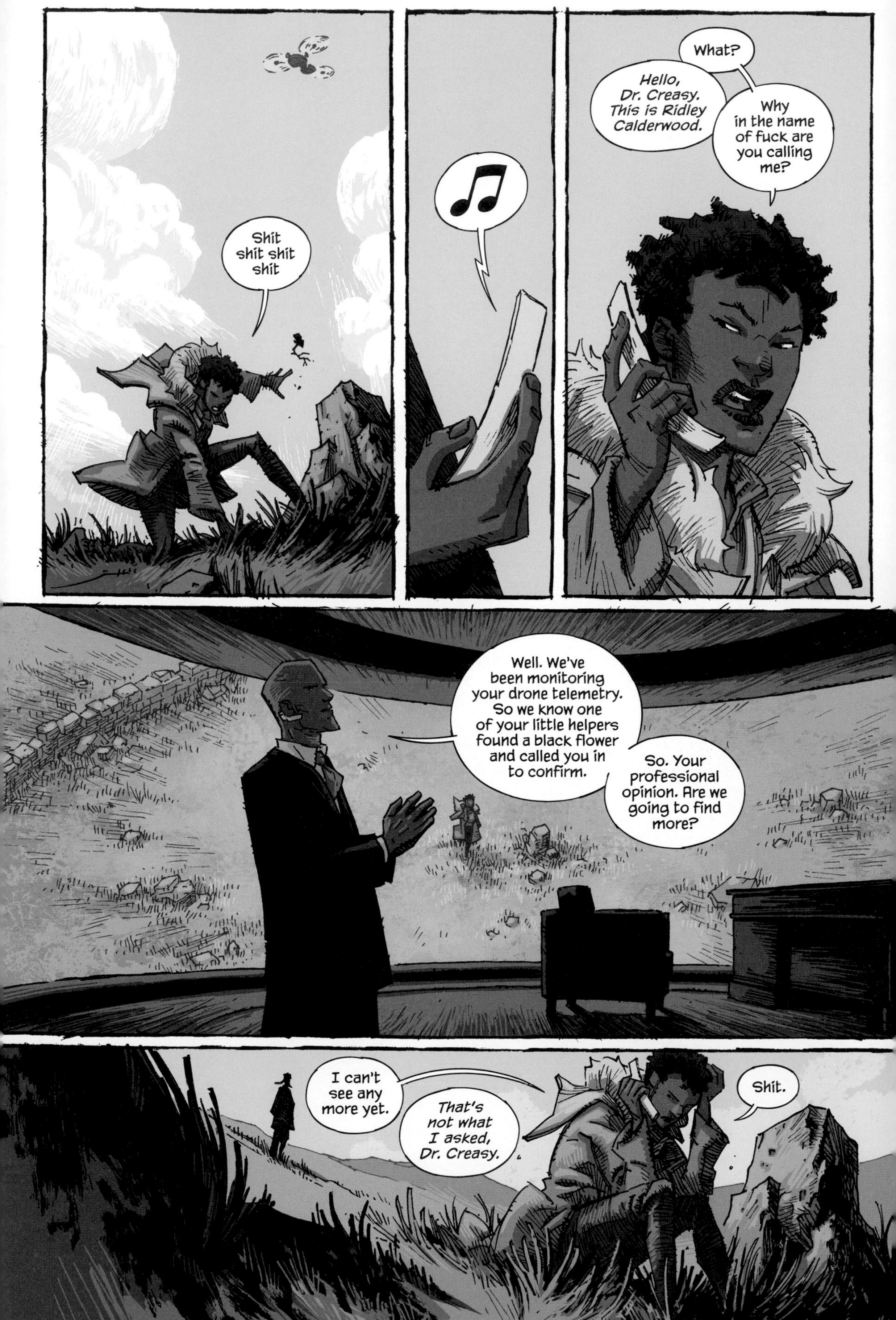

Shit shit shit shit
Hello, Dr. Creasy. This is Ridley Calderwood.
What?
Why in the name of fuck are you calling me?
Well. We've been monitoring your drone telemetry. So we know one of your little helpers found a black flower and called you in to confirm.
So. Your professional opinion. Are we going to find more?
I can't see any more yet.
That's not what I asked, Dr. Creasy.
Shit.

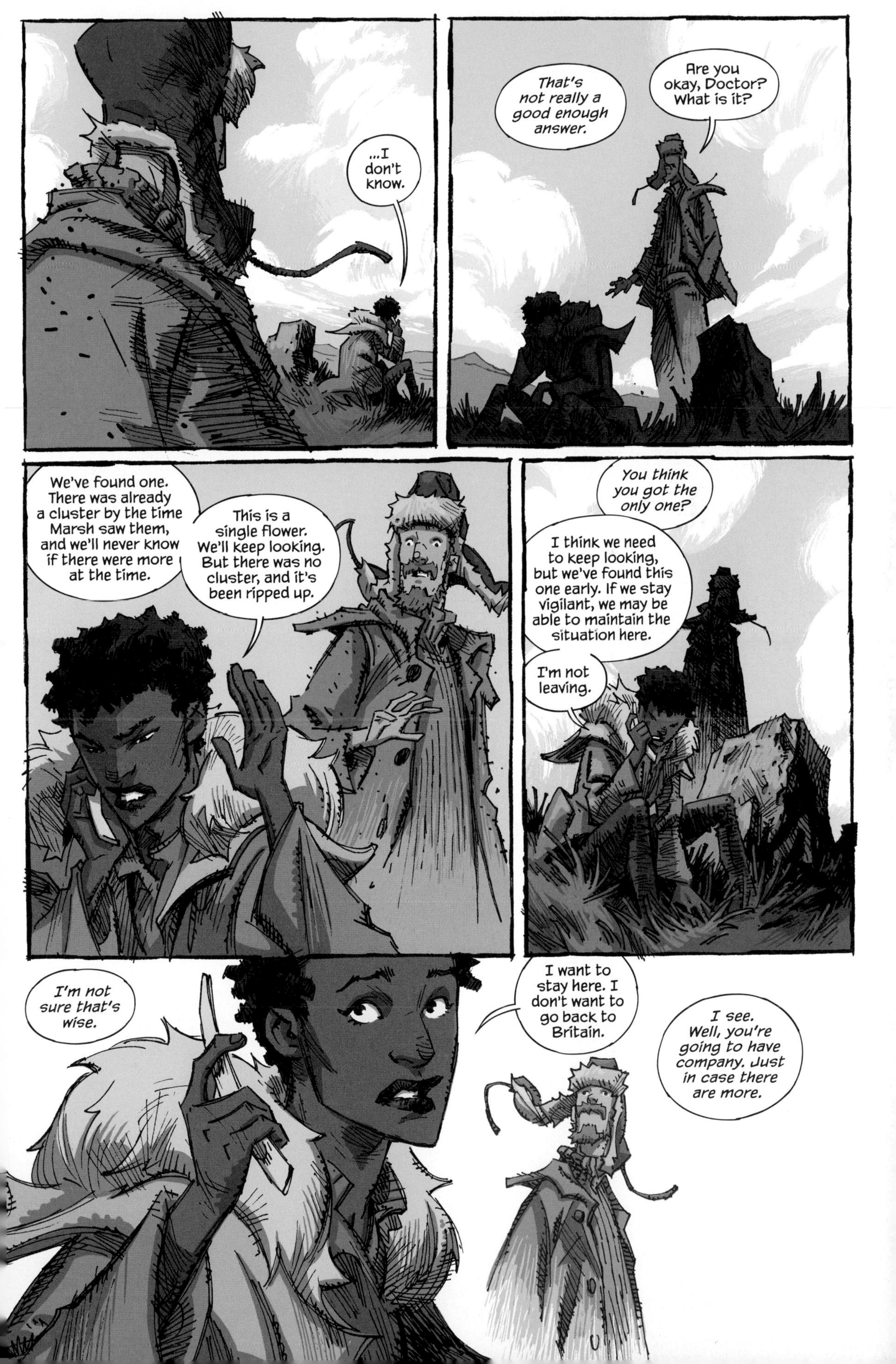
...I don't know.
That's not really a good enough answer.
Are you okay, Doctor? What is it?
We've found one. There was already a cluster by the time Marsh saw them, and we'll never know if there were more at the time.
This is a single flower. We'll keep looking. But there was no cluster, and it's been ripped up.
You think you got the only one?
I think we need to keep looking, but we've found this one early. If we stay vigilant, we may be able to maintain the situation here.
I'm not leaving.
I'm not sure that's wise.
I want to stay here. I don't want to go back to Britain.
I see. Well, you're going to have company. Just in case there are more.

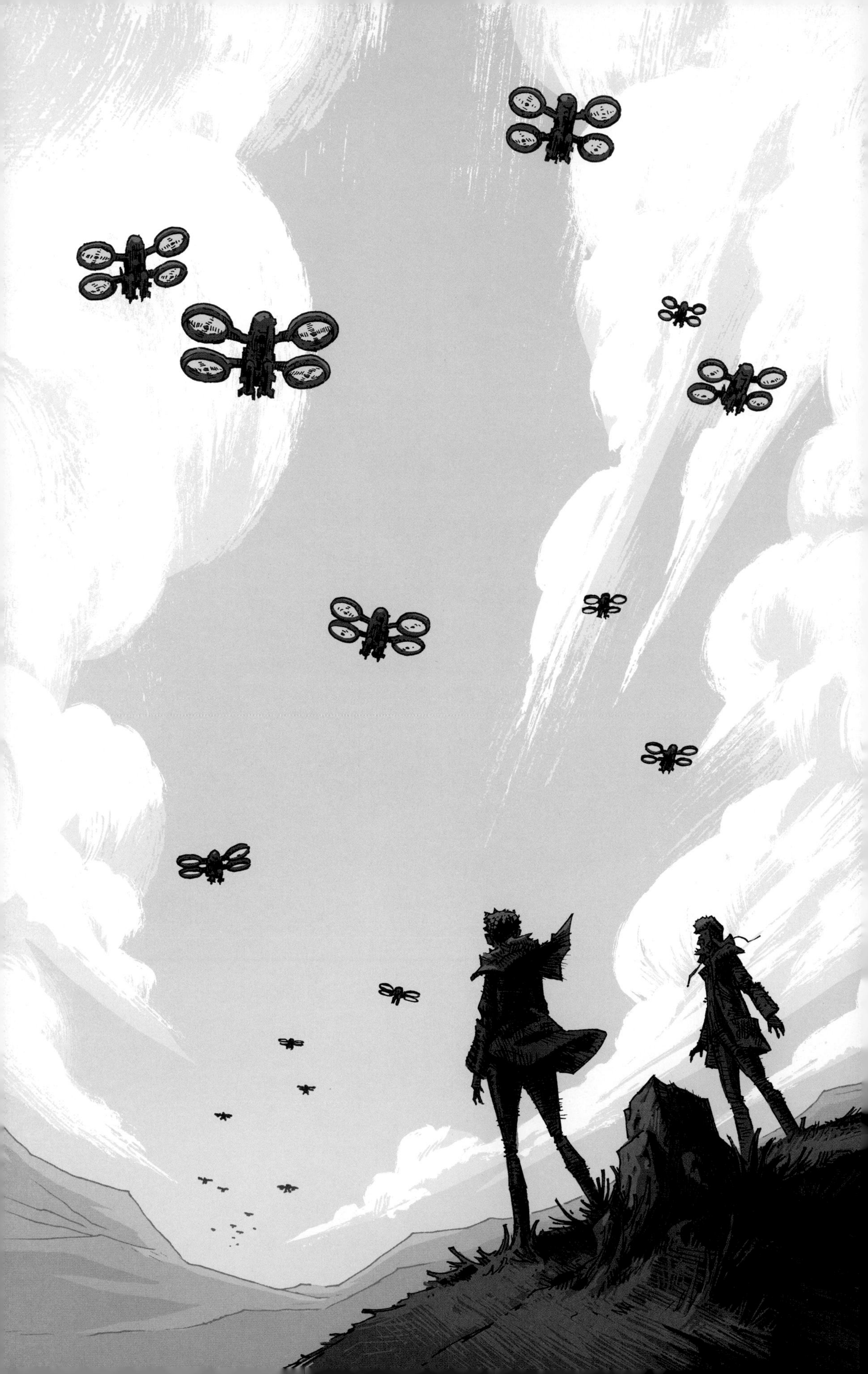

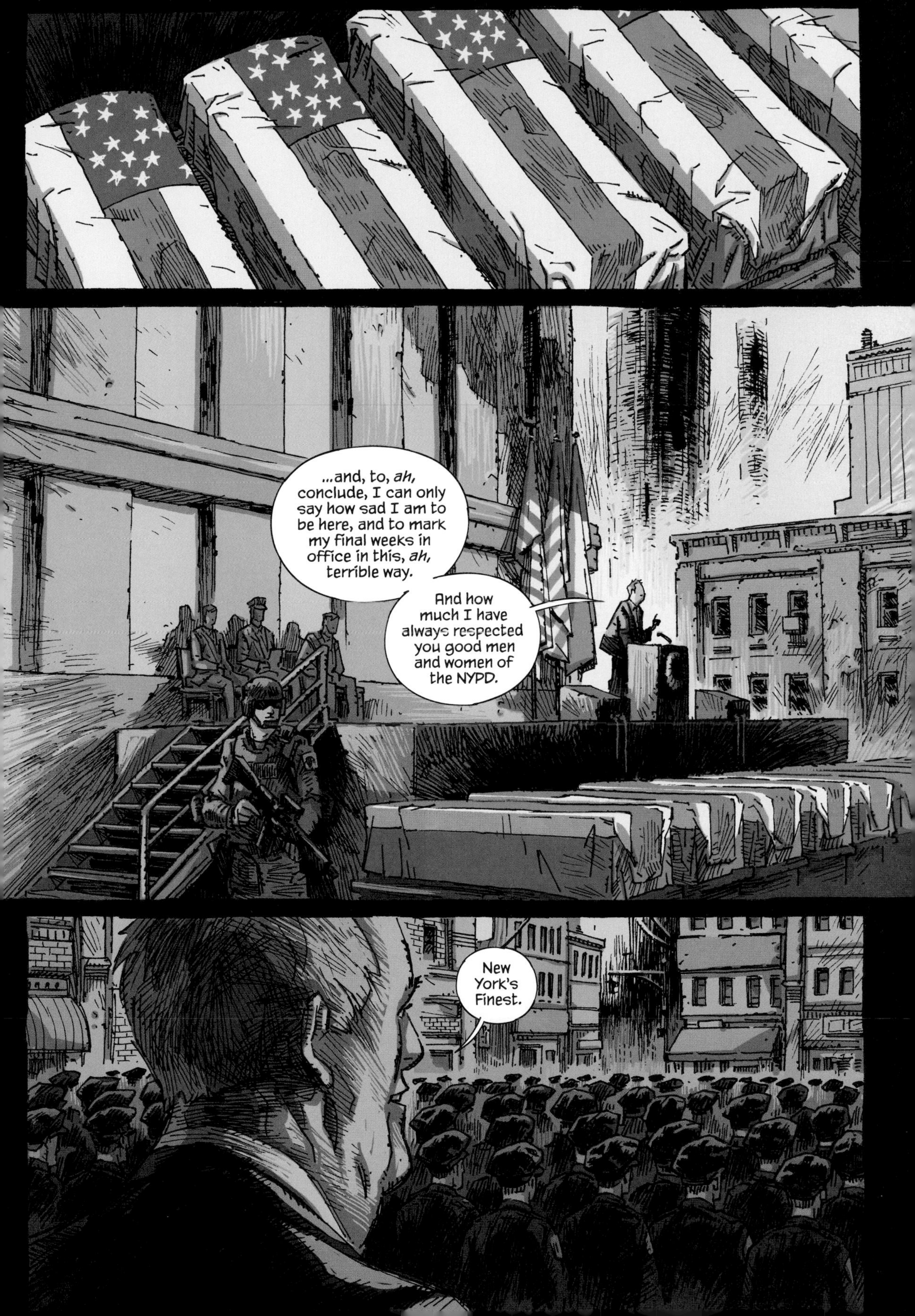
...and, to, *ah*, conclude, I can only say how sad I am to be here, and to mark my final weeks in office in this, *ah*, terrible way.
And how much I have always respected you good men and women of the NYPD.
New York's Finest.

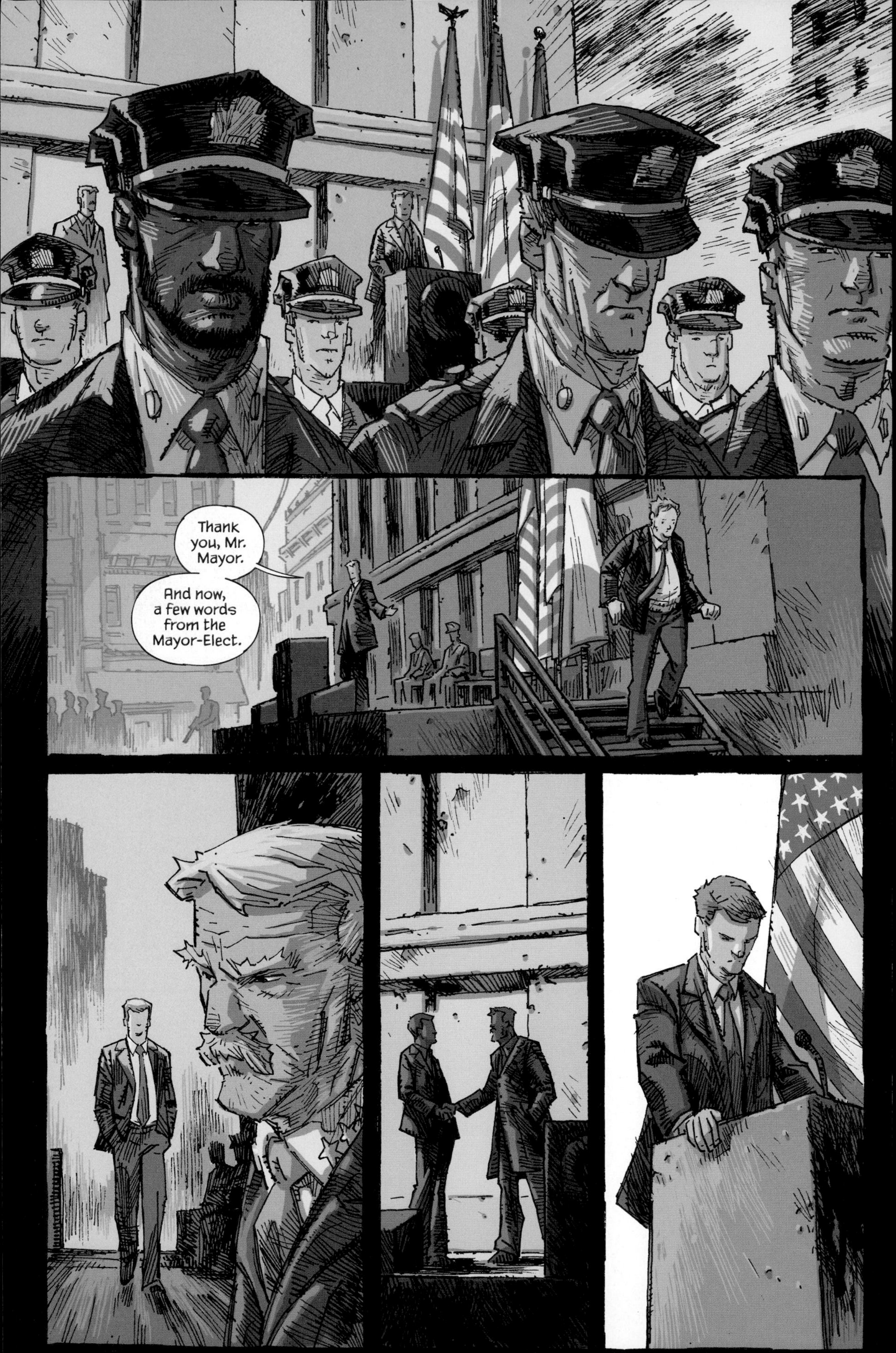
Thank you, Mr. Mayor.
And now, a few words from the Mayor-Elect.

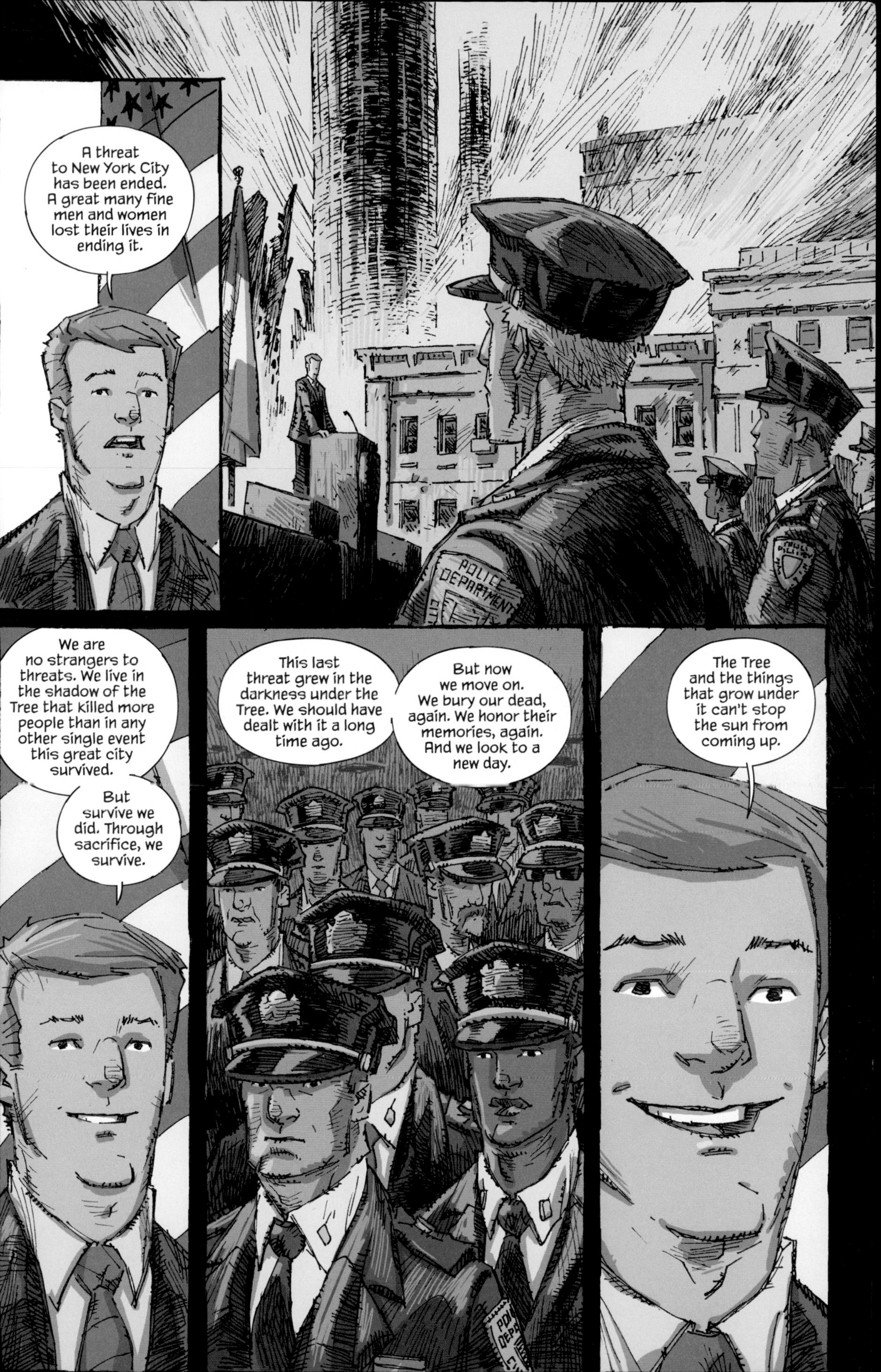
A threat to New York City has been ended. A great many fine men and women lost their lives in ending it.
POLICE DEPARTMENT
We are no strangers to threats. We live in the shadow of the Tree that killed more people than in any other single event this great city survived.
But survive we did. Through sacrifice, we survive.
This last threat grew in the darkness under the Tree. We should have dealt with it a long time ago.
But now we move on. We bury our dead, again. We honor their memories, again. And we look to a new day.
The Tree and the things that grow under it can't stop the sun from coming up.

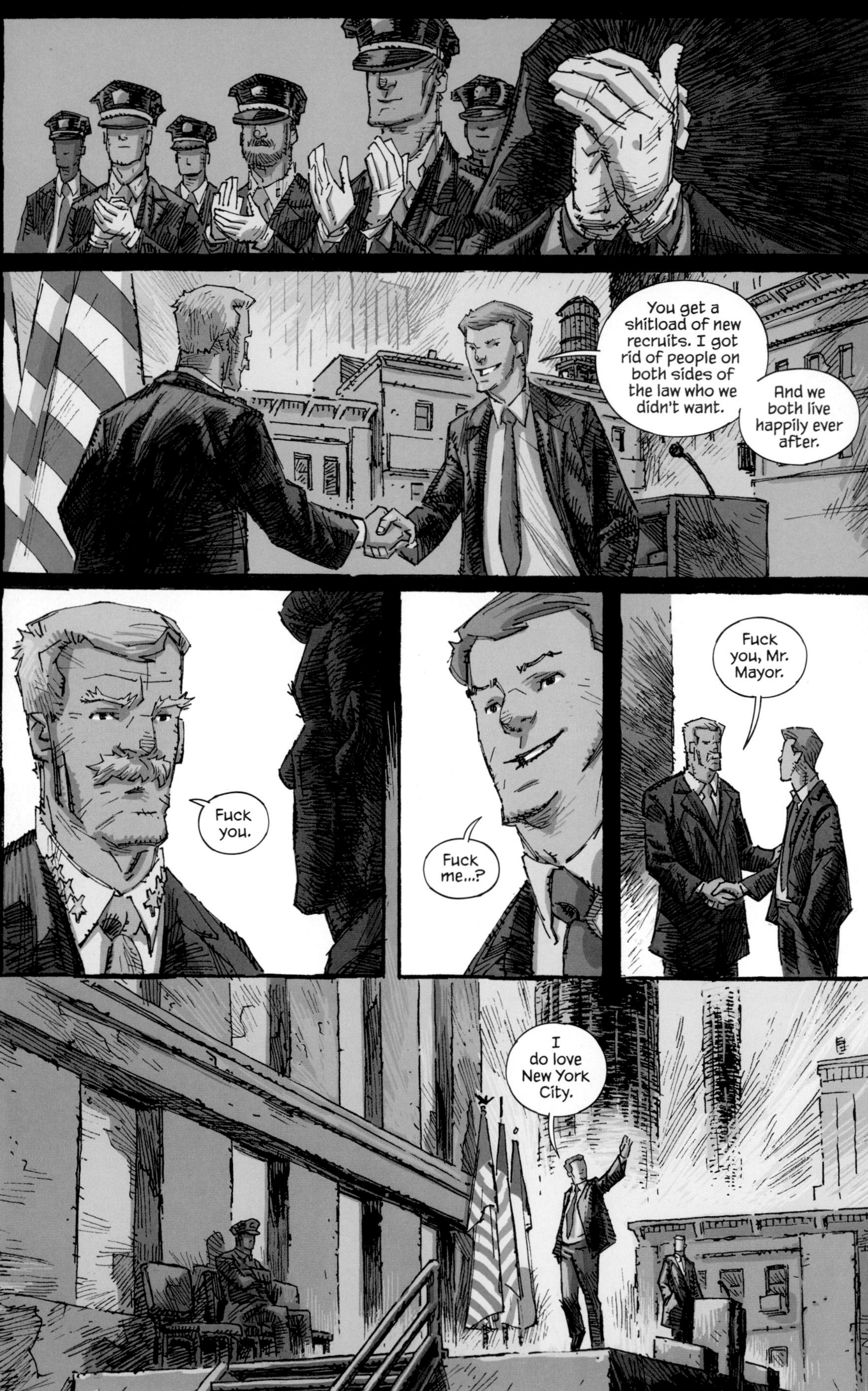
You get a shitload of new recruits. I got rid of people on both sides of the law who we didn't want.
And we both live happily ever after.
Fuck you.
Fuck me...?
Fuck you, Mr. Mayor.
I do love New York City.

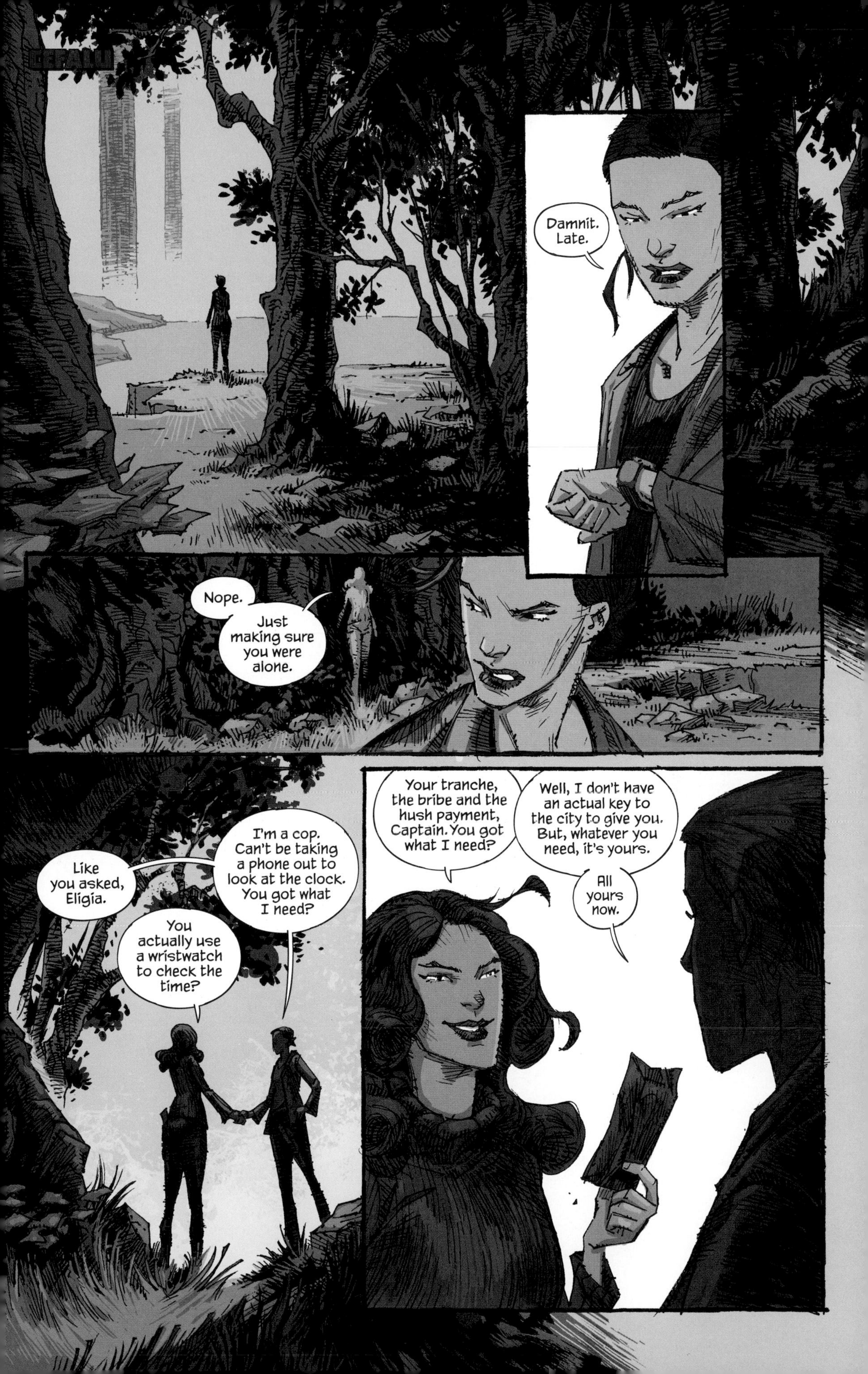
Damnit. Late.
Nope.
Just making sure you were alone.
Like you asked, Eligia.
I'm a cop. Can't be taking a phone out to look at the clock. You got what I need?
You actually use a wristwatch to check the time?
Your tranche, the bribe and the hush payment, Captain. You got what I need?
Well, I don't have an actual key to the city to give you. But, whatever you need, it's yours.
All yours now.

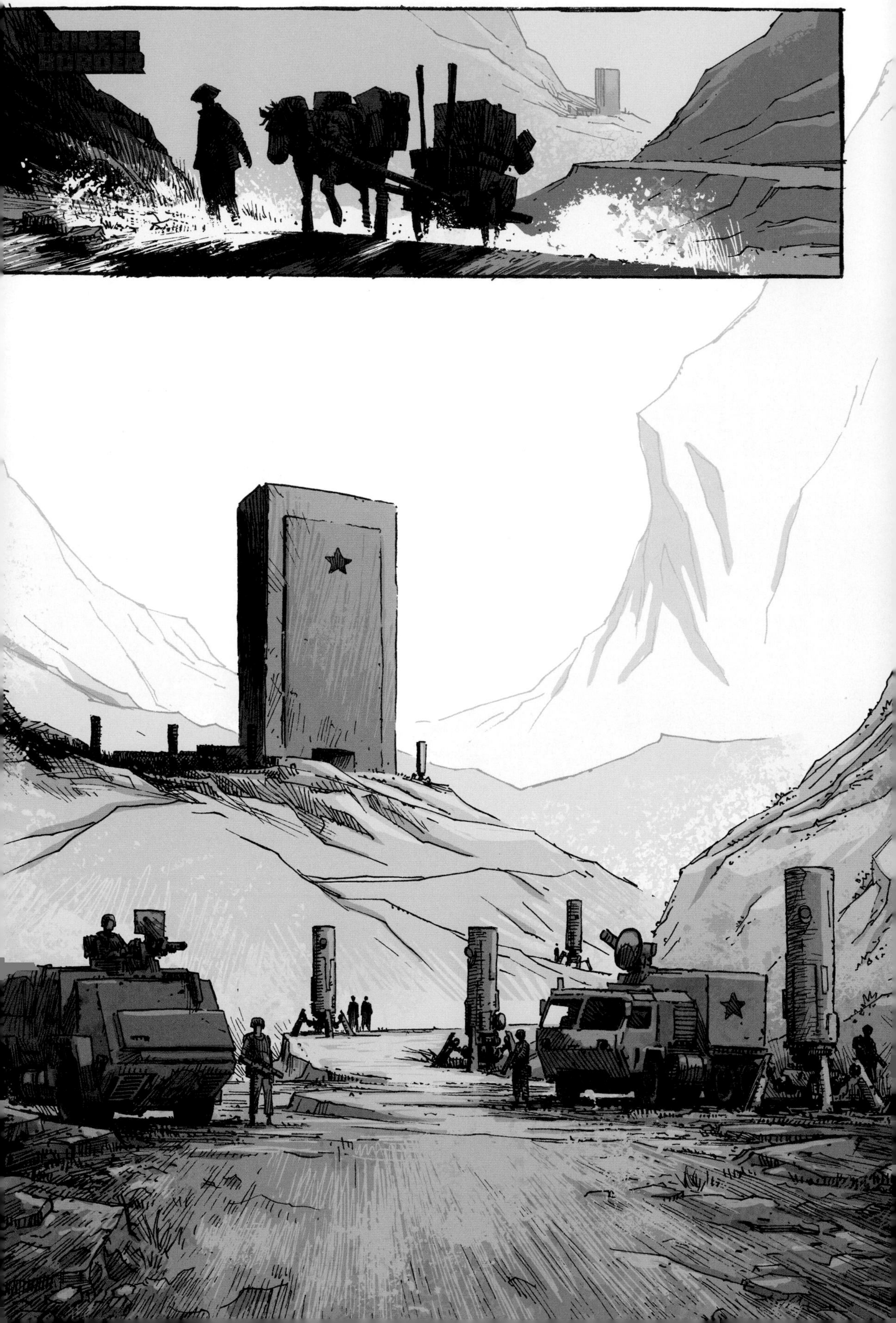
CHINESE
BORDER

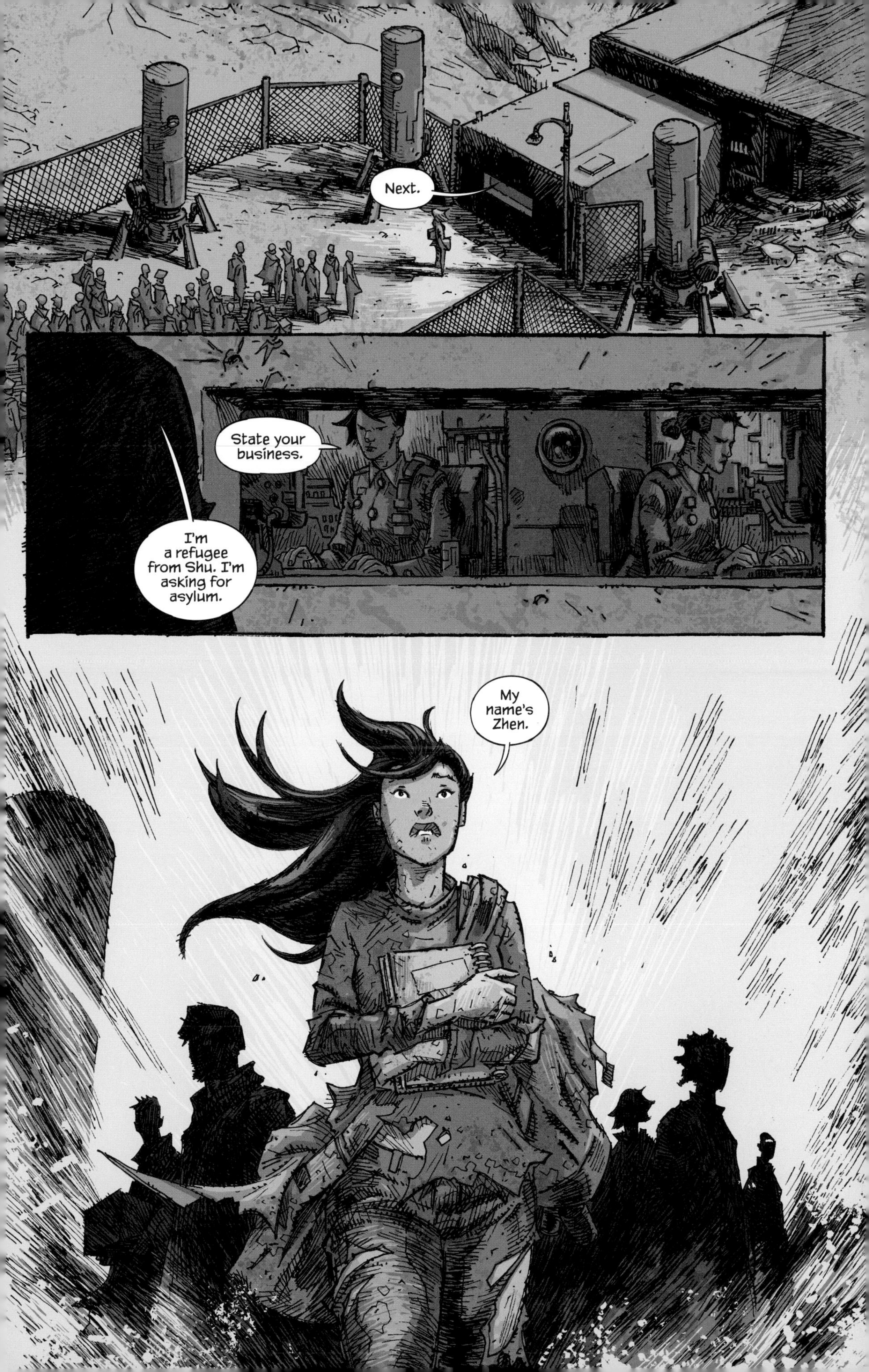
Next.
State your business.
I'm a refugee from Shu. I'm asking for asylum.
My name's Zhen.

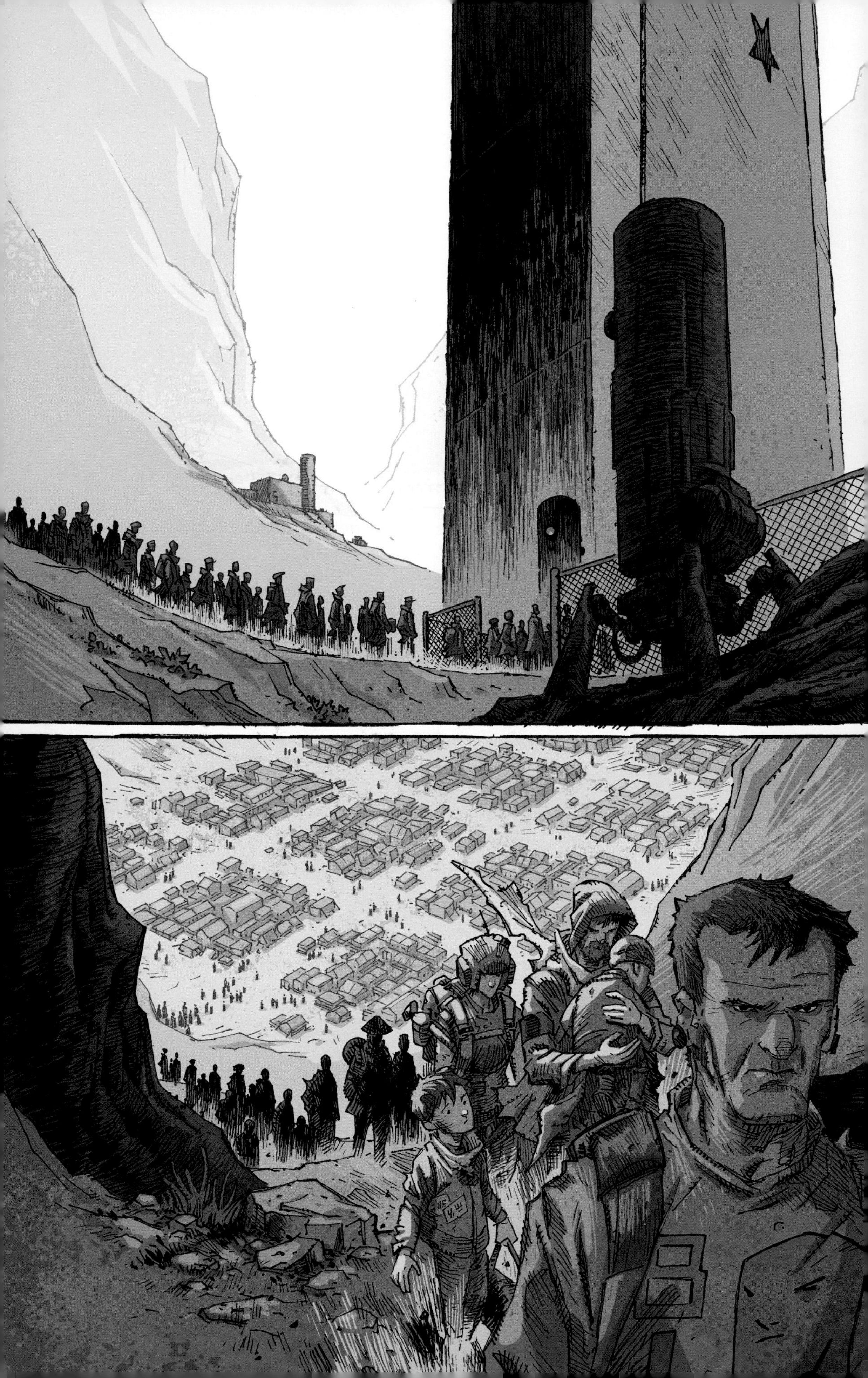

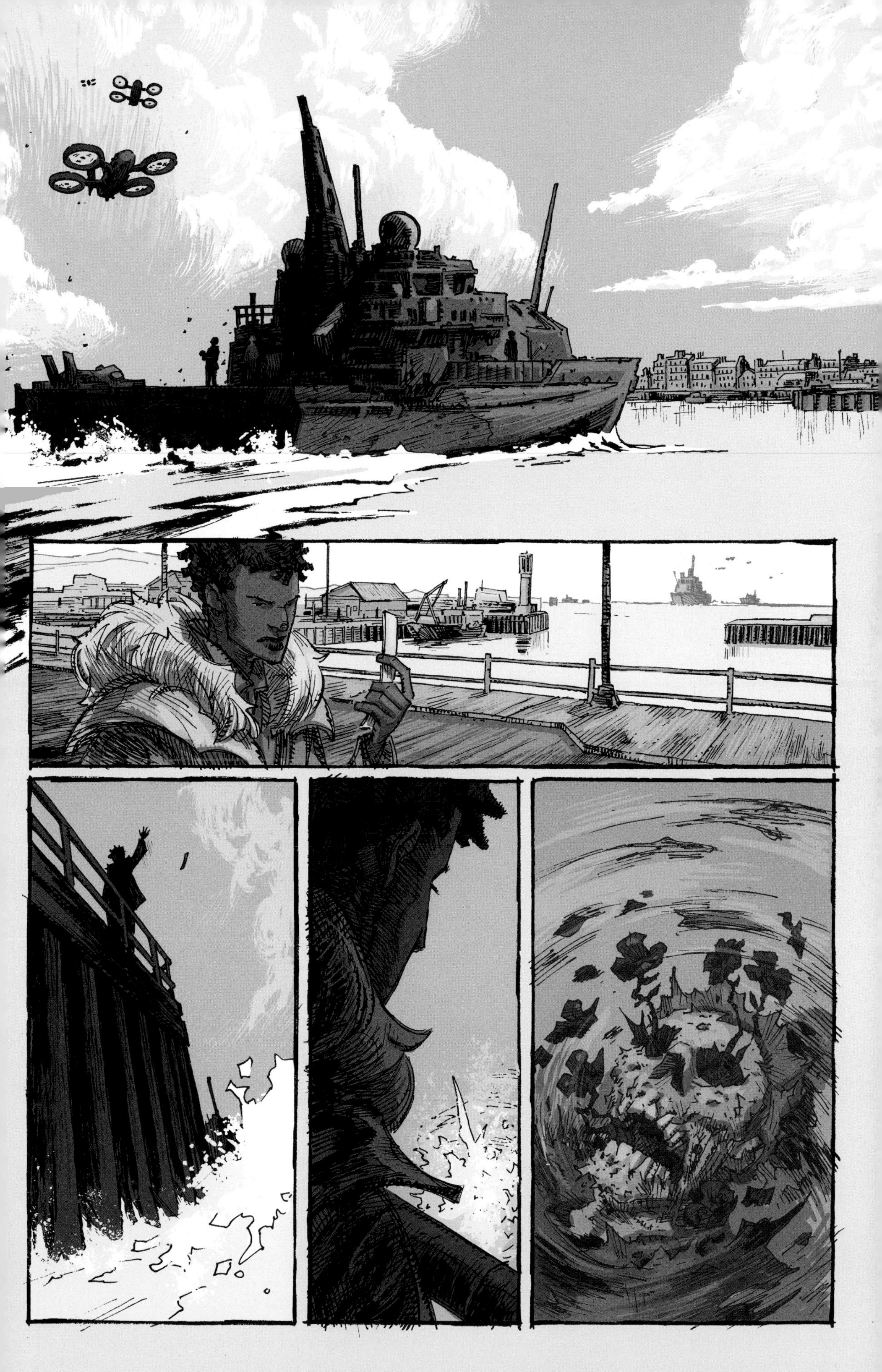

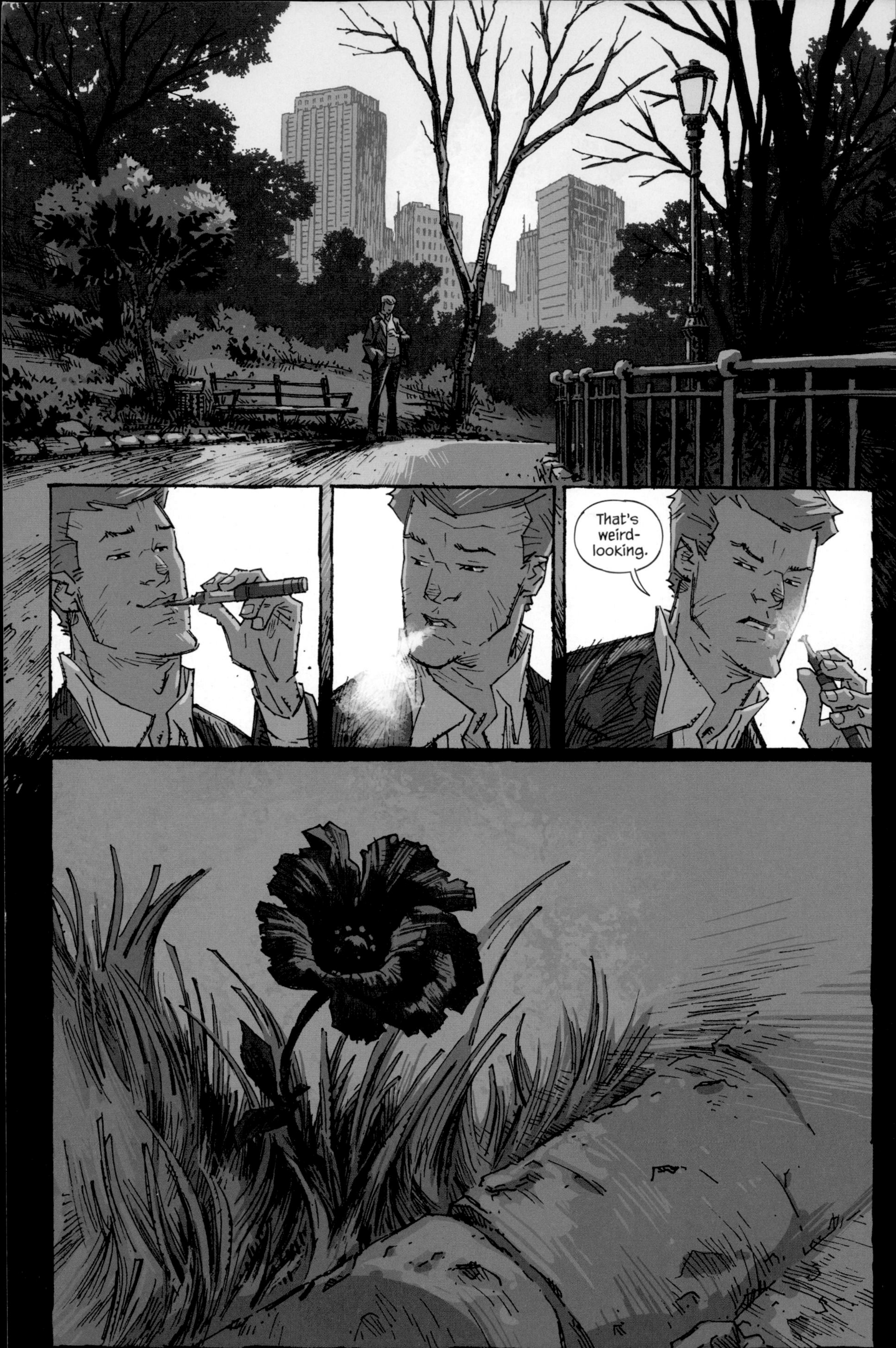
That's weird-looking.

NEXT
RULE OF THREE

SERIES COVERS

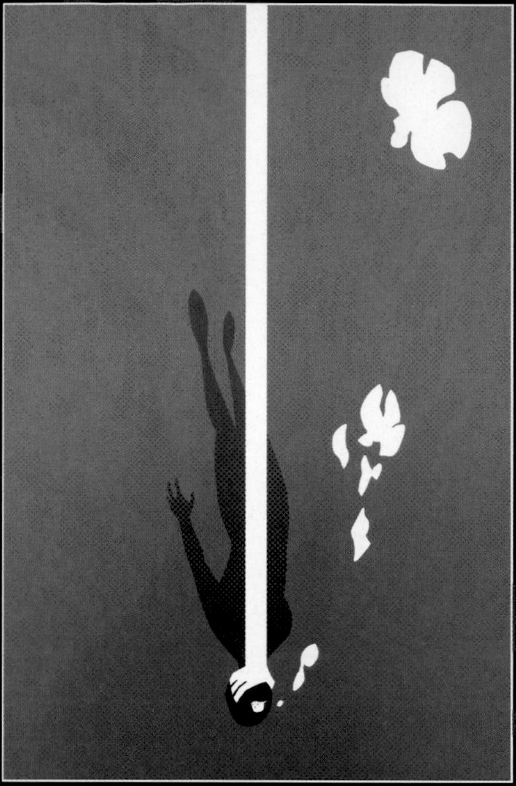

9

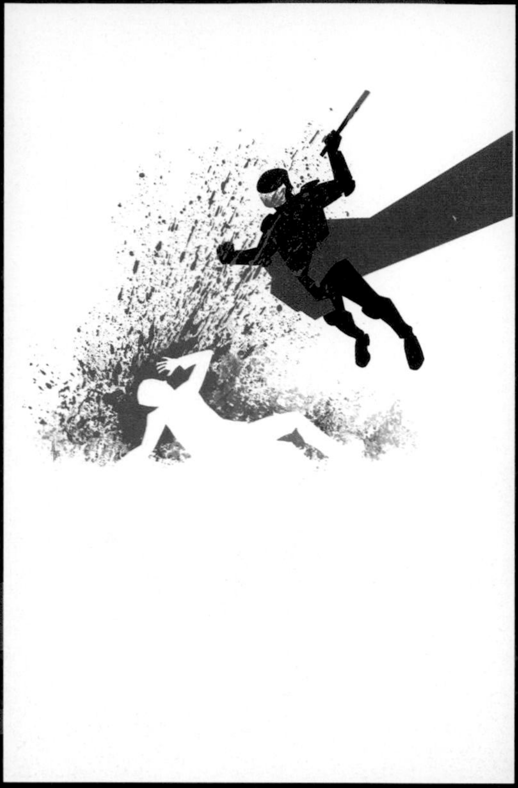

10

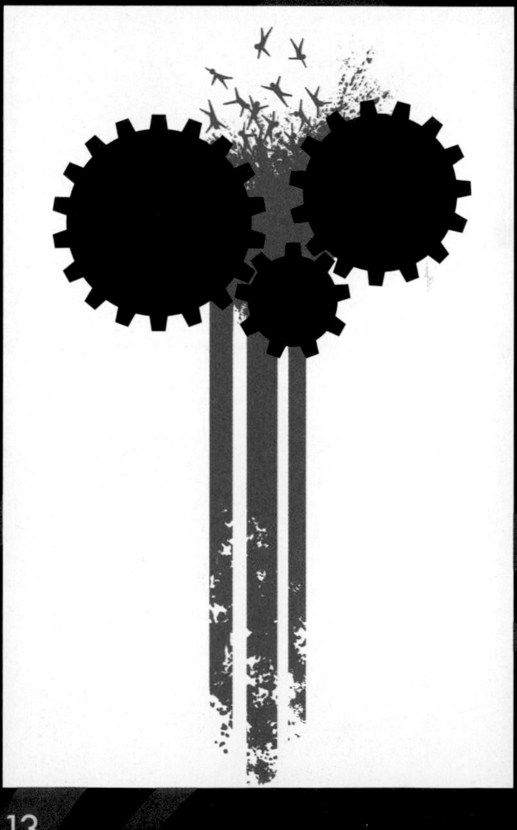

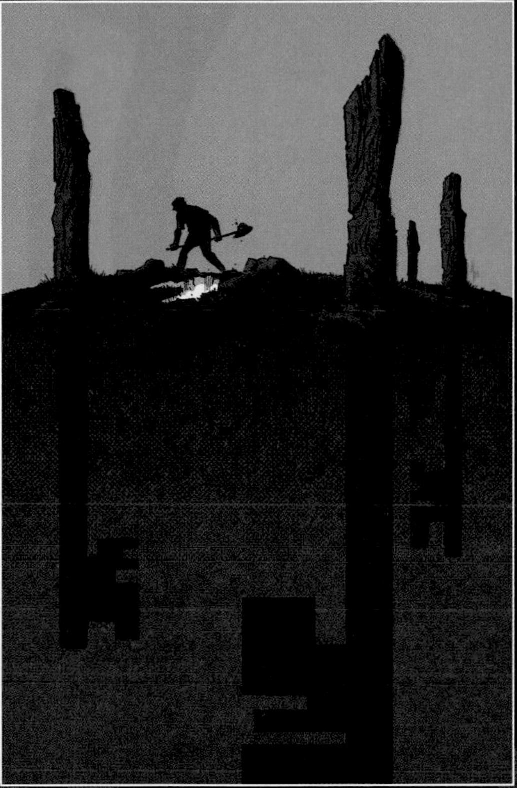

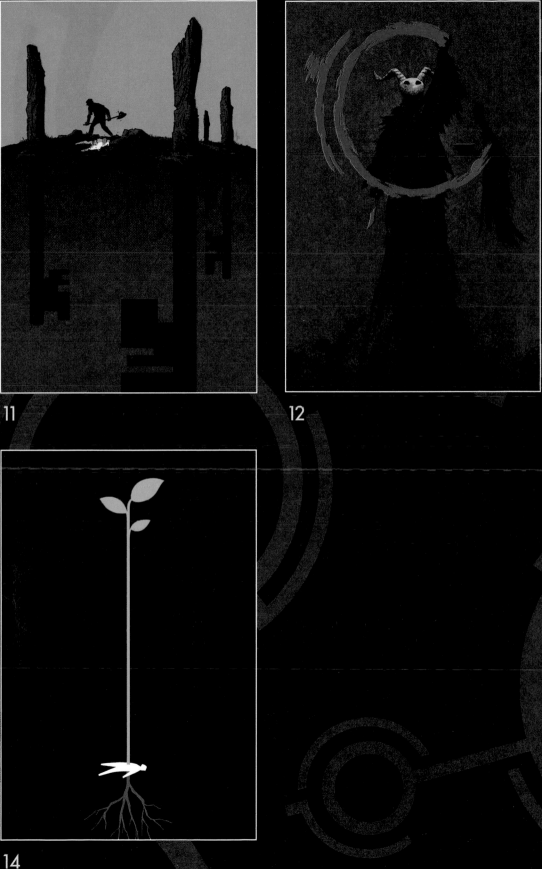

11

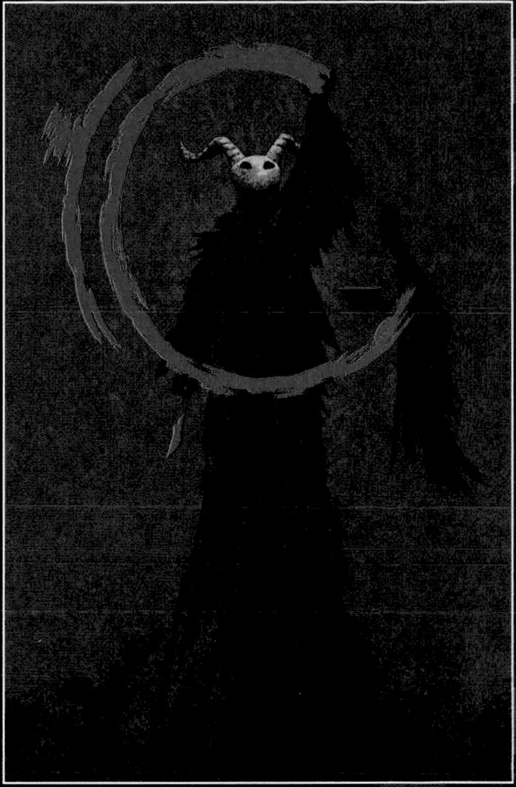

12

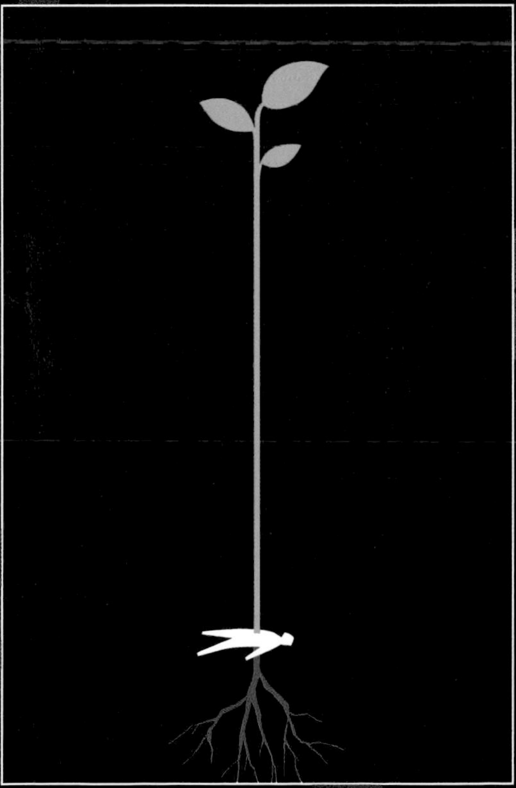

14

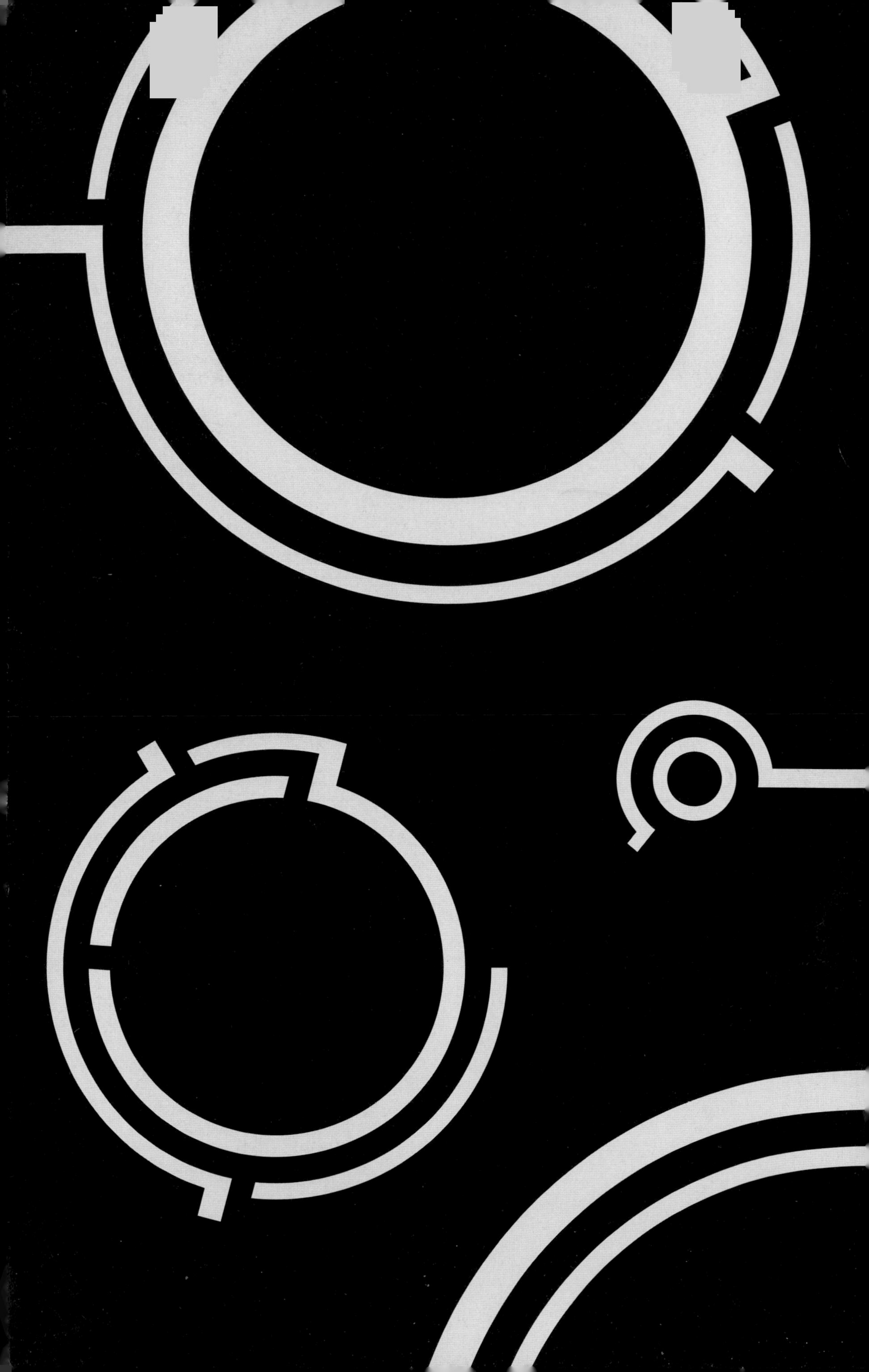